WITHDRAWN FROM DÚN LAOGHAIRE-RATHDOWN
COUNTY LIBRARY STOCK

IN MY OWN WORDS

www.transworldireland.ie

IN MY OWN WORDS
The Autobiography

Paul Galvin

WITHDRAWN FROM DÚN LAOGHAIRE-RATHDOWN
COUNTY LIBRARY STOCK

TRANSWORLD IRELAND

TRANSWORLD IRELAND
an imprint of The Random House Group Limited
20 Vauxhall Bridge Road, London SW1V 2SA
www.transworldbooks.co.uk

First published in 2014 by Transworld Ireland,
a division of Transworld Publishers

Copyright © Paul Galvin 2014

Paul Galvin has asserted his right under the Copyright, Designs
and Patents Act 1988 to be identified as the author of this work.

A CIP catalogue record for this book
is available from the British Library.

ISBN 9781848272057

This book is sold subject to the condition that it shall not,
by way of trade or otherwise, be lent, resold, hired out,
or otherwise circulated without the publisher's prior
consent in any form of binding or cover other than that
in which it is published and without a similar condition,
including this condition, being imposed on the
subsequent purchaser.

Addresses for Random House Group Ltd companies outside the UK
can be found at: www.randomhouse.co.uk
The Random House Group Ltd Reg. No. 954009

The Random House Group Limited supports the Forest Stewardship Council® (FSC®), the
leading international forest-certification organisation. Our books carrying the FSC label are
printed on FSC®-certified paper. FSC is the only forest-certification scheme supported by the
leading environmental organisations, including Greenpeace. Our paper procurement policy
can be found at www.randomhouse.co.uk/environment

Typeset in 12.5/15.5pt Ehrhardt by Falcon Oast Graphic Art Ltd.
Printed and bound in Great Britain by
Clays Ltd, Bungay, Suffolk

2 4 6 8 10 9 7 5 3 1

To my parents, who raised me to be the man I am.

To Louise, who makes me better than the man I am.

Contents

Foreword

What Are You Doing with Yourself?

I get asked a lot of questions. Nothing but questions. Some I can answer, some I can't. Of all the questions I get asked there's one that stumps me every time. 'What are you doing with yourself?' A lot of people ask me this. The tone of the question varies but is always telling. Some people are interested, some are ignorant, and others are genuinely confused. Sometimes the tone is actually plaintive. It might come with a furrowed brow, a shake of the head or a shallow sigh. Like I'm not doing enough somehow. I presume each time someone asks me, what am I doing with myself, they mean generally on a day-to-day basis, occupationally, and not what am I doing right at that particular moment in time. It is a question that somehow implies that because I'm not teaching any more, or not on the regular nine-to-five in an office with a job title, then everyone thinks I'm maybe ... I don't know ... at home doing nothing all day. 'What are you doing with yourself?' How do you answer that? Occasionally I wonder if there has been a story doing the rounds. That maybe I have done something outrageous and scandalous that I don't know about yet. I catch myself sometimes when I find I'm about to justify my existence to a stranger or even someone I vaguely know. Perhaps I should explain to them that I'm an existentialist. That I exist as an individual, a free agent, defined only by my own free will, by the whims of every action I decide to take.

So, what am I doing with myself? Well, I played football for Kerry for a while. Eleven years, that's one-third of my life. Sixty odd games, that's not enough of my life. Thousands of training sessions, that's way too much of my life. One football career that somehow was my whole life. Four red cards, that's not bad; three of them on the same weekend for three successive years, that is bad. A shop load of yellow cards, that's not bad either. No black cards, that's just great. Seven months of inter-county suspensions. Is that bad? Back-pats and brickbats, love and hate, Green and Gold. Heroes and have-a-go-heroes, real deals and unreal feelings. Great men and fake friends. Tough guys who said little, weak guys who said a lot, and results that said it all. The climb from the bottom, the fall from the top, the defiance to start again. A lot said, a lot done, but not all is said and done. Not yet. This is my story, these are my words, this is what I think. You are free to take these words any way you want, they'll still be mine after you're done with them. Yes, I have done some mad things. That doesn't make me a mad thing, though. Yes, I have strengths. That doesn't make me strong. Yes, I have weaknesses. Accepting them makes me strong. Yes, I am my own man. I've been my own man since the day my father told me to be. For that reason I am myself full-time. Yes I have faith. I pray to God every day to keep me. That was Mom's advice.

To those who take, or mistake, silence for weakness and take that weakness for opportunity, know this. Sometimes silence is strong. Sometimes silence is just patience, waiting for the right time to come. That time has come. Here's a little of what I've been doing with myself. I wrote this book.

What are you doing with yourself?

Prologue

'What is it, Paul?
 'What's driving you?'

I was sitting in the back of Liam O'Flaherty's pub in Listowel having presented medals to some underage kids. We were deep in 2006 and Kerry had won our second All Ireland in three years that September. We had lost two championship games in that period and a handful of league games. We were winning for fun. Stephen Stack, the former Kerry defender, had just asked me the questions above. I sat there, 26 years old, and I had no answer. Plenty of questions, but no answer. What Stephen was getting at, I think, was the source of my motivation, and maybe our motivation as a team. From where sprung the intensity that fired me on the field of play? What was it that stoked this all-consuming aggression within me, that brought out the best and worst in me? There had to be some root to it. Didn't there?

I tried to answer him but my reply was that of a man who had neither the time nor the maturity nor the self-awareness for that kind of introspection. Since I had eventually established myself in the Kerry team, I knew nothing but success. I drank it in and

1

belched out what didn't agree with me. Onwards. Next challenge, please. Never mind the challenger. I hadn't time to stop and ask myself questions.

I didn't care. Success was all I wanted. Winning was all that mattered. Kerry was all I respected. Even when I was a sub, a spare part with no hope of playing, it mattered more than it should have. I stood on the line in '03 when Tyrone tore down the walls of a footballing dynasty and went about using the rubble to build one of their own. I took it personally. I saw great men brought to their knees, and it hurt when it shouldn't have mattered that much. I was a sub. I stood a few yards away from Páidí Ó Sé on the sideline when he got banjoed by an old man and it was all I could do not to banjo the old man back. That was as close as I got. But I found something out about myself that day. I had fight in me. I wanted to be in the middle of it, as bad as it was for us. I learned later on that same fight came a bit too easily to me, and got me in trouble, but what can you do? Without that fight I wouldn't have got to where I wanted to go. You are what you are. You can't change that, right?

Having spent the Tyrone game warming up, I walked to the dressing room heartsick when the final whistle went. I had so much respect for all the lads, Darragh and Seamo and Hassett and Fitzy and Tomás and the rest that it upset me to see them beaten. I wanted to help. To fight. To be defiant. To protect Kerry. And if defeat was to be our lot, then let us lose, but let us go down fighting and let me go down with the men on the field, with sweat and blood on my jersey, with pride, with honour. Not standing on the line rubbernecking. No honour in that.

The question stayed with me as I drove home that night. 'What is it, Paul? What's driving you?'

*

What drove me? I didn't know. I always just played to win. I wanted medals, achievement, success. I wanted respect. Pure and simple. With me it was always pure but rarely that simple, and once I gave it some thought, the answer, or some kind of answer, was not far away. It was hidden in a recess of my brain. The temporal lobe. That's the part that stores emotion and memory. Emotion has a powerful impact on memory. Autobiographical memory consists of the episodic and the semantic. A lot of my memories tend to be episodic, linked to experiences, events, people.

I think back to a day when I was around 13 years old. I was standing at Ballinclogher Cross waiting for my drive to arrive. The Cross was a central part of my childhood. Ballinclogher, Baile an Chlochair as Gaeilge, 'the townland of the convent'. It lies on the main Tralee to Ballybunion road in the heart of north Kerry hurling country.

A quarry, on the right-hand side of the road as you head for Lixnaw village, was our playground as kids. We explored every part of it. Tunnels and caves in the quarry base at the back, and the sheer rock face at the front, provided just the right amount of danger necessary for any young lads' adventure. We'd spend some days hiding in the tunnels, burrowing underground like rats, others having races to climb to the top, a good 40 or 50 feet above us.

Years later the same quarry would glow in the fiery light of bonfires as we brought home County Minor Hurling Championships, County Under-21 Hurling Championships, County Senior Hurling Championships and County Football Championships. Sam Maguire has paid a few golden visits too.

This day I had been selected to play for the Kerry Under-14s. Have boots, will travel. Nerves darted around my stomach like bumblebees in a summer kitchen. I was buzzing.

The car arrives. There are four players inside plus a selector, who's driving. I get in, wishing I had a teammate from Lixnaw with me for company. I don't remember which players were there.

But I remember the driver. And his words. And his tone. And the look on his face.

'Oh, are you coming too?' he sneers.

I redden and mumble a reply. He's not finished yet, though.

'Along for the drive, is it?' he scoffs.

I say nothing. No one does. The silence is uncomfortable. The car drives on. The embarrassment I feel in front of the other players soon turns to defiance. This defiance consumes me the whole way to the game. Maybe it has never truly left me. Maybe it was always in me, a part of who I am. Maybe it's what's driving me.

We sit there in silence.

I find myself staring at the driver. I sit and I stare and I make a pledge. A pledge I would go on to make a few more times as I got older.

'F**ck you, old boy, I'll show you.'

1

Penny Lane

The sun always seemed to shine on Penny Lane. I'm still brown as a berry from it today. All my memories are of long, warm days, the evening sun casting long shadows, the wind at my back and the sound of my own commentary in my ears as I ran home, sidestepping imaginary opponents, scoring last-minute, match-winning goals and celebrating accordingly. But only in those parts of the road where I knew I couldn't be seen from neighbours' windows. From top to bottom, Penny Lane stretches for around half a mile dead straight. My only memory of my grandfather is of his silhouette walking away from me towards the top of Penny Lane one dusky evening. I was standing near the bottom, wondering where he was going. With all the life experience of a silhouette myself, I watched him disappear into the distance. I don't recall ever seeing him again.

It's funny the things we remember, out of all the life experiences we have. Why do we remember some things and not others? Why do we remember something as forgettable as an old man walking up a lane and not something as important as that same man talking to you or him being laid to rest?

I wonder about this. I think it's because memories have reasons. There are reasons we remember certain events or people, somewhere deep in our subconscious, and life reveals these reasons to us as we grow. For me, in writing this chapter, I can now relate my feelings for Penny Lane back to that sole memory of my grandfather walking away from me on that evening many years ago. I was maybe four or five. I can still see him clearly walking away but I find it hard to recall his face at the same time. I have many memories of my grandmother Nora. I was close to her. Everything seems smaller on Penny Lane now. The road isn't so long any more. I sit on walls I once had to climb. I see over ditches I once had to cut back with my hurley to see into. I know every hump and pothole along it. It still moves me to walk it.

How could it not? My laugh echoed so loudly around it when I was young that my best friend Trevor's mother, Mary, always knew when I was calling. It was that kind of place.

I lived at the end of Penny Lane, or the 'Boraheen' as we called it, on the edge of a forest which separates the parish of Lixnaw, where I lived, from Causeway, where I went to school. Between the last house, my uncle Martin's, and the forest, lay a bog. A bog right on our doorstep. Jesus.

If God had given me every natural amenity a young fella could wish for to occupy himself, then placing a blanket bog outside my door was his way of balancing the books. I learned quickly that the elders, folk like my dad, loved the bog. If they weren't talking about it at home, they were knee-deep in it, firing heavy, black sods with hairy heads at me.

My dad and Johnny Ryan, a local turf connoisseur, drank tea from Lucozade bottles, ate bacon sandwiches with brown sauce, swapped stories and cut turf. I listened and did what I was told until the day was down. I grew up on a bog and spent so much of my youth at the bog that I can safely be considered a 'bogger'. Being called a bogger was seen as an insult when I was in school, and even when I was in college. I never saw it as an insult. I call myself a bogger.

Dad was born and raised on a small farm halfway down Penny Lane. He is one of nine siblings and, like many others, left home at a young age to work. He spent years in Birmingham and stood on the Holte End every second week in support of Aston Villa before moving back home. He met my mother and they lived in Curraheen on the Tralee to Dingle road for a while before moving into a house at the bottom of Penny Lane. From there he worked for CIE for years. If he had stayed in Birmingham I'd have ended up playing for Aston Villa if he could have helped it. He is the only Villa supporter I know. The Kerry Branch of the Aston Villa Supporters' Club is still looking for members to join him. He was a dark, swarthy man when I was young. There was more sunshine in Ireland back then. Everyone seemed dark-skinned. I share his dark complexion now and some of his personality too. My first memory of being conscious of clothes is of looking at my dad's work uniform every day. It wasn't that I loved fashion from a young age or spoke about it or wanted a career in it. I didn't dream about it or speak about it at all. I dreamt about football and sport and playing for Man United, but I was always interested in fashion – the detail, the brands, the imagery – yet I didn't really know what it was. I had an eye for the detail of clothing, the names, reading the tags, the composition of the clothes, how the grey trim of my dad's V-neck matched the grey of his shirt. He wore a navy work uniform, navy slacks, a navy V-neck jumper with a grey trim and light grey shirt, with black or brown shoes. The thing I remember most is the tag on his trousers. It was orange with the letter 'F' written on it in stylized form. Later on I learned that this symbol represented the Farah clothing brand after finding a pair of trousers in a vintage clothes store in Dublin. I have three pairs of Farah trousers myself today.

My mother's family, the Moriartys, from Curraheen on the Tralee to Dingle road, are football mad. Her brother, my uncle John, is one of my favourite people. He is unique. He likes visitors but you only get a certain amount of time in his company. You must be able to read him to know when he has had enough of you. If you can't he might let you know, in his own way, that he has better things to be doing. I called to see him one day as I was passing. We spoke at the front gate for twenty minutes. That's a long time for John. I didn't read the signs this day anyway. I think that was because he was standing. When he was sitting you could read him better. He would start rubbing his knees as he sat. That was the first sign that he was getting sick of you. Then he would start moving his feet under the seat. That was the second sign. If he resorted to saying, 'Oh, cripes,' in response to your ramblings it was all over. He had switched off from you completely at that stage. I liked observing his mannerisms. This day he eventually took his leave from me. 'I better go from you, I've an egg boiling inside,' he said. I drove off laughing, thinking, 'I hope he likes hard-boiled eggs.'

Lots of my cousins on that side of the family played football with St Pats Blennerville. Séamus O'Sullivan, a master butcher in Tralee, played in the 1986 All Ireland minor final for Kerry. His brothers, Tommy and Derek, also played to a high level. My other cousins, Kevin and Declan Moriarty, played too. Their dad, Muiris, won a county championship with Kerins O'Rahillys in 1955. A first cousin of my mother's, Jack Falvey, played on the Kerry team of 1946 that beat Roscommon in the All Ireland final. He played wing-forward too.

I speak Irish fluently and I got that from my mother, who grew up close to an Irish-speaking area in West Kerry. The first time I heard the Irish language being spoken was out of her mouth at home. Mom grew up with Kerry football. I vaguely remember her watching the 1986 All Ireland final between Kerry and Tyrone. All her side of my family are football people. She instilled in me the importance of God and prayer in my life. I'm not sure what I was like as a child. When I was still in primary school I remember going to a dentist in Causeway for a check-up. For some reason I missed an initial appointment and had to re-schedule. This time was for real and I had two of my back teeth pulled. When I say pulled what I actually mean is they were slowly drawn from my jawline, creaking and cracking like an old tree stump being uprooted by rope from the back of a tractor. I lay there shocked that I could have teeth so big in my mouth. When the second one was withdrawn it must have been half an hour later. I sat there afterwards, pissed off at how sore it was but delighted because I knew there and then I would never sit through that again. Twenty-two years later I still haven't sat in a dentist's chair. I think I had my own ideas on life from a young age. I may have been a little bold, without being bad.

I laughed a lot when I was young, that's what I remember most.

Sport was the thing I was most serious about. Which begs the question, should sport be serious or fun? Growing up in the early '90s it was serious fun. We played everything we could: hurling, soccer, football, rounders, American football, rugby, sprinting, cycling, slow-bicycle races. Anything we could compete at. Penny Lane was our pitch and our world and all we knew. We walked it and talked, ran it and screamed, cycled it and hurled on it; we hid in its ditches and climbed its trees. We chased each other on it and laughed, we fell on it and cried, we fought on it and somehow grew up that bit quicker than if we'd never fought. We'd lie on it at night and watch for shooting stars. If they didn't light up we'd pretend we had seen them and then pretend the others had missed them and laugh some more. 'Look, look, look. Over there. See? See? See now? . . . Ah, too late. It's gone.' We'd look for the constellations and make up new names for them. Orion's Belt became Johnny Ryan's Belt and the Big Dipper became the Saucepan instead of the Plough, then we'd swear we saw spaceships and run home half-laughing, half-scared. We learned the ways of the world on the flat of our backs, looking up at the night sky. Trevor, Patrick, Alan and I lived on the road. They were my best friends. The O'Mahony boys, Thomas, James, Noel and Vinny, lived next door to me. Half a team of us.

Later we grew up and the world became a more serious place. We shouldered coffins into hearses and watched them carry our people on their final journeys up Penny Lane. Young and old passed on. Carried out of their own front doors, doors we knocked on as youngsters with enquiries sent from our mothers or fathers or brothers or sisters because that was how we communicated back then. We didn't have mobiles or email. I was about 14 before we got landline telephones. We knocked on front doors and left the message with the relevant neighbour. 'Mom said this, Dad wants to know that . . .' If we weren't carrying messages door to door we were standing in the same door jambs waiting for friends to gather themselves so we could be gone up the road to Kirby's field or further over to the Cross.

Because there were so many of us it was easy to organize games. Mostly soccer games. The O'Mahonys had a big back lawn which was the perfect pitch for us. There were plenty of other young lads living nearby, so we sometimes had to relocate to Kirby's field at the top of the road for more space. Every game was competitive. There were days when I went off home steaming, having lost, but I always came back for more the following day. And I wasn't alone. Éamonn Fitzmaurice was very competitive back then and still is. We all were.

We often had enough for two teams. Us lads on Penny Lane, the McKennas, O'Mahonys and I, were often joined by the boys over the road, the Fitzmaurices, Éamonn and Ciaran, and Mossie Kelliher. Further back down the road in Killahan, Abbeydorney, lived more McKennas, Mark and Brian, who would often join us for games. We were full-time sportsmen.

Because I lived at the bottom of the road the lads would some-times have to wait for me halfway up if we were going over to Ballinclogher Cross to catch a bus to a game or just to go to the shop. If I was ever late they might walk on a bit so I'd be further behind them. To keep myself entertained and involved I'd puck stones at them from behind, maybe 40 or 50 yards away, to slow them down. They would have to duck and take cover so then I could catch up. Eventually they cottoned on and just kept walking. They knew the chances of being hit were slim so they'd continue walking just to best me. They'd each raise the bas of their hurley to the back of their heads for protection when they heard the smack of a stone on my hurley, and keep walking. If a stone whizzed by particularly close to someone's head they would stop and roar back, laughing. 'Hi, that was close, boy!!' and a volley of stones would come flying back in retaliation. If you were daring enough and could see one early enough you'd stand there and try to meet it on the volley. When we weren't playing we were always up to something. Ballinclogher Cross became a meeting point for kids in our area.

We would head over looking for something to do to give us a laugh. When we got a little older we went further afield to the sports field in Lixnaw. Hermitage Park lies on the banks of the River Brick as you drive towards Listowel. At the top of the pitch stands Hermitage Castle. We'd cycle the three miles over on our racers with our hurleys in tow and spend the day hurling on the field and climbing the castle. Hermitage Park was the place we all started out playing hurling with Lixnaw. But we came from Ballinclogher Cross. The Cross was our first port of call.

When winter came, and the excavated limestone at the base of the quarry filled with water, we'd sail on large slabs of aeroboard that we took from Trevor's house. His dad, Moss, is a builder. The rock face was high and sheer and at one point near the top it forced us out and around a rock projection that we really had to cling to so as not to fall. The fall would have been 30 feet or so to the bottom. No one ever fell. The tunnels at the base were narrow and full of old shoes for some reason. Locals told us the shoes belonged to Black and Tan soldiers who used the quarry as a base during the English occupation. They were forced out and left the shoes behind them. I'm not sure I'd go into them now as an adult, but as kids you do these things in the name of adventure.

The sailing was the one hobby that got us in trouble – the water was quite deep and there were a few days when we fell off the aeroboard and got drenched. The game was to see how many of us could get on the aeroboard at the same time and set sail. There might be four or five of us trying to fit on. The lake, or turlough, was quite big and would take you a few minutes to travel from one side to the other. We'd all be on the same team as we sailed out towards the middle, talking to each other and making sure everyone was in the right position to balance the aeroboard out so we wouldn't capsize. Because we never really knew how deep it was around the middle we would steady up and begin to concentrate. Patrick was usually first officer and sailed it with a paling stick we'd picked up in a field nearby. So he'd be in the middle guiding us and Trevor, Alan and I, and sometimes Mark and Brian, would be strategically placed around him so as to balance the weight and steady the ship. The craic would start once we neared dry land again on the other side. Then it became every man for himself. The talking stopped. Anything said would betray the speaker who was thinking of only one thing. Getting off without getting dipped. When everyone went quiet you knew you were getting close to tipping point. The first to go was always the safest bet to reach dry land. He had the weight of the others behind him to give him leverage. The rest were hostages to fortune. The laughing would start when the first man jumped ship. We'd all roar and shout and laugh and grab each other for safety or leverage but mostly just so if we did have to take a dip we wouldn't be going in alone. Between the laughing and the wrestling and the giddiness of trying to save ourselves we all went home with wet shoes and socks, if not drenched from head to toe. If the day was sunny we'd hang around the quarry for a while and welt our socks off rocks and leave them to dry.

Boating wasn't our only adventure sport. The Cross, located on the busy main Tralee to Ballybunion road, sees a high volume of traffic pass daily at high speed. We would take fistfuls of calf nuts from cattle troughs nearby and wait for nightfall. Then we'd assume our positions behind walls, trees, hedges, ditches – anything that would conceal us – and wait for oncoming cars. As they passed, we'd unleash a flurry of calf nuts from all angles and wait in hope for the brake lights to swallow up the darkness, reverse lights to follow suit and the driver to begin the search.

With that we were off and the chase was on. Young boys' greatest thrill. We knew our terrain, the only clue our pursuers might have as to our whereabouts would be our laughs piercing the air. Sometimes we'd laugh on purpose. The closer they got, the giddier we became. Later on we were a bit more daring and did it by day.

It was a Saturday and Trevor, Patrick, Alan and I were ducked behind a wall at the Cross. We bought our weapons in Betty's shop down the road. You could get twenty golf-ball chewing gums for 20 pence back then. They were hard enough to make a driver stop, but not so hard as to do any damage to a car. Golf-ball throwing gums I called them. We'd buy twenty each and head back up to the Cross. Patrick was the oldest. He had mastered the art of lying down with his ear to the ground, listening to the road for oncoming traffic. We stood over him waiting for news. The rumble of an oncoming car, he reckoned. We ran for cover and waited. It was time.

Sure enough a car passed by. We'd fire a volley of chewing gums. The familiar sounds, 'rat-a-tat-tat', followed by the screech of brakes. This day the driver was local. He knew his terrain as well as we did. He got out. I stayed put right behind the wall.

Trevor took off back over the fields for home. The car followed, watching him from the road. The laughing quickly turned to that sick feeling you got when you knew you were in trouble. Trevor had to give up the chase. Caught. Voices were raised and all sorts of threats were made. Mothers, fathers, guards, teachers and the parish priest would all be told. We'd do well to be left up the altar for our confirmation. We stayed hidden. 'Who is with you?' demanded the driver. 'I know there are more with you. Where are they?'

Trevor toughed it out. He said nothing until the driver gave up and drove off. He walked home. We all came out of hiding and walked home too, feeling sorry for ourselves, looking over our shoulders and hiding from any cars we heard coming in the distance. We gave up that game of chase pretty quickly.

2

School Days

My first time running on to Croke Park for a game was thanks to my primary school. Lixnaw Boys won the Primary Game hurling tournament in Kerry and I went on to be picked to represent Kerry as part of the Mini-7s Primary Game initiative. A player from the winning school in each county was picked to play a 7-a-side hurling game in Croke Park at half-time in the senior game. In 1992 we got the All Ireland hurling semi-final between Cork and Down. I was around 12 years old and selected as a midfielder for Down. I still have the Down number 4 jersey at home that I wore on the day. Raymond, my brother, went on to play for Clare in the Mini-7s a few years later. We were given strict instructions as to the protocol once we walked out on the field. I forgot myself and ended up walking off on my own before I realized and got back in line. I was mesmerized by the place and started looking around me: the crowd, the size of the stands, the noise, the grass, the lines on the field, the divots dug up by the players. There were humps and hollows on the playing surface back then. It was a very enjoyable experience, although it was over quickly. We had less than ten minutes to play. On the train on the way home I got Tony O'Sullivan's autograph. He was a class wing-forward for Cork at the time. He signed my programme, and I still have it somewhere at home. It was a lesson for me later in life in how to deal with kids who look for photos or autographs. You would hate to let anyone down.

Growing up in Lixnaw and going to Lixnaw Boys National School was a great start to life for me in a sporting and educational sense. It is a learned place. There are an amazing number of teachers in the parish, for some reason. I can think of about fifteen off the top of my head. I was immersed in sport and surrounded by peers who were talented but also ambitious academically. That's a great advantage to have in life, growing up. John McAuliffe, my teacher all through primary school, left a lasting impression on every boy who passed through the school, particularly in a sporting sense. He is a very popular figure in Lixnaw and Finuge. A tall, rangy man with a larger than life character and great pride in his school and students. He took an interest in everyone and is now principal, taking over from John Joe Cantillon who was principal when I was there. When I started off in Lixnaw the senior boys played soccer in the schoolyard with a plastic bottle or a small rock. As junior students we'd watch on until someone would hit the deck roaring after the rock flew off a boot and cracked them on the shin. That was a great laugh for us younger lads, watching an older lad on the ground roaring in pain. We'd have to turn away and pretend to be wrestling or play-fighting so the older boys wouldn't see us laughing. Really we'd be hoping to get on for a game. I'd ask to play with whatever team might be losing to see if I might turn it around. The older boys were moody. Some days I got on, some days I didn't.

At one end the goals were chalked on the red-brick gable of the school building; we used the bike shed at the other. When I got to sixth class we had a full grass pitch at the back of the school and John Mac had organized mini-league GAA competitions. Peter Lenihan, a local man who played for Kerry, joined the school as a trainee teacher and continued them for the year he was there. John's passion for sport was infectious. He was competitive and that rubbed off on all of us. You would always try to impress him as a result. He loved to try to chip a dead ball up off the ground into his hands if it came near him. That was his trick and he liked to show us his skill any chance he got. Every Friday we got to walk to the local community centre to play 5-a-side indoor soccer. That was the highlight of our week. Firstly we were out of class, secondly we were playing soccer and thirdly we got to walk right past the convent where all the local girls went to school. Twice. Those were the good days. The bad days came whenever rain started to fall on a Friday lunchtime and the soccer was cancelled. More class, no soccer and no walk past the convent.

Quizzes were John's other speciality. We had regular class quizzes. As good a way as any to teach and learn. He also coached us at underage level in Finuge. His passion on the side-line was obvious but he was also big on discipline, both in the class and on the field. He always pushed me to be a writer because of the English essays I wrote for him in class. You really should listen to your teachers.

Our time at Lixnaw Boys was short (though it felt long at the time). After John McAuliffe the next mentor I had was Éamonn Fitzmaurice, father of Éamonn Óg. He trained the Lixnaw under-14 hurling team. Even at a young age he was able to capture me in the dressing room with his words. He was passionate and intelligent. I found him inspirational, and that is a rare quality in my experience. We would have done anything for him on the field. Éamonn was príomhoide in GaelCholáiste Thrá Lí and I was tempted to go there for his influence.

In the end I moved on to Causeway comp. Going from an all-boys school to a co-ed school was a real arrival.

John O'Regan was the principal in my time. (I bump into him now and again. He always has a positive message.) His vice-principal was a man whose importance in the history of the GAA (and Kerry GAA in particular) I didn't fully appreciate at the time. Gerald McKenna was the Kerry County Board chairman for the duration of the Golden Years and the man who appointed Mick O'Dwyer manager in 1975. You never would have thought it. He never carried himself with the kind of self-importance you might expect from a man whose decision-making led to Kerry's domination of the game for an unprecedented number of years, in the process creating legends who are still the reference points for anyone playing the game today. Gerald lives in the heart of hurling country in Ballyduff village, not far from Lixnaw, and taught mainly English in school when his vice-principal duties allowed. He was more likely to quote Shakespeare than refer to anything he may have said or done with Micko, Jacko or Páidí back in the day. Any time we meet today we always enjoy great chats. Not long ago I was presenting some medals in the national school in Ballyduff and decided to call on him in the village. I put out some feelers first as I hadn't seen him in some time and didn't want to be landing unannounced. His son was present so I asked him to ask Gerald if I could call for tea. The response was typical Gerald McKenna. Firm and resounding. 'Tell that man he doesn't ever have to ask for permission to visit me.' I ended up staying for two hours chatting about everything from school and education to my career and inevitably Kerry football and the great characters we both knew. Gerald is a man of excellent opinion and is still very tuned in to the game on every level. He doesn't suffer fools or curry favour, and would still make an excellent officer or administrator if he so wished. He reminded me lately that I was never inside his door for disciplinary reasons in school. I wasn't either. I was too focused on other things in school to be a trouble maker, plus I had too much respect for Gerald, John O'Regan and the PE teachers in the school to be causing bother. One of the PE teachers was a Lixnaw man called Willie Dowling, father of two of my good friends, Scruff and Red. Gerry Whyte was head of PE. Another honest man who gave great service to the GAA. On my first day in Causeway Gerry appeared at the door of my classroom. He asked if I was in the room. I put my hand up. Gerry looked down at me, nodded and walked away again. I wondered if I was in trouble but he was just putting a face to the name as it turned out. The head of PE seeking me out on my first day gave me confidence.

John Leahy from Listowel was everyone's favourite teacher. He drove me to a hurling game in Limerick one day and en route stopped off at the newly opened Manchester United superstore in the city. He pulled up outside and went in. When he returned he had the United fanzine and a pen in his hand. He scribbled something on the front of the fanzine and handed it to me. I was a second-year at the time. I looked at the front of the fanzine. 'Bryan Robson' it read by way of autograph. I looked up at him quizzically. John looked back. 'Can't you tell all the lads you met Bryan Robson today?' he said. I did too. He knew I was a big United fan. That was the kind of guy he was. When I left Causeway for UCC he urged me to play Fitzgibbon Cup hurling. I didn't get around to that unfortunately. Although from Listowel, hurling was John's game.

In hurling Causeway competed at a high level. I remember marking Ben O'Connor against Charleville in an under-16 game one day. We hurled against a very strong Killenaule side in a Munster under-16 final in Rathkeale another day. I was only around 14 at the time. Eugene O'Neill and Liam Cahill, who would go on to win All Ireland medals with Tipp in 2000, both played and they beat us on a terrible day. I was part of two All Ireland winning Kerry Techs hurling teams in my time in Causeway. We beat Wexford in an under-16 final back around '93 or '94. That medal counts every bit as much to me as any football medal. In football we won the All Ireland Vocational Schools in 1997 with Kerry Techs. The previous year four of us from the school were involved in the Kerry Techs team. Liam Boyle, Trevor McKenna, Enda Galvin and myself. The three lads made the panel and I was cut. I put the disappointment to work for the Causeway school team. The defiance in me came out. My instinctive reaction was to prove the selectors wrong and get back on the panel. From when I was young I always reacted well to a challenge or setback, which I am grateful for.

Willie Dowling was our school team manager and a selector with the Kerry Techs. I'd have to show him my response on the field for the school. We got to the Munster under-16 final against Coachford Community School in Fitzgerald Stadium a few weeks later. That was the first time I can remember going out on the field feeling like I had a point to prove. I heaped pressure on myself to perform. Knowing the Kerry Techs selectors would be watching gave me a lot of motivation. We won the Munster final and I kicked 7 points – 5 from play, 2 from frees. When the final whistle went I felt a weight off my shoulders. A week later I was called back to the Kerry Techs panel for a semi-final against Donegal. That pressure I felt at a young age was good for me. It focused me. It would visit me a few times in my senior career too. I was always sure of my performance when I felt its weight upon me. You can't rely on it every time you play, though. It wears off you as you get older or you begin to achieve things. Motivation then comes from different places. Better to play and train with natural enthusiasm in the name of seeing how much you can win and how good you can become. I could see why I hadn't been selected for the Techs. I was a small corner-forward and they had plenty of those. I didn't do particularly well in trial games. I hadn't done enough to be selected. A year later in 1997 I played all year at corner-forward for the Techs. We won the All Ireland that May, beating Tyrone in the final in Páirc Uí Chaoimh. There were three of us from Causeway on the team – Trevor McKenna, Enda Galvin and myself – and Tom O'Sullivan was there, who I would go on to play senior with for Kerry.

Later that summer I played Kerry minor football under Charlie Nelligan. I remember the morning he called on my parents' landline to ask me to join the squad. Charlie's was one of the names that stuck with you from the Golden Years. Charlie Nelligan. It rolled off Micheál Ó hEithir's tongue, which meant it rolled off everyone else's tongue too. We beat Cork in Tralee and Limerick in the Munster final the same day Kerry beat Clare in the senior final. I scored two goals and we went on to Croke Park where we drew with Mickey Harte's Tyrone, before losing the replay 0–23 to 0–21 in Parnell Park.

I had a goal chance in the first half of the drawn game but hit the post. I waited for another chance. Like the rain it came from the sky. A high ball rebounded off the top of the post at the Hill 16 end in the second half. I fisted it to the net only for it to be disallowed for a square ball. I felt I had let the team, especially

22

Charlie Nelligan, down. Mikey Sheehy was a selector along with Derry Crowley (Johnny's father), Junior Murphy, and Sean Walsh from Moyvane who went on to become County Board Chairman and served as Chairman of the Munster Council. Sean had a thing for Grenson shoes, which impressed me. Only a cultured man would know anything about Grenson shoes. He is the most stylish man in the GAA. Officially. Charlie was a players' man. He loved to mix it up with fellas on the training ground. He plays in a trad band these days with the same spirit he brought to football and the Kerry jersey.

Martin Beckett from Dr Crokes was one of our best players on that minor team. He quickly progressed to under-21 level winning an All Ireland the following year. He had all the tools to be a senior All Ireland winner for Kerry until he was sadly killed in a car accident later in 1998. Attending his funeral was surreal. I had met him in Tralee during the Rose of Tralee festival not long before the accident. I can still remember the conversation. He told me he was going to Spain on holidays soon. It was on his way home that the accident happened. He was ahead of his time in many ways. On the field he was always one step ahead, anticipating everything as a defender. Off the field he was a step ahead too. He wore Air Jordans and bomber jackets and bleached his hair. Of that minor team Noel and Tadhg Kennelly and I went on to win senior All Irelands. Martin Beckett would have made it four I have no doubt.

Playing with the Kerry Techs and Kerry minors was my priority in 1997. Study wasn't a priority. I wanted to repeat the Leaving Cert for a few reasons. One was I hadn't studied much the first year. It was a dry run. Secondly, I had no idea what I wanted to do after school. A job? College? I hadn't even thought about it. All I thought about was sport. Repeating suited me. A gang of us knew we would be repeating so there was no pressure at all on us doing the Leaving in 1997. We set ourselves up the first year and finished the job the second.

One day in my repeat year I was sitting in Irish class. Our teacher, Timmy Leahy, came in. He was in great form as usual, which always put me in good form. He was a very happy man, always telling stories but always getting the message across too. I like languages, particularly grammar. I sat there listening to Timmy dissect the declensions of the noun in Irish. Everyone hated that stuff. I loved it. I liked deconstructing sentences, looking at the origins of verbs and examining the changes in form that happen as you construct the sentence again. I already understood grammar. That was the hardest part of teaching and learning the subject. I could speak it fluently from when I was young. Timmy was a great advert for teaching it. I decided to be an Irish teacher that morning.

In terms of sport, Causeway Comprehensive was the place I learned how to win. I extended myself every time I trained. Éamonn Fitzmaurice's drive at the club was matched by Willie Dowling's at school. Our under-16 football team trained so regularly after school, and Willie was so demanding a trainer, that we learned to compete for every minute. We always felt we'd win and we were dogged in that belief. All the coaches I had in my formative years – John McAuliffe, Éamonn Fitzmaurice Snr, Willie Dowling, Billy Curtin with the Kerry Techs, Charlie Nelligan with the minors and later on Jack O'Connor – had one common quality. They were all very demanding. Your best effort was a basic requirement. Only effort beyond the bounds of necessity or normality might earn you outright praise, and I think in essence that is what players at any level strive for or should strive for, the praise of a manager you respect for doing something extraordinary on the field for your team. That is what I always strived for. Willie Dowling tells the story of the day he turned around during a training game to find myself and his son Scruff wrestling on the ground. I can't remember what it was over. Scruff says it was because he didn't track a runner and I was on his case. Willie remembers it because we were on the same team at the time. He played on and left us to sort it out. That was the kind of environment I grew up in. We were fighters. We were competitive because we had to be. It was drilled into us.

3

North Kerry – Rebel Stronghold

It's hardly surprising that we are fighters in North Kerry. It is rebel country. A bastion of independence during the time of military struggle in Ireland. This might also explain why it is hurling country, despite there being little to no hurling in the rest of the county. North Kerry seems to breed a particular type of individual. Directional men. No different to the rest of Kerry, perhaps, but North Kerry is synonymous with fighting and rebellion. The area has been a stronghold of the game going back to 1894, when Kerry won the All Ireland in hurling. The whole team came from the North. Éamonn Fitzmaurice's great-grandfather, Moss Fitzmaurice, played on that team. Hurling has somehow survived as the main sport in the area since then. Why? For the same reason that the Irish language survives in West Kerry and in enclaves and outposts around Ireland. People don't want to give in. They don't want to let tradition die. It binds them with their place, their people and their past. There are young lads all over North Kerry, my own club included, who would much rather play hurling than football. I can understand that to an extent, though I will never understand the lack of ambition or guts to go for football if you plainly have the ability.

Proximity to strong hurling counties like Cork, Limerick and Clare is also a factor. We regularly played challenge games in Limerick, Clare and Cork. When we won the county hurling championship in 2005 Eamon Cregan was our manager and Anthony Daly managed the opposition, Kilmoyley. His Clare team were my favourite team to watch, growing up. They were uncompromising ground-breakers. Speaking of ground-breakers, one of Ireland's greatest men comes from my parish. John Byrne came from Kilflynn and broke a lot of new ground as he went. He built The Galtymore dancehall in Cricklewood, a refuge and meeting place for many a lonely Irishman and woman, and many other places of prominence in Ireland and the UK. Through construction he put money in men's pockets and food on women's tables and fostered families of expats. He came back home at the request of Sean Lemass and helped revitalize the Irish economy with his vision. I had seen a TV programme about him called *Damhsa Na Deoraí* on TG4 before I eventually met him in Kerry through his daughter Joanne. Afterwards I was telling Joanne about this great programme I saw on this man from Lixnaw, before realizing I had just met the same man.

When I was younger, hurling was the game I played most. There was a wall across the road from our house, it was the side gable of a neighbour's turf shed and every evening after school I would practise against it at a rapid pace, left and right side, one touch against the wall, over and over. The amount of practice I did when I was young means that today I can pick up a hurley after six months or more and it still feels very natural to me. The rhythm rapidly returns to my wrists. Soccer was my favourite game though. I flirted with it after a local scout saw me play in the school yard as he watched from the roadway. Mike Holly brought me to Listowel Celtic where I first met the

Kennellys, Noel and Tadhg, who would later become Kerry teammates. Getting to games was difficult, though, and the soccer clashed with GAA games, so I didn't play with Listowel for long.

I grew up watching the local county hurling championship games in Tralee. The Neilus Flynn Cup is the holy grail in Kerry hurling, even taking precedence over the county hurling team much of the time. Because the hurling jurisdiction is so small and parochial the local rivalries were becoming a little too intimate. The sliotar could be a right distraction if two close neighbours met on a bad day. A few years back the county board brought in outside referees in the hope that the players might lose interest in each other and be seduced by a mysterious stranger from Cork or Limerick. It worked a treat, which goes to show that most of us men really are elementary. I grew up with a desire to win county championships for Lixnaw, but no real desire to play with the Kerry hurlers. I'd have more desire to play for the Kerry hurlers nowadays, just to win a medal at senior inter-county hurling level.

Lixnaw is my parish and my hurling club; Ballinclogher is my townland and my home. Finuge is the football side of the parish, about 8 miles from where I grew up. Green and Gold has been the story of my sporting life. Every team I ever played for wore those colours: Lixnaw, Finuge, Feale Rangers and Kerry. UCC were an honourable exception. We wore red and white hoops in 1999. But even then there is a synergy: had Ballinclogher – my father's team when he played – stayed in existence my colours would have been red and white hoops too, like the old Cork goalkeeper's jersey. Ballinclogher were known as 'the Holy Terrors'. They could have been a Jihadist faction with a name like that. Somehow Frank Cummins lined out for them one day under a false name, wearing a helmet. I had to wonder who was fooling who there. It would be hard to mistake a man of Frank Cummins' ability, false name and helmet or not. I enjoyed listening to the stories my father's generation would tell about their playing days. Their nickname was well-earned.

Traditionally Lixnaw haven't done so well in the Kerry Championship, winning only seven titles. My generation has won three of those. The top team traditionally in Kerry has been Ballyduff, the club who formed a large portion of that Kerry hurling team who won an All Ireland hurling title in 1894. When I was growing up they were the dominant team. Lixnaw lost a few finals to them in the early '90s when the two Hennessys, John and Mike, were in their prime. They were two fine hurlers. They're both referees now and good ones at that. There were great characters in Kerry hurling when I was growing up. Todd Nolan played for our neighbours Crotta O'Neills. He was a flamboyant player and liked to entertain the gallery. He was a lethal free-taker. He lined up a free near the sideline in a championship game in Austin Stack Park one day. There was a child on the sideline eating an ice-cream cone. Todd walked over and took a bite of it before lining up the free and putting it over the bar. In 1997 we won our first major hurling honour in Kerry, which was a minor county championship medal against Abbeydorney. My first senior game for Lixnaw was in 1996. We played Ardfert in Stacks Park. The first ball I got was in the corner where the stand meets the John Mitchels end. I got out in front, collected and turned towards the sideline away from my man. As I ran for goal a swipe of a hurley split my helmet over my left ear. I fell to the ground and spilled the ball. My man recovered it as I checked that my ear was still there. I figured he cleared it too, as I could just about hear the roar of the crowd over the ringing noise in my left ear. I was like a small bird who had flown into a glass pane, lying on the ground wondering what the hell just happened, dazed and confused more than hurt. I looked towards the ref, then my man, then the ref again. No free. That was an education. I learned quickly.

4

Loosening the Limbs

The first All Ireland medal I won in Croke Park was for hurling. We had won B All Irelands at under-16 and minor level but the under-21 All Ireland win against Kildare in 1998 was different. Maurice Leahy, Mr Kerry Hurling, was manager, and a friend of mine, Sean Flaherty from Lixnaw, was his right-hand man. The players were all sound guys. We had played against each other for years, and almost all of us had been to Causeway Comprehensive. When you have friends involved, people you respect in charge, winning is better. The minor football experience of 1997 stood to me. I was disappointed with my contribution for the Kerry minor footballers when I last played there so I wanted to put that right. The u-21 hurling final was almost exactly twelve months later. The game was fixed for the weekend of the All Ireland senior hurling semi-finals. We headed for Dublin on the train from Tralee. To most of us it was new. I had the minor experience from the year before. We gathered from all parts of North Kerry and some parts of South Kerry too. Ballyduff, Lixnaw, Abbeydorney, Ardfert, Kilflynn, Ballyheigue, Causeway and Kilmoyley. Kenmare in the south provided our best player. T. P. O'Connor was an unstoppable underage hurler. His club-mates Séamus MacGearailt and Jimmy Wharton provided us with a goalie, a full-back and some town swagger that us North Kerry boys might have lacked.

Heading to Croke Park we had plenty going for us. We wouldn't be found wanting for toughness or attitude. We got the train up and settled into the Grand Hotel in Malahide around 6 o'clock on a continental August evening. Maurice Leahy, our trainer, advised us to go off for a stroll on the promenade to loosen our limbs before a team meeting at 9 o'clock. The majority of the panel, loose men from the bogs and forests of North Kerry, stalked down the main street in Malahide laughing with excitement. The sea air got the better of some. The 'disco music' in Gibney's overpowered others. Limbs well loosened, a few went in for a look. A few more followed. They weren't looking for long. A pint was ordered, followed by another. By 8.30 p.m. throats were loose too, and limbs were loose like Elvis. Having had the experience of travelling and preparing and playing with the minor footballers a year earlier this was an eye-opener for me. Drinking wouldn't have been contemplated with the minors. I left wondering how much we'd be beaten by the following day. The last thing I saw as I left Gibney's was one of our main players sitting on a timber barrel in the middle of the bar, with a can of cider in one hand and a blonde girl in the other. It wasn't draped around her in that attentive way it might be when you've just met a girl and you're putting in the hard yards hoping to charm her, but thrown lazily over her shoulder in a way that was just showing her off to the lads. The pleased look on his face was funny. It said, 'Well, this evening has turned out pretty well for me anyway, lads.' I wasn't laughing at the time. An All Ireland was about to be pissed away. I went back to a room of eight or nine players and a furious manager for a team meeting that turned into an inquest. I kept my head down and said nothing. Fellas rolled back in dribs and drabs, a good few pints consumed, limbs so loose they could be knotted. We hit for Croke Park the next day, all arses and elbows. If we lost there would be some questions asked. If we won there would be some stories told.

The game was fixed for 5 p.m. because the Clare–Offaly senior semi-final would be over by then. So we took to the field from the old dressing rooms at the corner of the Hogan and Canal End and we were met by a sea of Offaly supporters. I initially thought Offaly had won, but as we tried to warm up it was clear that the emotions being vented were not those of the victorious but those of the damned. As we manœuvred our way around them, and in between them, more and more poured on to the field. They weren't going anywhere. I asked one man what had happened. He mentioned that the ref had blown the game up early and they were sitting down on the pitch in protest. We imagined they would be moved on. But no – they wanted a replay. The Offaly fans sat down to make a stand and soon large tracts of Croke Park were covered in bodies. It was a great act of rebellion. Stewards tried to usher them off. They shouted and cajoled and harassed and pleaded for them to move: 'WE ASK ALL PATRONS TO PLEASE LEAVE THE PLAYING FIELD AS THE U-21 FINAL IS ABOUT TO COMMENCE,' they bellowed from loudspeakers, but the faithful weren't for departing. I admired their loyalty to their county. It was something to feel their passion and spirit at such close quarters. How could you not be inspired as an Offaly player? They had plenty of inspirational men on the team as it was. The people had spoken.

I stood there watching and I pleaded with them too. They didn't know our backstory, how half our team got loose in

Gibney's the previous evening. Please, lads. This was our big day. Our All Ireland final. We might never get this chance again. Please, please, please . . . stay where ye are.

Our game was cancelled. We won the replay a week later. Considering the display they gave on the day I have no doubt Kildare would have hosed us the first day had it been played. I bagged 2–02 and won my first All Ireland medal in Croke Park. History will show Offaly got their replay and went on to win the '98 All Ireland. What history won't show is they won a loose-limbed Kerry team an All Ireland too. Poetic justice after 1982? I like to think so.

5

Mad to Make It

In a game where players don't get paid, playing in Croke Park is a bonus incentive and medals are currency. 1998 threw up an All Ireland hurling final against Kildare. Feale Rangers also won the under-21 football county championship. The finals were coming thick and fast. 1999 was a windfall: the county senior hurling championship in Kerry, the county senior football in Cork, the Munster Senior Football Club Championship, the under-21 county hurling, the under-21 county football, and a losing county football final in Kerry – all within the space of a few weeks. You would need to be winning a medal a year for all the training to be worthwhile. In '99 we won five major ones and lost out on a sixth by a point or two. When you're 20 years old and playing on strong teams it feels easy – winning everything in sight makes it easier still. The challenge I found in later stages of my career was dealing with not winning things, which sounds silly, I know, but when you have a period in your career like 1998 and 1999 you expect to win again and again. The only one that slipped away in 1999 was the Kerry senior championship with Feale Rangers, when we were beaten by a point by the great East Kerry side led by Séamus Moynihan. Seamo went on to captain Kerry to Sam the following year. He was in his prime back around then, a force of nature at centre-back. Off the field you couldn't meet a better guy, always up for the craic when the game was won.

The story of 1999 was UCC, both locally in Cork and Kerry, and nationally. It all started with a chat with a doctor. Not just any old doctor but Dr Con Murphy, patriarch of UCC and Cork GAA. One day in his surgery, coming towards the end of my first college year, we got to talking about the Cork County Championship. Con asked me if I would get involved. Considering that it would be taking place over the summer months I wasn't sure. I'd be in Kerry, with club commitments of my own. I hadn't really considered it. I told Con I'd see what Éamonn was doing. He was eligible but was doing a Masters in European Integration at the University of Limerick at this stage. If he was going to play I would probably go along. Con told me to tell Éamonn he was playing whether he liked it or not. Éamonn opened the door for me in many ways in football. He led the way with UCC and Kerry.

In 1999 I had just completed my first year and was what would be termed in North Kerry a 'nippy corner-forward' on the Freshers' team. I hadn't anticipated what would happen on this senior adventure, the friends I would make, the success we would have and the craic we would enjoy. Des Cullinane was our manager. He was shrewd. Éamonn was our best player, Kerry's centre-back and our centre-back. He felt a sense of loyalty towards the college, especially when his close college friends, Micheál Ó Cróinín, Seán Mac an'tSíthigh and Alan Quirke, were involved too. He was our leader and carried himself like an inter-county footballer.

Damien Reidy from Limerick was to his left, and we became

good friends in college, as we were in the same geography class too. Damien was a class footballer with good pace and kicking ability off either foot. I would eventually join himself and Éamonn in the half-back line, but, initially, I was a sub for the first few rounds. The campaign started against Bantry Blues down in Castlehaven. They were a really strong side at the time, with several Cork footballers. We drew the first day and won the replay. I didn't start the drawn game but Des picked me for the replay, if memory serves me. We beat Aghada at their place and faced a good Ballincollig side in the semi-final in Páirc Uí Chaoimh, winning a high-scoring game. I had settled in at number 5 by now and, along with Éamonn and Damien, formed a strong half-back platform for the team. Micheál Ó Sé and Gary Stack were a high-fielding and hard-working midfield. At 6 foot 5 inches Gary, from my neighbouring club Listowel, was what would be termed in North Kerry 'the complete opposite of a nippy corner-forward'. His physicality and experience were vital for us. The final would be a showdown with the mighty Nemo Rangers.

Nemo were hot favourites with the team they had. Colin Corkery, Martin Cronin, Joe Kavanagh, Stephen O'Brien were just some of the names amongst other talented younger players. Billy Morgan was in charge, along with Dinny Allen, so they were extra formidable. By now we had been dubbed UCK in the media because of all the Kerry players we had (twelve on the first fifteen), although at that stage we only had Éamonn on the Kerry senior team and a handful of other inter-county players from other counties. The rest of us were novices. We didn't have the experience or quality of Nemo on paper. What we had was lots of football, lots of enthusiasm and a sense of adventure. We didn't really care who we played. We were students and played like it, fearless but smart. One of our best players was our corner-back, Fionán Kelliher from Milltown. He was on the Kerry panel around that time and played wearing a bandana around his head to keep his hair in place. I enjoyed playing with fellas like Fionán. He was easy-going. The team was like that too. Even though we were all driven the campaign was relaxed and enjoyable. We were playing by our own rules. We drew the first day against Nemo and went to the Western Star on Western Road afterwards, as they were our sponsors. We were having a few pints when word came through that the replay was fixed for the following Sunday. It was around 8 o'clock by now and we'd already had a few beers. I had found the game tough. When I heard about the replay I was keen to head off home, so I collared Éamonn by the bar having a few pints with Micheál Ó Cróinín, our captain. I was anxious to get tuned in for the replay so I told the boys we should head home. The two boys were our most experienced players and if they called matters to a close the rest would follow. My suggestion was met with a stony silence and looks of bemusement from the lads. I got the message. Tonight was to be enjoyed. If I was going home I'd be going home alone. I took a look around me at the scene. Fellas were standing on the tables and chairs and on the bar, singing songs and throwing beer mats, a favourite pastime of Éamonn's. There would be no prizes for going home. I joined the party. Tomorrow would look after itself and so would the replay.

The replay did indeed look after itself. We won. Beating a team of Nemo Rangers' stature meant something more. Éamonn had a big game, Damien Reidy got Man of the Match, and I played OK alongside them in the half-back line. Up front Ian Twiss from Milltown got a decisive goal, Liam Murphy from Gneeveguilla tormented them and Billy Sheehan from Austin Stacks was lively too. Because of the big Kerry contingent we were well supported from all over the county. The game was tight throughout. We led for a lot of it but Nemo came back at us. Stephen O'Brien scored a goal to bring them right back with about ten to go. I ended up corner-back in the second half. With minutes remaining Nemo broke through the middle to the Blackrock End goals. Sean O'Brien penetrated to create a two-v-one between himself, Colin Corkery and Seán Sheehy our full-back. Knowing the esteem with which Colin Corkery was held at the time I figured he would pass. I gambled and left my man in the corner early. I could make it to Corkery, but I wouldn't have made it to O'Brien. He slipped it towards Corkery on the edge of the square. As he did I darted in from behind him and intercepted. I took the ball across goals and slipped it to Éamonn who cleared the danger. I hadn't played as well as I would have liked on the day but I felt I had contributed something in that moment. We achieved something special in 1999. A Cork County Championship medal wasn't easily won, especially not against the calibre of teams we beat. We had a great few days after. Our college song rang out all over College Road. Back at the Western Star we were bullet-proof. There was a banquet for both teams the following day, sponsored by TSB bank in the Rochestown Park. Both the hotel and TSB must have been thrilled with the result. Forty-odd thirsty scholars descending on the place for a free bar. Just what a class hotel and high-powered financial institution had in mind for a Monday afternoon. I woke in Gillabbey Street, hopped downstairs to find a few of the boys waiting for me, and headed back down for the Star. I lived with Keith Moynihan from Annascaul. He was on the team too. We were thick as thieves on a diet of chicken tikka.

Witnessing first-hand how the club behaved the day after that replay you were left with nothing but admiration for Nemo.

They stuck together and attended the 'Man of the Match' function, which can't have been easy. It was no surprise to see them roar back and win the championship the following year. By the evening it was time to get out. As we were leaving the hotel, to go back to town, one of the lads spotted a party van in the car park full of accessories. It was unlocked, so about ten of us piled into the back and started messing with balloons, bugles, poppers, hats and badges – you name it, it was there. We decorated ourselves for the night ahead. As we were about to get out we heard the driver's door open and slam shut, and the van took off. We thought it was the owner who had returned. We started roaring and banging on the sides of the van for the driver to leave us out. We thought we would end up in some warehouse on the outskirts of Cork City. Then we realized the van was speeding around the hotel car park mounting speed ramps. One of our own lads had spotted the keys in the ignition and had started it up. We were thrown around the back until the rally driving stopped and we returned to the pits, then got out and ran before anyone caught us. The party van was parked. The party continued.

We went on to win the Munster Club Championship, drawing against Rathcormac of Waterford, winning the replay and repeating that sequence against Doonbeg in the final. The replay was a memorable day in many ways: we played some superb football, showing all the skills of the game and plenty of toughness too. We needed it. Doonbeg were never short of toughness themselves. We were probably lucky to get the draw, but there was no doubt on the second day. Doonbeg adopted a more physical approach but it didn't serve them very well, having two men sent off as we won 1–18 to 0–8. Our biggest player, Eamon Hanrahan, 6 foot 7 inches, was taken out by a punch from a Doonbeg player, who was then sent off. 'Tiny' (as we called him – more evidence of the fertility of the student mind when it came to creating nicknames), hit the deck anyway. He is so big it took him about thirty seconds to eventually topple. All night we shouted, 'Timberrrrrrrrrrrrrrrrrr!!' whenever we saw him. The physicality of the Doonbeg boys was something I would see many more times from Clare teams over the years. I played well enough and won Man of the Match on the day. Later that year I won the AIB Munster Club Footballer of the Year, which was a great honour. At the reception in AIB Ballsbridge I met with some of the other winners there. Oisín McConville from Crossmaglen Rangers, Kieran McGeeney of Na Fianna, and Barry Heffernan from Crossmolina in football; Brian Whelehan, Eugene Cloonan and Jackie Carson in hurling. Cloonan was an interesting guy: he was so talented, yet appeared so shy and kept to himself on the night. What a hurler he was, though.

By the time the All Ireland semi-final came around in 2000 I had damaged my shoulder quite badly in a challenge game. We played CIT in the Mardyke in preparation for the semi-final and I tore the ligaments in my A/C joint and partially dislocated my right shoulder. I remember the crunching noise and the pain, but because I had gone for the hit I couldn't go down, so I played on for a while before coming off. I knew I had done some damage but you try to convince yourself otherwise – until you have no choice. It was bad timing. As I left the dressing room I got a call from Páidí Ó Sé, who wanted me to tog out for a league game against Roscommon the following Sunday. This was my first ever call up to the senior panel. It was early 2000. This was the story of my early Kerry days: it didn't come easily. I told Páidí I wasn't sure, as I had just done something to my shoulder. This was not something he wanted to hear. There was silence on the line. 'It mightn't be too bad though . . . I'll see what Dr Con says.' More silence. 'I'd say I'll be fine . . .' More silence. 'Look it, get that right. Leave it off. I'll be in touch again.' The conversation was short. You wouldn't get too many chances with Páidí. I played the semi-final against Crossmaglen with the aid of an injection. We met a great side, who picked us off. I kicked one point but conceded two to Jim McConville. It was the end of an adventure, one which brought us medals and memories, laughs and luck, and earned us nicknames – and some not so pleasant names as well. I learned a lot from college life in an academic and a sporting context, and made great friends and memories that I still enjoy. Losing the Sigerson Cup final as captain of UCC in 2002 is a memory I don't enjoy. It was very disappointing. Eamon Ryan, our coach, was a brilliant guy.

I learned that though most of us were boys, football at that level was a man's game, and to survive and win you had to be tougher than tough. My football education in the Farm, the Mardyke, the Sigerson Cup and the Cork County Championship was testing, but I graduated. Were it not for UCC I might never have played for Kerry. It was the start of the voyage that brought me to the attention of Páidí and the Kerry senior selectors, but just as importantly to the attention of other Kerry footballers like Éamonn Fitz, Séamus Moynihan and Tomás Ó Sé, senior players whose references are very important for younger players. Established players vouching for an up-and-coming player goes a long way in the eyes of a manager. Sometimes the most important thing you can do is show your peers what you're all about. I have learned more from my various teammates over the years than anyone, and earning their respect in return is the greatest prize I have won in sport. The shoulder injury I picked up along the way proved critical in terms of me making the breakthrough too. It would be sixteen months before I finally got the problem sorted. In the ten months after I damaged it I trained away with physiotherapy and continued playing with strapping. I played wing-back for the Kerry under-21s later in 2000 and tore the A/C ligaments again. I ploughed on with more physio because at 20 or 21 all you want to do is play and win as much as you can while the going is good. There were several medals up for grabs every year. It came to a head down at UCC's training ground, the Farm, one day in early October of 2000. I showed it to Dr Con Murphy, the UCC team doctor. I hadn't been sleeping well – when I lay on my right side the bone would click out of the socket. Con told me to take my top off. I did, and he played around with my arm. The bone was slipping in and out. Con prescribed surgery there and then. I was glad of it at that stage. I had taken it to the limit. Mr Maha Lingam performed surgery in December almost a year on from the injury. The recovery period was six months, during which time I decided that my comeback would be with a view to the Kerry senior team. I was set on it – to the point where I couldn't think of anything else. I was lucky that one of my best friends, Eddie Harnett, is a physio. I could call on him any time for treatment or new methods of strengthening my shoulder and upper body. Without his guidance I wouldn't have come back as strong. He is a progressive thinker, and was employing methods back then that other physios adopted much later. A strain of madness came over me as I was out of the game. There was nothing I wouldn't do to make it with Kerry. One night out in Cork sticks in my memory.

I was in the Bailey in the centre of Cork City. The old Bailey is a pub run by a Kerryman, amongst others. Before it was renovated there was a small central bar area that ran 360 degrees so that you could stand at the counter and still be facing people on the other side of the bar. To the left of the counter were the stairs to the toilets, narrow and wooden. The toilets were old and stale. I was out with a few buddies from college. They were pretty much the same buddies I always had from home – we just moved things to Cork. It was a Sunday night. The year was 2000. There had been National League games played earlier in the day. The National League was none of my business, I was a good way off being any kind of inter-county footballer. My rehab was underway. For that reason I wasn't drinking. Across the bar from me a few of the Cork lads were out for a few pints after their league game. Those were the days when you could do that. I can't remember who exactly was there but I lost interest in my friends and everyone else in the place. All I could think about was the Cork lads, enjoying themselves after a game. That's what it was all about. I wanted a Kerry jersey on my back. Then I wanted medals. All Ireland medals, Munster medals, National League medals; anything and everything that was going, I wanted it. The Cork boys had every reason to be out for a pint. They'd won a game earlier that day. It had been a while since I played a game never mind won one. My mind was working overtime: my next rehab session, my next training session, the date I would return to playing – a date that was still a good many months off. Making it with Kerry was more important to me than anything else. There were nights I would wake at 3 a.m. and 4 a.m. to do my rehab exercises. Scruff, my room-mate, would be sound asleep; I'd be on the floor doing stabilization exercises. An extra session at that time would strengthen me and speed up my rehab significantly. I lifted weights on the makeshift bench I set up on the bedroom floor in the middle of the night, then I would do dumbbell presses, bent-over rows, press-ups and theraband exercises. Anything I needed to do I would do it. If I was told to do an exercise five times I did it ten times. If I was told to do it three times a week I did it every day. I was obsessed with recovery and coming back stronger than before. Where I was weak I would be strong. That was a message I would hear many times more over my career. Where the opposition think you are weak be at your strongest. I messed my shoulder up badly by refusing to accept it was hurt. I played on it for almost a year. The situation went on so long I swore I would never be injured again. Getting back was one thing; getting to where I wanted to go was another. I knew exactly where I wanted to go. To the top of the game. For now the top of the stairs would do. I went upstairs to the toilets in the Bailey and into a cubicle. One hundred sit-ups and a hundred press-ups later I re-emerged. What had I proved? I don't know. Something. Nothing. Everything. One thing was clear. I was absolutely mad to make it.

6

Just Enough Education to Perform

Study took a back seat for me in college in comparison to my Leaving Cert year. I attended lectures but regular study was left closer to exam time, as is the case with a lot of students. In the first year you picked four subjects, two majors and two minors. I picked Irish and geography as majors, archaeology and Léann Dúchais as minors. I initially picked French then swapped it for Léann Dúchais, I think, which is the study of Irish folklore stories. Archaeology was a strange one too. I'm really not sure why I chose to do that.

I wasn't as interested in college study. 1999, in particular, was all about football. The games kept coming and they took easy precedence over lectures. A few good buddies of mine looked out for me when it came to lecture notes if I happened to miss any lectures, especially Ger Murphy, my cousin, who was in a few of my classes. Ger is a great friend and character, and back then he was a great man to share notes and generally find short-cuts or loopholes in the system. He went on to get his degree and become a guard. If anyone is the epitome of the cute Kerry man it is Ger. For that reason I take particular pleasure in catching him out with crank phone calls. I have caught him with a few. There was one concerning a greyhound that went almost every day for a week until I handed myself in. I have mastered a range of accents that even a university-educated guard can't crack. Ger's dad, Mike, and my father were great friends, until Mike passed away. Ger and myself have become great friends as well since.

On my first day in UCC I sat in on the introductory Irish lecture in the science building on campus. The idea of finding the science building to attend an Irish lecture only added to the sense of confusion we were all experiencing. Then again there is little in life as receptive to information as a fresher student on his first day, so I wasn't long finding my way. I walked up the side aisle to the back of the lecture theatre and took a seat as close to the back of the room as possible. I happened to sit right next to a guy called Keith Moynihan, who I knew vaguely through a mutual friend, Ciaran Fitzmaurice. We were in the same classes, except for geography, and on the same Freshers' football team. Neither of us had a pen on our first day. This could have been construed as a bad omen for our academic aspirations but, like any earnest scholars, we didn't focus on the problem but worked together on the solution. We borrowed a pen from a girl sitting next to us in that lecture and used it between the three of us to take notes. We've been on the same page ever since.

Leaving home to go to university is a big move in anyone's life. Being able to adapt is important. I was lucky in that there were a good few of my classmates in Causeway going to Cork, either UCC or CIT, so there were some familiar faces on Galvin's bus every Sunday evening: Scruff, Trevor, Keith, Ciaran Fitzmaurice, Karl McCarthy and Anthony Whelan made for good company. Ciaran and I moved into digs on Highfield Avenue, off the Model Farm Road, with a lovely woman called Betty O'Sullivan who looked after us like we were her own. Betty lost a son in a road accident and I think she enjoyed our company. We often spoke with her late on Sunday nights after we arrived up from Kerry, and she would tell us all about life in Cork. We ate like kings and slept in comfort every night. It was an urban area, though peaceful. Paddy Casey's song 'Sweet Suburban Sky' always reminds me of Highfield Avenue. It was a song I listened to a lot in that first year. At the bottom of Highfield Avenue there was a wall. From there at night-time you could see the night sky brushed orange by thousands of city street lights. The only light you saw at night in Lixnaw came from the moon – after that there were the dots of speckled light you might see from the handful of homesteads on the hills around the parish. We didn't have street lights in the country. I had gone from rural to urban living. Highfield Avenue backed on to the Bishopstown GAA club. Over the same wall lay a smaller juvenile playing pitch, off the main pitch. I would spend evenings in the dark practising my kicking or doing extra training and running drills under those same street lights.

The main improvement I felt from my time in college was a physical one gained in the Mardyke gym in Cork City. My ball skills were always good but my physique needed work to make it at inter-county level. I worked really hard on my body. Thanks to Eddie Harnett, I came back from the shoulder operation twice as strong and ready for the step up to inter-county. Away from football and training I enjoyed life in Cork. Ciaran and I had a good laugh living in Highfield. A cousin of my dad's, Thomas Murphy, lived at the top of the avenue, and across the road on Bishopstown Avenue lived Dr Con Murphy, although in first year I didn't really know him. With plenty of good memories Ciaran and I moved on from Betty's house. I moved in with Keith on Gillabbey Street the following year, sharing a room with my old school friend Scruff. In primary school Patrick Dowling, aka Scruff, was in a bad accident, stepping off the school bus straight into a van. He spent weeks in hospital in a coma. John McAuliffe started a few morning classes with prayers for him. Scruff pulled through in the end, and the world is a better place for that. He suffered a badly broken leg in the accident. Years later he told me the story of his time in hospital. He awoke from a three-week coma with his right leg in torsion and severe pain in his left. For three weeks his good leg had been put in a cast and his broken left leg lay untouched beside him. Once I knew it was OK to, I laughed, and luckily Scruff has a good sense of humour. We both needed a sense of humour at times in Gillabbey Street. Our room was like a thrift shop. You could just about make out the beds hidden under books and notes, behind weights and barbells, clothes and shoes.

One of my best memories from college is of a geography field trip we took to Paris. It wasn't my first time there but it was definitely a new experience. I hardly knew anyone except for Ger Murphy, my cousin. We quickly got to know a tall, funny guy from Cork called Gary Wade. Gary and I hit it off after he passed some remark at the start of an introductory talk. I was the only one who laughed. We both wondered why no one else was laughing until we realized the talk was underway and everyone else was trying to listen. It's funny how you get to know people. That trip to Paris brought me a new circle of friends.

College life was good to me. I learned some, obviously. The most important thing I learned in college was adaptability. I had to adapt to a new environment, new people, new subjects, new demands, and a new position on the field. On my very first day I had to adapt to the fact that I had no pen. A man called Max

McKeown says in his book, *Adaptability: the Art of Winning in an Age of Uncertainty*, that all failure is a failure to adapt, all success is successful adaptation. I can relate to that. Students are nothing if not adaptable. From that point of view I was a good student.

Graduation from UCC meant looking at postgraduate qualifications. I applied for the Higher Diploma in Education and got it. My teacher training took me to Douglas Community School and then on to Críost Rí for my first teaching job, fresh out of college. This graduation to working life meant a graduation in living arrangements too. We left Gillabbey Street after four years and went to live by the sea. We rented a house on the Lough. Our previous landlord Tim MacCarthy was extremely good to us, which was a blessing. He is a regular at Kerry matches and one of life's good guys.

Joining the workforce as a teacher was a novelty. I was on the more conventional, socially acceptable path in those days. Get an education, then a job, then a mortgage, settle down with a nice girl, marry and have kids. I wasn't mature enough to see another way of life back then. As soon as that maturity grew in me I realized that there were other ways to live. Realizing that the more conventional way of life wasn't for me was great. I taught for nearly ten years, which was plenty. At first the independence and job security was great; earning the kind of money I was on as a young substitute teacher was an eye-opener – 800 or 900 quid a week wasn't unusual if you had enough hours' teaching combined with hours' covering free classes for other teachers. By the end I was earning just over half that amount on almost full hours in the Sem. There have been two or three further cuts to teachers' pay since I left.

Life was very comfortable back then, no doubt. Once Kerry started winning All Irelands it got better. Sean Flaherty, my old friend from Lixnaw, was a customer of Des Adams, the Renault dealer in Tralee, and between them they arranged a Renault Mégane for me to drive as an ambassador. The deal lasted longer than any of us expected. Des's head of sales was Noel O'Connor, a big Kerry fan from Causeway. I ended up buying Noel's house off him a few years later. Críost Rí was a great place to work. The kids were full of character and a bit of devilment. The staffroom was lively too. There was a good mix of young and experienced teachers. My boss at the time there was a man called Tomás O'Caoimh, a former Christian Brother. Tomo was like the kids in many ways: full of devilment too. He'd see me coming along the corridor and break into a grin. Then he would do anything from shadow-box me to reciting a poem. I'd stand there and laugh. I never thought it appropriate to spar with him. He was a man who really enjoyed his job. He seemed to enjoy small things, like dressing up in fine suits every day. Fashion has that power for some people. That trans-formative power to alter or enhance someone's mood. To some, fashion is frivolous (and that is fine too) but it goes deeper than that for others, and that should be respected not laughed at. It can be a symbol of status that can bring happiness and con-fidence. Tomo loved his suits and especially his ties. If he wasn't in the mood to perform he would call me to one side and turn his tie over to show me the label on the back. 'See that? Ralph. 100 per cent silk. Savile's.' Then he'd walk off. He might throw a look over his shoulder to see my reaction and start laughing. I'd tell him I didn't like the colour just to take some of the steam out of him. He was a unique character.

I did my first bit of coaching in Críost Rí with the school under-14 team. We won the Simcox Cup, which is a Cork schools championship. They were such a talented bunch that they didn't need much coaching. The following year I got involved with a hurling team. Michael Hassett, a roguish colleague from Tipperary, coaxed me into it and we had great craic together.

The staffroom in Críost Rí was a good place. I looked forward to going to work every day. Aidan Moynihan, who I knew from the club football scene in Kerry, was there before me, as was Micheál Ó Sé from my Kerry minor and college ball days, so settling in was easy. John Paul Sheehan was another pal of mine from Castletownbere. Fergus Fitzmaurice, a friend of mine from Lixnaw, joined to do his teacher training. Críost Rí was home from home. Outside of the lads the man I got on best with was Mick Evans. He was the boss when it came to GAA in Críost Rí, training the senior football team for years and winning the Corn Uí Mhuirí. Outside of the football he was a great support, and a sounding board for me and all staff from a professional point of view. He is a man of absolute integrity who would do anything to help you. You don't forget people like that. People like Mick and Billy Reidy, a Maths teacher at the time, were great men for a hop-ball. Nothing was off-limits. Mick is now principal of the North Mon secondary school on Cork's northside and has seen student numbers boom since he took charge. Jim Cremin, a Nemo stalwart, was another whose company I enjoyed. He would tell me great stories about local characters from Nemo Rangers, the Capwell area, and former colleagues in Críost Rí. Jim and Billy Morgan are great friends of mine. Billy was one of those characters I admired from afar, though he was the enemy being manager of Cork at that time. I have enjoyed his company and that of Colman Corrigan, one of his lieutenants, a few times over the years and always felt at ease.

Cork was good to me for many a year. I got my first taste of life living away from home, learned how to cook, clean, work, pay bills and take responsibility for myself; it gave me an education and my first real job. Getting to know Cork people was interesting. I listened more than I spoke, and that pays with Cork people. You can learn a lot from them. I admire their wit and their chippy nature. My formative years, as a player and a person, were spent there. I'm not one for having heroes or idols but the two sportsmen I most admire are both Corkmen, Roy Keane and Ronan O'Gara. I might have made a good Corkman too: dual player with a bit of an attitude. I grew up in Cork in many ways. I learned what it took to be a top inter-county footballer. It was while teaching in Críost Rí that I eventually made the breakthrough for Kerry.

That breakthrough took a while. It didn't come as easily as it should have. Twenty-four years old is late enough to the party, but that wasn't without its advantages. I learned during that time – 2000, 2001 and 2002 – what it was like to be a supporter. I felt the passion of the fan. Later on, as a player, I often thought back to how I felt on the terraces watching Kerry play. That is why being booed never bothered me; I understood that that was just the passion of the fan. For some reason I do elicit strong emotion in people. I watched Kerry play enough times to know I definitely wanted to be on the field and not in the stands. I went to the final in 2000 against Galway and got a sense of what it was like for the players at the post-match reception. Éamonn had won his first senior All Ireland at centre-back. A gang of us from Lixnaw went up to support him and went on to Leopardstown for the reception afterwards. That definitely whetted my appetite.

The All Ireland semi-final against Meath in 2001 stands out for the opposite reason. My cousin Rich was home from New York and we went to the game together. He played football as a youngster in Rockland County and travelled to Ireland for the Féile in the early nineties. We were both excited to see Kerry play. From the middle of the Cusack Stand we watched Meath massacre our county. In 2002 I was on the panel and actually made my league debut against Leitrim in March. Torn ankle ligaments in May put me out for two months, so I watched that year's final from home when Armagh beat us. Those two defeats left their mark on me even though I wasn't playing. Kerry were brought to their knees. I was close enough to smell the action. In 2003 I wanted a taste.

7

'Go in There and Work Like F**k . . . and Whatever You Do, Don't Kick the Ball'

I'm standing beside Páidí on the sideline in Fitzgerald Stadium. It's July 2003. Munster Final. It's hot in the kitchen. Out on the pitch Limerick are putting it up to us. Again. Páidí has his left hand on my right shoulder. He's facing the pitch as he directly instructs me, all five fingers on his right hand extended as he presses his palm away from him towards the pitch with each word for emphasis, like he's bouncing a basketball. As the play develops in front of us he rises up on his tippy-toes. His head is out on a stalk, his polo shirt is un-buttoned, his collar is upturned and he's sweating. He's wired. Wired in like he was as a player. Absolutely in tune with the game and with his players, even the subs. We're down to 14 men and there's not much in the game with 15 minutes to go. I know what he wants from me, what he needs, to go in and work like a madman, win ball for us, win it back from them when they have it, win breaks and win tackles and bring some energy and intensity to our game. I can do that. And I suppose, more importantly, I know what he doesn't want: for me to kick the ball and risk giving it away. He was very clear on that. Possession was king with Páidí. Two things would happen after I went on. I'd raise the intensity levels . . . and I'd kick the f**king ball. I go on wing-forward on the stand side playing towards the dressing-room goals. The very first ball I get, I turn and look inside. Cinnéide moves out from full-forward towards the 13 position. I pop it about 25 yards into his chest. He wins it and gives it back to me. I move it back infield with a hand-pass. Páidí's not very far away from me on the sideline. I keep moving, for fear I'd find myself standing beside him again.

This incident stuck in my head after the game. There were a few lessons in it for me. Páidí was sharp, because at the time my kicking was not up to scratch. In training I was liable to give it away. I could win it anywhere, anyhow. Keeping it was an issue. He knew that. Even though I probably knew it myself I didn't want to accept it. So I kicked the ball. He had no problem delivering the message either, which is something you always appreciate, especially in a manager. What's more he was pragmatic enough to accept I had qualities that he needed on the day, so he simply told me not to do what wasn't needed. I thought that was smart management, even if I didn't like hearing it at the time. If you can't accept straight talking on where your strengths and weaknesses lie and where you must improve then you're never going to be a top player. If you hide from that kind of straight talk you're unlikely to develop. Even though I was a good kicker, technically, I was liable to give it away by not keeping it simple or not being composed on the ball. Even a year later in 2004 when we won an All Ireland my kicking still wasn't up to scratch. By 2005 I had improved and by 2006 I was happy with it. From there to the end of my career kicking was my biggest strength.

To get it to the level where I felt it was the best it could be took practice. I would drive to the Finuge pitch on non-training days and kick hundreds of balls. I'd stop by the Corridans' house and grab a bag of footballs from Maurice, Pat or Jack, whoever had brought them home from training the previous night, and go to the pitch to practise. It was amazing the difference those few kicks could make the following night at Kerry training. Instead of going to training to practise or improve you were going to execute what you'd already been practising alone. That approach served me well in my career. I never waited for a Tuesday or Thursday to train and improve. I did that every other day and went training to execute and per-form and carry out the manager's instructions at the highest level I could. An hour's practice on non-training nights makes you feel more comfortable and confident in your ability to deliver a ball anywhere you want to put it. The few hours a week you spend on the training field alone aren't going to improve you to a level where you're at the very top of your game. The other thing I learned from that cameo was that I saw everything as a challenge back then, and I had a defiance which meant I couldn't accept what Páidí perceived to be a weakness in my game without doing something about it. I had to face up to it. Where they think you are weak you must be at your strongest. It wasn't a criticism at all, really, it was coaching. We went on to win the Limerick game and the Roscommon quarter-final game before we came upon Tyrone for the semi-final. The Munster final was the only action I saw that year. Looking back now I can see what Páidí saw. Someone who was raw but risky. Although I felt I had something to offer, for sure, I can understand now why Páidí was hesitant. The sideline is nowhere to be in Croke Park but that's where I was for Tyrone in 2003. An onlooker for a car crash none of us really saw coming. We knew they were good but Tyrone hit us with a force Croke Park hadn't seen in a long time. Maybe ever. I say 'us' but really I wasn't part of it. I sat on the sideline rubbernecking as the stands shook. Being outdone in Croke Park like that wasn't easy to accept. Being a sub wasn't easy to accept either. I wanted responsibility. To be in amongst the bodies, doing my bit to help the men out there. Still, I was close enough to the action. Close enough to see it unfold. Close enough to feel the intensity. By the end there wasn't much honour left for any Kerryman that day. The battle lines had been re-drawn. In fact they had been erased. The whole field was a battle zone from where I stood. We went home to regroup. If there was a reason, outside of my own personality, for my uncompromising nature in a Kerry jersey, I'll give you three: 2001, 2002, 2003. I had the taste I was after. I was hungry for more. If it was a war they wanted, a war they would get.

Páidí and I weren't as close as he was with Éamonn Fitz, who was one of his lieutenants. Strong physically, but most importantly strong mentally, Éamonn was responsible and dependable. Add in a good kicking game and an ability to win breaks – he was just Páidí's type. In later years I got to know Páidí a bit better. We both regarded each other with an equal degree of respect and bemusement. Neither of us quite knew what to make of the other, which made our conversations more like verbal jousting, each trying to figure out whether there was more to what was being said or to take it at face value. Usually there wasn't, but you could never be sure. When we ran out of things to say to each other Páidí would say, 'You're a great character,' to fill in the gap. Again, I had to examine this. I took it to mean I was a bit eccentric, which I suppose I couldn't argue with. Some people might say Páidí was eccentric too. I enjoyed his company. Not long before he died I called back west to see him. We had some enjoyable conversations. We would speak about football, of course, but I liked to draw him out about art and photography too. He had an eye for a good photo and promoted artists locally. I sat with him and Ger Loughnane in TG4 one day as we waited to film a quiz show *as Gaeilge* back around the tail end of 2010. The lads asked about my plans for the new year. I was a bit disillusioned with the game at that point. I wasn't sure of my plans for 2011. The lads' backs were up on hearing this. They felt that I had been harshly treated and that I should return to play more determined than ever. I could sense something of both men's greatness there and then. They were born defiant.

8

What is Greatness?

Fitzgerald Stadium. July 2004. Munster final. The time is somewhere around 3 p.m. The sun is shining so brightly and it's so hot that every breath I take dries my mouth out. I can't swallow. There's a pace and intensity to the game that leaves me breathless. I need air, but not as much as I need water. There's a guy following me around the field. He's hopping off me, telling me, 'Ye're fucked,' as they rattle off another score and reel us in closer and closer to the bank. They'll catch us pretty soon at this rate. We'll be nicely done too if they do. Burned to a cinder, more like. The Kerry public will take care of that and the rest of the country will eat us without salt. We won't get much grace and we won't deserve any. We might get some disgrace all right, but there should be no disgrace in it if we lose. We're playing a proper championship team. Still, we're at home, in Killarney. We can't allow defeat.

This is the first time I've experienced the type of 'man-marking' I would come to expect in later years, especially in the Munster Championship.

There's a water boy coming on every few minutes chirping at me too. He's roaring at my man, pushing his buttons, egging him on. 'Give it to hiiimm!!!!' He thinks he's on the terrace. He's sunburned and sweating and it looks like that's where he belongs. I ignore him. He sprays water down my back and legs before giving it to my opponent. I ignore him some more. Galleryman. All he wants is a roar from the crowd and an alter- cation that will earn him a few free pints later that night. He wants to be a somebody. Good luck to him. I keep my focus. My man isn't much better, trying it on off the ball, hopping off me, tripping me up, talking nonsense, roaring and shouting. During a break in play he ploughs into me with a shoulder from behind. I throw back an elbow into his ribs. He goes down. The crowd get up, his teammates too. They surround the ref, shouting at him to take action. Four or five of them are making a scene. It's like they were waiting for this to happen. Mick Curley takes it all in, takes his time, goes to the linesman and correctly books me. Darragh Ó Sé comes over and has a word: 'Steady up, we need you here.' That focused me again. I admired his presence of mind never losing sight of the bigger picture. I nearly gave Limerick what they wanted, but for a strong referee in Mick Curley. We were steeped to get a draw in Limerick the first day. This Munster final replay is anyone's with 15 minutes left. If we don't do something to arrest the momentum that has begun to go the other way we're done for. The Big Mo, your best friend and your worst enemy. No worse enemy there can be in sport: not a man-marker, nor a water boy, a referee, nor a lines- man, the conditions nor conditioning, tradition nor the lack of it.

It's hard to define exactly what momentum is, or when it comes to bear on a game. It just manifests itself at a given stage when someone acts. It can be slipping through your fingers, deserting you, siding with the opposition – until someone rises up in defiance, makes a stand, and wrestles it back. The great players have the composure to read what's happening at the time and the balls to do something about it.

A Limerick kickout from the scoreboard end. That's where the sun is blazing from too. I'm at the stand side of the pitch, using my hand to screen my eyes as I look in towards the goal. 'This is the one,' I tell myself, a vital possession is on the way. Time to act. Win it. Out it comes, long and high towards the middle of the field. I wasn't the only one with my hands full that day. Darragh had it all on too. No better man to find a way to get the upper hand some way or other. And no better man again to act when a game is in the melting pot. I wait for the break, trying to stay loose. The worst thing you can do under a break is tense up. Stay loose, ready to pounce in whichever direction, left or right, high or low. Sometimes there's just no way of telling which way the ball will fall. Winning it comes down to the speed of your reactions, or the keenness of your instincts, or the size of your heart. There was no break this time. As the ball descends, Darragh ascends. He catches it about a foot above me. I'm crouched underneath him as he goes up. Limerick men strain to get near him. I can see the white soles of his Copa Mundials. I can see the determination etched across his face, the power coursing through his arms – and momentum itself turning its back on Limerick and rejoining the Kerry team. He claims the ball, and with it, control of the game. Momentum is fickle. I feel a surge as the crowd take in Darragh's catch. As they roar I take off and run and run and run. I spend the rest of the game running. And tackling. And working. And doing whatever else I have to do to get us over the line. The adrenaline drove me on to the end. We went on to win a raging Munster final, a battle that steeled us and primed us to win the All Ireland in '04. That Limerick side were close. As close as any team came to winning a Munster

Championship. They gave us the toughest games we had that year, but we were a team on a mission. We weren't short of tough characters: William Kirby, Liam Hassett, Johnny Crowley, Éamonn Fitz, Tomás, Aidan O'Mahony, Darragh. We were bold and hardy. We needed to be to face down that Limerick team.

I got my first taste of what it was like to be distracted by my opponents, on and off the field, that day. Water boys were getting in on the act. I got my first taste of the real heat of championship football. It was searing. I liked it. I liked the pressure, the intensity, the requirement to stay highly concentrated. I liked the crowds and the noise. I liked the fact that, despite the crowds and the noise, sometimes all I could hear was the sound of my own breathing – in and out, in and out – like I was sucking air in through my ears as I trawled my reserves of fitness to recover and go again. I had learned that crunching my abs, really clenching my core muscles deep in around my spine, somehow helped me to recover quicker. Twenty seconds I gave myself. That was enough. I liked that at certain times it was just about survival. I liked hiding the fact that at stages I was more vulnerable than any one of the thousands watching could imagine: weak, tired, my lungs screaming for oxygen to give to my muscles. Hiding that weakness was my strength. I never let it show. More importantly I learned that momentum can take 30, 40, 50 or 60 minutes to build, brick by brick, inch by inch, run by run, tackle by tackle, break by break, score by score – and can be lost in one second, to a lapse in concentration or to a leader.

Who was the greatest player I played with over my career? I don't know. Gooch? Tomás? Marc? Mike Mac? Seamo? Éamonn Fitz? Declan? Star? William Kirby? Hassett? How do you choose? What is greatness anyway? I don't know who the greatest player I played with is, but maybe Darragh was the most influential because he could grab momentum by the throat and change its mind. That, in my book, is greatness.

I have a great belief in Kerry football. If there is a single cause for that belief it is the 2004 All Ireland win. If you take the win in the context of the three previous seasons then it was a more notable achievement than people think, and one that I often referred to internally over my career. When you consider where Kerry football was at late in 2003, coming off the back of a hammering by Meath in the 2001 All Ireland semi-final, the 2002 final loss to Armagh and the destruction by Tyrone in 2003, there was ground to make up. We were at a crossroads. The signage was confusing. We knew where we wanted to go. How to get there was the question? Which direction to take? Winning an All Ireland was a long shot. Luckily Jack O'Connor had a roadmap for the journey. Even so our first route took us down a dead-end. We lost our very first league game of 2004 against Longford in Pearse Park. If winning the All Ireland was a long shot in late 2003, by the first weekend in February 2004 it was a long shot in the dark. The previous three seasons' defeats could have finished Kerry for years, yet didn't. We started the 2004 league campaign in the worst manner possible, which could have thrown us off course, yet didn't. We went the rest of the year unbeaten and won the All Ireland final without our two best players, Darragh Ó Sé and Séamus Moynihan. Out of the experience gained on that 2004 journey I formed a set of reference points that I still use today.

After a year or two of knocking on the door I got the nod from Jack O'Connor. He had taken over from Páidí in the winter of 2003. The circumstances of the changeover were messy. I made my debut for Kerry under Páidí but never made the breakthrough. Still, I was grateful to him for giving me a look at it. I learned plenty in that year. By the time Jack took over I was 24 years old. Not exactly straight out of minor. At our January 2004 training camp in La Santa, Spain he spotted me sitting on the side of a pool recovering from a session. Those early sessions under Jack were information-heavy as well as labour-intensive. Jack had to get his message across on the training field. Pat Flanagan had drilled us on the basics of our running technique. There was a lot to take in. Jack came over and sat beside me and told me I had what he was looking for, and a jersey was mine if I was able to show him I had the balls to wear it and the brains to do what he wanted. He had a system in mind and needed players to suit. That was all the encouragement I needed. It was an example of Jack's man-management skills: he could connect with players. I played every game throughout the league and played well. My job was simple – basic, but necessary for the team to function. I would only learn later on in my career just how necessary. The fundamentals had to be looked after every day we played. Taking care of them gave us consistency and a platform to play on. If I didn't take care of the fundamentals the team would splutter. That was my job. Jack was happy with me and how I was carrying out that job. We went on to win the league. That was important. We beat a high-quality Galway side in the final. Pádraic Joyce, one of the best forwards of the last quarter of a century, Michael Donnellan, a favourite player of mine, and, likewise, Declan Meehan, were just three of the Galway players who had won All Ireland medals three years earlier. These three were top-drawer foot-ballers. I marked Meehan in that league final. He was at his peak back then and the best player I marked in my career by a distance. He was fast but he was also strong, aggressive and really good on the ball, which meant he was the type of player that occupied half-forwards rather than the other way around. He was also the cleanest player I marked. He was too busy dictating games to be negative. I learned a bit that day. Dictating games was exactly what I wanted to do. Back then I was all intensity. A few minutes into the final I tackled three Galway players in rapid succession. In the process, I accidentally dislocated Mike Frank Russell's elbow. Mike Frank Russell was like Gooch back then, a rare bird. I was a rare bird myself. I'm just not sure which type.

I had a good league campaign overall. And a medal at the end of it. Everyone said the serious business started with the championship. I couldn't see the difference myself. It was all serious business to me. By the time we went to Clare in the first round I was ready to crack on. I was taken off 10 minutes after half-time having played poorly. The following day out was against Cork in Killarney. After Clare the defiance kicked in. I trained even harder. Killarney. Cork. Perfect. I was dropped for that. When the team was picked I was so disappointed after training that I couldn't eat my dinner in the Gleneagle. I sat across from Johnny Culloty, our selector, who sensed my disappointment. Gentleman that he is he made small talk, and told me I'd be back in again for the next game. Johnny is from that easy, old Kerry stock that carry themselves with easy class and confidence. He is a man I have a lot of respect for. We would often chat about hurling. Johnny hurled for Kerry and has a great knowledge of the game. We won that game against Cork. I came on as a sub and got ready for a Munster final against Limerick. I got back in for that as Johnny promised and was named at centre-forward. This would finally be the day I announced myself on the big stage. I was ready. We drew in Limerick. Just about. My man got Man of the Match even though I was one of our better players. We won the replay in

Killarney. So by the quarter-final in August 2004 this was my track record. It was rookie stuff. Hardly inspiring. Somehow it did just that. Inspired me to do better.

That quarter-final was against the Dubs in Croker. This was the day I finally found my feet and discovered what the game was all about – why we did what we did, trained the way we did, strove the way we strove. I remember the moment when I felt it, the excitement of the occasion, the feeling of belonging. It happened at half-time, just as we arrived back on the field for the second half. There wasn't a ball or opponent in sight. We were out on the field first. I had played well enough in the first half. The scores were level at half-time. It took the Dubs a while to come back out for the second half. As we waited I stood at the Hogan stand side of the field, playing towards the Hill. It was in rapture. One of those sights and atmospheres that are rare in GAA. Rock 'n' roll. The Dubs supporters rocked and they rolled and punched the air with every word, their hands flitting like a shoal of fish in a sea of blue. They sang in unison: 'Come . . . on . . . you . . . boys . . . in blue, comeonyouboysinblue, come on you boys, comeonyouboysinblue!!! . . .' I stood there looking up at this concert. I found myself filling with energy, and as the words grew louder the rhythm grew faster and I found myself singing along in my head: 'Come . . . on . . . you . . . boys . . . in blue, comeonyouboysinblue, come on you boys, comeonyouboysinblue!!! . . .' I loved it. I was thinking the very same thing as those Dublin fans up on the Hill: 'Come on out and let's get it on.' I've loved playing the Dubs in Croker ever since. Right up to my last day against them. I wasn't prolific in my career, but I got more scores against Dublin than any other team in league and championship. I always used the atmosphere as energy. Just like the Dublin players did. If you aren't in some way inspired by the atmosphere in Croke Park playing against

Dublin you will struggle. We embraced it and used it against them.

They came out and we went on to win 1–15 to 1–8. I got my first senior score in Croker that day, taking a pass from Éamonn Fitz to make it even better. The Holy Terrors. I grew into my role as a ball winner, break winner, tackler and link man from there. That moment at half-time seemed to flick a switch in me. I was turned on. In the semi against Derry I was better again, and for the final against Mayo it all came together for the team. When that happens everyone looks good. Jack had an ability to predict games. The morning of the 2004 final he broke the game down to a tee. He predicted what would happen, how exactly we would beat Mayo. We beat them pretty close to how he said we would. He picked Johnny Crowley on the basis that the Mayo lads wouldn't be used to working with men of Johnny's size in training, considering the size of the Mayo forwards. I marked Peader Gardiner that day. He liked to attack so I had to be defensively sound. I enjoyed that work. When the final whistle went the field was overtaken by our tribe. One of the first people I saw sprinting towards me was my friend and club-mate Fergus Fitzmaurice. It is hard to describe that kind of joy. It never lasted long for me, and I'm glad of that because if it did I might never have won another medal. I made my way to the stand and watched as Cinnéide raised Sam towards the sky. With that he raised us all to a new place and he raised the spirit of a county that twelve months previously had its belly on the floor and its face in the mud. I thought of my cousin, Conor Smyth, my uncle Jack and all the great Kerry players of the past reaching down from above for a touch of the silverware as Cinnéide raised it. He was a great captain all year. His speech captured both the essence of the place he came from and the essence of Kerry. Cinnéide is a man of integrity and intelligence. He isn't someone who is dictated to. He follows his own agenda. 'Whatever it takes,' was his mantra all year. He would say it to me before every game. That mantra made perfect sense to me. That was how I saw things too.

Having had three setbacks at the beginning of the championship I finished with three strong displays winning an All Ireland and an All Star. There couldn't be more difference between my first three championship games in '04 and my last three. That became a reference point for me for the rest of my career. If I ever needed to give myself perspective I thought back to 2004. I told myself I got better the longer the year went on, regardless of circumstances or setbacks. If you tell yourself something enough you will believe it. If you believe it you become it. That was my belief. I never lost faith in myself. Circumstances will get tough – so get tougher than the circumstances. You can only do that by asking yourself tough questions. The truth is the truth. You're better off knowing it than not. I looked at my performances in my first three championship games and realized I could do much better. So I focused on doing better. By the last three games I did much better. Find positive reference points, look for them, write them down and return to them whenever you need to steady the ship.

I started out raw and hungry, suffered a few setbacks along the way that didn't break me, and came out the other end with a league medal, a Munster medal, an All Ireland medal, an All Star and invaluable experience that would stand to me going forward if ever the going got tough.

Winning that All Ireland was special. We had a great laugh in the days that followed. Back to Cinnéide country, West Kerry. Bonfires and trad sessions roared. We paraded in Dingle and then on to An Bóthar pub in Cuas. Years earlier I listened to trad sessions in An Bóthar as an Irish summer student. For a band of the younger lads like Aidan O'Mahony, Marc, Gooch, Declan and myself, it was a time that would bond us. Gooch gave a special display in the final as he would do many more times. For older guys like Darragh, Fitzy, Hassett and Seamo it was special for a different reason. 2001, '02 and '03 had been hard on them, but they had the invisible strength of character that some people just can't see. So they overcame those defeats and triumphed again. We started the year with Declan O'Keeffe in goal – by the end he had departed. I had learned a lot from Deco, travelling with him from Cork in my early years. I was always taking things in back then; full of questions. I still question everything today. Deco was good to talk to and good craic too. One night on the way home from training he drove through Macroom hanging out the driver's window of his car singing 'Billy Jean' at the top of his voice. That in itself was funny, but throw in Deco's accent and his singing voice and it became funnier still. He was showing his age too, knowing all the words to 'Billy Jean'. We finished the year with Diarmuid Murphy in goal. I roomed with him on holidays in Australia. When Murph stalked the dressing room before going out you knew all we had to do was score because he wouldn't concede much. I travelled from Cork a good bit with Johnny Crowley too, another teak-tough man in every way. He carried a quiet pride with him too. Until he reached the arena. Then the pride burst out of him and he could run straight through grown men. His recall for the 2004 final was un-expected, maybe, but turned out great.

I found a baseline for myself in 2004. I never worried if I wasn't flying early in the championship. The other reason I use 2004 as a reference point for everything is that winning of the final without Darragh and Seamo. In sport everything is possible.

Kerry football has given me a lot of opportunity in life, for which I'm grateful. Aside from the few medals, I have travelled and seen the world and laughed way more than one man should. That first All Ireland was horse's fun. I went to Dublin one night shortly after with Eddie Harnett. Ed is bolder than a brass band. Great man to dance too. We were staying in the old Burlington Hotel this night. When we got back after our night out the residents' bar was heaving. We strolled in nonchalantly. I spotted an r'n'b singer from the UK called Lemar near the bar. He had just dropped a big single called '50/50' and was touring. I liked the song at the time, so I turned to Ed.

'Hey, Ed, there's your man Lemar over.'

'Who?'

'Lemar . . . the singer.'

'What does he sing?'

'Ah, Jesus, Ed, you know that song "50/50"?'

'No. Sing it for me . . .'

'Ah, you know it all right. The chorus goes, "Right about now I'm 50/50."'

'Sing it for me I said . . .'

'I just did . . . "Right about now I'm 50/50."'

'Never heard of it. I'll tell you one thing though, you sing the very same way as you talk. Will Lemar have a drink?'

'Nah, leave him off.'

I was too late. Ed made a track for Lemar, who was flanked by a large bouncer. I followed.

'Lemar, how's things? I love that "50/50" song, man. What are you having to drink?'

'Oh fanks, mate, O'im aw'ight.'

'You'll have something, Lemar . . .'

'Nah fanks, mate. O'im off ta bed. Fanks.'

Lemar, very clearly, didn't want a drink.

'Lemar, I'm buying you a drink now, so what will it be?'

By now Lemar was getting vexed. So was his security. He asked for a Coke just to get rid of us.

'A Coke? Lemar, I'm not buying you a Coke. You'll have a brandy and Coke.'

By now I'd been trying to keep decorum by telling him how much I liked '50/50'. I repeated the only lyric I could think of over and over. I was absolutely plaguing him. 'Great tune that, Lemar, man. ". . . Right about now I'm 50/50 . . ."' He was less than impressed. I was flat out trying to think of another lyric to throw at him but nothing came. Completely blank. And I wouldn't mind but I genuinely liked the song. I went to the jacks to see if inspiration might visit while I took a slash. There was no epiphany. I was walking back across the lobby of the Burlo to the residents' bar when I heard some commotion. I looked to my right. Ed was at the door of a lift. He was trying his best to prevent it from closing with one hand. In the other he was holding a brandy and Coke, trying to force it in the lift door before it closed. In the background I could see the whites of Lemar's eyes. He looked distressed. His 7-foot bouncer looked distressed too. Not as distressed as our Ed, though. The bouncer was trying to prevent Ed from getting the drink in. Ed changed tack and decided to take the moral high ground. 'DRINK THE F**CKIN' THING NOW AFTER I BUYING IT FOR YOU, LEMAR!!!' he pleaded. He lost the battle with the lift door. It closed on him and disappeared. Ed stood there staring at the floor number. It stopped at 7. He made for the stairs to give Lemar the drink he didn't ask for. I intercepted him. We went back to the bar to give out about how difficult popstars can be.

Aside from the craic of winning, things like All Stars are also a nice recognition for hard work. I won three in my career and only went on one All Star tour ever. That was to Hong Kong in January 2005. Gooch, Tom Sullivan, Murph, William Kirby and I went from Kerry. It was worth going for the craic we had. You can do things you could never do at home, like sit in a tiny karaoke bar with ten strangers and sing all night. More so, it was worth going for the experience I gained, and the knowledge that what goes on tour doesn't always stay on tour. Sometimes what goes on tour comes home with you. Coming home from Hong Kong I was sure of one thing: Tyrone were well into their preparations for 2005 already. Their focus was evident. They played the exhibition game in Hong Kong like it was a championship game. There was something different about them.

I'm standing in the function room of a hotel near Causeway Bay, Hong Kong. I've just been benching weights with Enda McNulty and Francie Bellew. I challenged the lads to a lift off because they beat us in 2002. I wanted to show them I was strong. We went at it while trying not to laugh. Never laugh while benching. Once you start it's impossible to stop, and more impossible to lift. Darragh and I could never lift weights together for that reason. Once the benching stopped the messing started. I threw a medicine ball at Enda, then Francie threw a medicine ball at me. The three of us then kicked medicine balls around the gym until we couldn't rise a leg with the laughing. Then we left the gym and took our seats for dinner again. The Chinese ambassador to Ireland was waiting for us. We were the 2004 All Stars. The trip to Hong Kong was my first and last. Communications minister Noel Dempsey is sitting nearby with the ambassador's family. I wrote to Noel a short time later asking how exactly does a Meathman from Nobber communicate with a Chinese man's family in Hong Kong. Noel wrote back a note explaining how he had mastered the art of communication in many languages.

I retake my seat. I see Mickey Harte is standing nearby. 'Interesting guy,' I think to myself. I go over to him and say hello. He says hello. 'What do you look for in a player, Mickey?' I ask him. Mickey looks at me for a second. Though he has a deep, thoughtful look on his face the answer is instant. He knows exactly what he looks for in a player. He says two words that have stayed with me since. 'Something different.' I went back to my seat thinking, 'I knew he was an interesting man.' I went back home thinking Tyrone were up to something.

9

Club Versus Country

Home is where the heart is? My home parish is so big you'd want a few hearts to cover all of it. Or one very big heart. From Ballinclogher on the far western flank of Lixnaw parish to Finuge, nearly ten miles to the east. There are four GAA clubs in the parish – Lixnaw hurlers and Finuge footballers on one side; Crotta hurlers and St Senans footballers on the other. I feel a bond to the people of Finuge and to the place of Lixnaw. Finuge has a lot of heart. Especially on the field. Too much heart at times, maybe. It isn't a town, it isn't even a village; Finuge is essentially a crossroads. It sits less than two miles from Listowel town. Even if you didn't blink you could still miss it. On the Listowel side of the Cross you'll find the sports-field, O'Sullivan Park, and Teach Siamsa. On the Lixnaw side of the Cross you'll find McCarthy's pub and a handful of houses. That's about all you will find in terms of landmarks. If you look through the cupboards in a few of the houses which nucleate the crossroads, though, you'll find plenty of All Ireland medals. Starting out playing football with Finuge I was coached by good men: John McAuliffe, Dan Joy, Christy Killeen, Paul Kennelly. I was lucky enough to be exposed to All

Ireland winners. Minister Jimmy Deenihan started it all as part of the great Kerry teams of the '70s and '80s. Jimmy is a great hero to us all and is a good friend of mine. He captained Kerry to the 1981 All Ireland. I always enjoy his company and listen to his advice. One of my earliest memories of visiting Finuge for football is of Jimmy coming to speak at our training session. We were under-14, maybe. He was wearing Adidas boots with a purple and orange trim and a huge tongue, plus an awful shell suit. I still slag him about that.

After Jimmy finished playing and took to politics Eamon Breen was inspired to follow his lead with Kerry. I remember the first time I saw Breen play. It was in the early '90s and at the time Brick Rangers from neighbouring Abbeydorney had a big representation on the Kerry panel: Bernard McElligott, Conor Kearney, Pat Slattery and Tom O'Connell were either on the team or on the panel. The sides met in a Novice Championship game in Finuge. It was as if Breen played them on his own: he caught ball, carried ball, tackled, and kicked scores. He acquired a broken nose somewhere along the way too. The game went to extra-time. At the end of ordinary time I happened to be in the Finuge dressing room and saw him at close quarters. He was a warrior.

Éamonn Fitz was the next to win All Irelands. He has All Irelands at every level, though he keeps them on the other side of the parish in Ballinclogher. Éamonn led the way for my generation. He went to college and played for Kerry, which meant he stood out to us. He has All Irelands at minor, under-21 and senior. When he finished with Kerry he gave some great years back to the club. Enda Galvin (no relation) won an All Ireland in 2000. I made my mark in 2004. Maurice Corridan was there in 2009 with me. We were shown the way from an early age. When you have leadership like that in your club from a young age you can consider yourself lucky. That's why, despite a few approaches from a number of Dublin clubs, I have always stayed with my club. I was a bit annoyed when one Dublin-based newspaper wrote a front-page story on my transfer to the St Vincents club in early 2011 even though there was no foundation in the story. The journalist contacted my club secretary asking how they felt about me leaving. Vincents were the one club who didn't approach me. At least not officially. I had a lot of explaining to do to my own club-mates and officials when the story broke down in Kerry. Transferring never really appealed to me, even when I was driving all those miles to Finuge for training. It meant I was going home, down to my friends and family. That means more than a quick buck. The only enticement I do feel is the possibility of winning an All Ireland senior club title. That is more a probability than a possibility with the strength of the Dublin clubs these days. I'm sure the Dublin clubs will dominate the senior All Ireland Club Championship for the next few years. The thought of another All Ireland medal seduces me from time to time, and my mind wanders. Which club? Where is it based? Who plays with them? Who is the manager? How did they do last year? All hypothetical.

The guys who played for Finuge and achieved for Kerry before me inspired me – and I hope that my own career with Kerry will inspire some young lads in our club today to aim for the same thing. Finuge's tradition of producing Kerry foot-ballers is important. It has garnered fifteen All Ireland senior medals and six All Ireland under-21 medals. When I started out playing senior with Finuge in 1996 we were a Novice Championship team and playing Division 5 league football. In 2013 we played senior championship football in Kerry for the first time and got promoted to Division 1.

How good are we? Maybe not senior Division 1 standard but

definitely intermediate Division 2 standard. The journey from the bottom to the top, or near to the top, took us all over Kerry and Ireland. That very first game for Finuge, back in early 1996, was against Brosna. I was full-forward. I had 1–07 scored from full forward. Towards the end, my marker fouled me and left me on the floor. As the ref ran in, blowing his whistle, my opponent was all apologies. The sincerity of him disarmed me and the referee. He reached down in a conciliatory way to tap me on the head. Or so I thought. On the blind side of the ref he grabbed a fistful of my cheek and tried to lift me while smiling and apologizing. No one saw it. I had to laugh afterwards. We had a few fellas of our own who could leave their mark on you too. Eamon Breen nearly took the head off me in training one day. I was well able for it. If I got a chance at all I'd give it back.

We won the County Novice Championship back in 1996 when a few young lads came through straight from minor level to play. Enda Galvin, Trevor McKenna and myself played in that Novice final against Jack O'Connor's Dromid Pearses in Beaufort. It was a terrible day. I was only 16 at the time. We won a battle of a game, the kind of game that, if you play enough like that, shapes you as a footballer. We played a lot of these games growing up. Eamon and Éamonn were our main men. The younger lads brought some energy and devilment. Trevor at full-back, Enda at wing-forward and me at corner-forward. Jack was Dromid's main player back then. He played centre-forward. He was very competitive. He was the manager of the Kerry under-21s at the time. Éamonn Fitz was one of his players. We knew we were in a game when he hit Éamonn Fitz hard early on. I remember thinking, 'You'd have to be tough to play for the Kerry under-21 manager if he was taking on one of his own players.' Especially Éamonn Fitz, who was probably the strongest player on the field. Still, it was an example as to how ruthless you had to be at the top level. I liked being around people with that kind of hard edge. Jack and Éamonn shared the same outlook on the field. Both were bloody-minded. The personality of the Finuge team I started out in was a great advantage to me. Age didn't matter. The older lads would look out for you, but if you were out there at all you had to deliver and be able to look after yourself too. A rollicking was never too far away if you weren't doing the business; a shot of a fist from an opponent was never far away if you were.

We won the North Kerry Championship in December 1996. That was probably more important to us than the Novice win. Trevor and I turned up for the final in Listowel not knowing what to expect. Listowel was nearly 15 miles away from where we lived. We definitely weren't expecting what we got. A crowd of several thousand in the stand, a band playing on the field as we warmed up, a full parade followed by three-quarters of 'Amhrán na bhFiann'. That's when we knew we were in a big game: we only got three-quarters of 'Amhrán na bhFiann' – for the last quarter the din of noise was enough to cause people to lose the run of themselves. As far as we knew we had a club final to play, a North Kerry final. I guess we associated the senior finals with a minor final we played a year earlier. We learned quickly that North Kerry senior finals were a law unto themselves. Our opponents Moyvane were a law unto themselves too. In the best possible sense. They had a team similar to ours: a few very good, tough older players and some talented younger ones, although they didn't have anyone like Eamon or Éamonn they weren't far off that level. What they had in spades was durability and a tradition of winning North Kerry finals. We drew the first day. Trevor and I learned fast. We were now playing against men not boys. Enda Galvin would have known more about what to expect. He grew up watching North Kerry finals the same way Trevor and I grew up watching county hurling finals. For the replay the following week we were ready. The terms of engagement had changed a little. I got a few scores in the drawn game, so as I took my place for the replay I had a new man marking me. He was younger and faster than my opponent the first day. We lined up side by side for the anthem. We reached that crescendo where the music gets lost in the noise from the crowd. It hadn't finished when I got a crack of a fist into the face from behind. Instinctively, without turning around, I drew one back. The anthem played on. Both of us stood our ground. No one budged. No umpire or linesman raised a flag and no one in the crowd batted an eyelid. I didn't care. He started it. I finished it. An eye for an eye. The scores were still level. When the anthem finished I turned to face my opponent. He had a shiner in return for his punch. That was the end of the punches. We won and I got Man of the Match, scoring 1–02. That was my first introduction to North Kerry championship football. The school of hard knocks. No problem. Call any time.

The county Novice win brought us to junior level in Kerry. It took us eight years to win that. We lost a few finals and semi-finals along the way before eventually winning it in 2004, followed by the Munster Championship against Aghabullogue from Cork in Fitzgerald Stadium. In February 2005 we won the All Ireland Junior Championship, beating Stewartstown from Tyrone in Portlaoise. We play like a family in Finuge which is no surprise considering the number of brothers and relations on the team. We are tight. We enjoyed that win together. In some ways I wondered if winning it stalled us, though – it was another eight years before we won the intermediate championship, in 2012. At the same time junior and intermediate-level football is very competitive in Kerry. By 2004 Maurice Leahy, better known as a hurling coach in Kerry, had taken over as manager. He is also an excellent football coach. Maurice was the first coach outside of Lixnaw who took an interest in my development from a young age. Without him in Finuge I don't think we would have been as successful in that time. He was a guy you would try to impress every time you trained.

After the club win in 2005 I returned to the Kerry squad ready to mount another attack on Sam. I had scored 1–07 against Stewartstown in the final. I wanted to move on to the next level at inter-county football. Some people have no time for league football although that mindset has changed over recent years. Back in 2005 it was beginning to acquire an added significance: eventual league winners regularly ended up championship winners. Any year we won the league with Kerry we went on to win the All Ireland. I always felt league football was important and enjoyed the continuity you got from playing games week on week. You could get a definite feel for the hard edge of opposition teams who thought of autumn while playing in spring. I never understood how people couldn't see the importance of league games. I played many more important league games than championship games. If we won the league I was always very sure of our prospects for Sam. I can't say winning the Munster Championship gave me the same assurance. Depending on the draw you could nearly predict Munster. The league was unpredictable. There was always some sorting out to be done. Teams were always lining us up. We had to be right on our games every day. By the end of it you would have a good indication as to where you were at. The championship can be difficult to handle from a continuity point of view, playing only once a month. Later in my career I found it hard to balance the long breaks between games. There seemed to be way more training than playing. It's hard to reconcile playing sixty, seventy or eighty championship games (it tells you something about the standing of the league competition when league appearances are never accounted for at the end of a player's career) over a ten-, twelve- or fifteen-year period. I returned to the Kerry team to play Tyrone in the league in Killarney. You could tell they were a team on a mission that day. They'd started the mission in Hong Kong, I was sure.

By the summer of '05 the club campaign had caught up with me. I'd gone straight through from November '03 to the spring of '05 without a break. By June I hit a wall. We beat Cork in Páirc Uí Chaoimh in the Munster final. It was one of my poorest displays for Kerry. By July I was left out of the starting team for the All Ireland quarter-final against Mayo. Jack left me out. He told me to be sure and react the right way as I was walking out on the field before training. I told him there was only one way I would go and that was up. I said that to put it up to myself and make sure I responded in a strong manner. Sometimes it's good to say things aloud to challenge yourself. I was more emotional and bloody-minded about the game back then, and reacted accordingly. Everything was a challenge. Even though he was right to leave me out I was cross. When you're starting out and mad to make it it's the greatest offence to be left out of a game. Ultimately the only way to show any manager who you are is on the field of play.

It was around this time Jack introduced the psychologist Declan Coyle to the group. Some players had difficulty with this arrangement. I kept an open mind. Early in the summer I was struggling a bit. I put it down to fatigue. I did chat to Declan at the time and found him helpful. He taught me that how you think every day is a decision you make. I had never considered my thoughts like that before. Such a pragmatic premise. You decide how you think. I took it on board and decided how I would think every day from then on. I would say I am a pragmatic thinker. Some older players were more closed to Declan's methods. I can understand that too. When you're older you have your own wits that you depend on. Later on in my career I became like that too. Self-possessed and self-dependent. I would still listen out for new voices, angles or approaches to the game but I was past listening to psychologists unless it was on my own terms and I knew what I wanted to achieve from the process beforehand. I liked to change things up with regard to how I prepared. Outside of that I found Declan a nice man.

Being left out turned out to be the best thing that could have happened to me. It stung me and gave me the impetus to improve. I kicked three points after coming on as a sub and, more importantly, showed the work rate that maybe Jack felt was missing from my game. I tackled hard, dominating the breakdown and setting up play. It was a mixture of defiance at being dropped and freshness having not trained so much in the build-up. Less training suited me, especially in the summer. I could get fit really quickly. Staying on the right side of fit and fresh was the issue I faced as the summer progressed. Lots of heavy training didn't suit my body at all. Jack would give me the odd session off if I was going particularly well. Some fellas feel they have to do every session – I never minded missing one here and there. It kept me sharp. The '05 semi-final threw up Cork. Our Croke Park rivalry was beginning to intensify around now. This was only the second time we would play each other in Croker. These were extra-demanding games but extra enjoyable for the same reason. Once you won. The pressure I felt coming up to Cork games in Croke Park or Killarney was always keen because there was more at stake. That feeling was always good for me. We beat them in that '05 semi-final. Another three points against Cork had me set up for the final against Tyrone. We hadn't lost a championship game in the two years I had been playing. Going into the '05 final I didn't see that changing.

Tyrone proved themselves a great side on the day. That was probably the best team I played against if you look at the quality and character spread throughout. All Ireland finals come with a guarantee of excitement. 'Expect the unexpected,' I would tell myself going in. Every year would throw up something out of left field. The unexpected drama and excitement of All Ireland final day only adds to the occasion for the spectators – but as a player you can't be moved by that. Sure enough the 2005 final threw up the unexpected. We started well. The intensity was ferocious. I put a ball in over the top which Gooch flicked to Cinnéide for a goal. A few minutes later I was one-on-one defending a high ball on the edge of our square, which Peter Canavan eventually passed to the net. A few of our backs had gone upfield and, as Tyrone countered, I saw some free men in front of our goal, so I sprinted back to cover. We got caught by a sucker punch. I had repeated my form from 2004 by not starting the championship very well but finishing it very strongly.

Every All Ireland final we played in threw up some surprise or side-winder as it unfolded. You had to be prepared for any eventuality. The one eventuality you never prepared for was losing. I still remember the shock of losing that game. In the dressing room after the game Tomás told a journalist we'd be back to win it the following year. I couldn't see beyond the 70 minutes that had just happened, myself.

I sat in my hotel room alone for an hour afterwards trying to process the defeat. The loss goes a bit deeper than just the result or the medal. You lose out on a lot of fun and memories and moments too. Someone else is having the laughs. That was what used to kill me. Throwing on your suit and getting on with things is the only solution. For some it was the end of the road. Cinnéide and Liam Hassett retired. Hassett helped me along at the start of my career. He told me in 2004 that he was only minding the jersey for me. Not many men are big enough to say things like that. We lost our last game together.

All was not lost though. The club were waiting at home. Hurling became the priority for a few weeks. Lixnaw won the county hurling title against Abbeydorney. I scored 0–5 from play to take some of the disappointment away from losing my first All Ireland final. We lit bonfires near to my house at Ballinclogher Cross that night, and we grew that bit closer as a result of winning. 2005 started with winning an All Ireland against a Tyrone team and finished with losing an All Ireland to a Tyrone team. Kerry were back at a crossroads too, but there were no bonfires at this one. We were looking for directions again.

10

Always a Way

By 2006 I was still happily living and working in Cork. Coláiste Chríost Rí was my place of work. You'd hardly find it if you didn't know where it was, tucked up Capwell Road in the middle of a residential area. The large, square, red-brick building stood tall, but it didn't stand out for some reason. It seemed hidden. You'd pass it without noticing if you didn't know it was there. Rows of houses flanked it. The only space there seemed to be around the school was at the back of it, where there was a large green playing field. Football and athletics were honed on that green. Críost Rí have a fine tradition in both. In January of that year I trained with Cork City FC. I knew a few of the players from UCC. They trained in the evening at Deerpark National School, next door to my house on the Lough. The fitness work I undertook over a four-to-six week period was some of the best training I ever did, and stood to me for the year. Soccer players are unbelievably fit. It's a different type of fitness to GAA players, less about physical strength and endurance and more about speed, intensity and recovery. Speed of recovery was the big difference I found between the two sports. In soccer you were rarely out of the

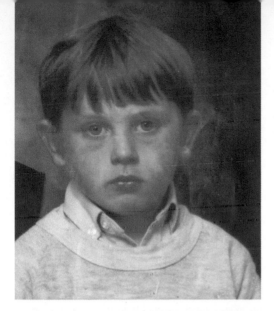

Left: Me on my first day at school in Lixnaw.

Below: *(L–R)* Ciara, Ray and Mom, Catriona, me and Tina. I used to love those New Balance trainers, a gift from my godmother Nora.

Bottom: The whole family. Dad is a big Aston Villa fan. You can see the collar of my Man United jersey under my jumper.

Above left: All the family at my Communion in May 1988. *Back L–R*: Mom, Raymond, Dad; *front*: Tina, me, Catriona, Ciara. I don't look too impressed.

Above right: And again, with childhood friends Vincent O'Mahony (*left*) and Trevor McKenna (*middle*).

Below: Best friends: with my grandmother Nora at my confirmation in April 1992. We were very close.

Above: Starting out: lining out front row (*centre*), for Finuge under-12s in Mountcoal. John McAuliffe (*right*) and Dan Joy (*left*) were our trainers.

Below: Boys will be boys. The Lixnaw Boys NS team which won the Kerry Mini 7s competition. I'm front row, second from right. I was then selected to represent Kerry in Croke Park.

MINI SEVENS

Above: Mini 10s? There were ten of us on the Mini 7s team. We played at half-time in the Cork Down All Ireland hurling semi-final in 1992. I'm back row, second from left – I still have the jersey.

Left: Up the Cats: we've always admired the manliness of Kilkenny hurling in Kerry. I got to play against the Kilkenny Vocational Schools in Fitzgerald Stadium back in my teens. The stadium is where it all begins and ends.

Below: Hometown glory. Winning with the club is special. We were lucky to win county championships at every grade with Lixnaw up to senior. This was an under-21 win from 1997 – I'm at the back on the right.

Above: Point made: winning the Munster under-16 schools championship was the first time I remember really challenging myself to perform. I kicked seven points from midfield and was recalled to the Kerry Techs panel. My old PE teacher, Gerry Whyte, presented the cup.

Right: Speeeech!! Captaining Finuge at minor level. On the left with the glasses is my late uncle Jack. The amateur hecklers have my buddy Scruff face-palming while Maurice Corridan (*back right*), was on the 2009 All Ireland winning Kerry panel.

Below: Number one: my first All Ireland medal in Croke Park was for hurling in 1998. We beat Kildare after the original fixture was postponed due to a pitch invasion. Little did Kildare know about our walkabout in Malahide the previous weekend. My childhood friend Trevor McKenna is to my immediate right.

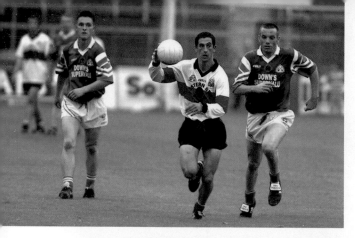

Left: On the break: playing wing-back for UCC in the 1999 Cork County Championship semi-final. It was a position I felt most comfortable playing.

Below: Going bandanas! Fionán Kelliher and Éamonn celebrate at the final whistle in the Munster Club final 1999. Fionán did things his own way. His paisley bandana was a first in GAA.

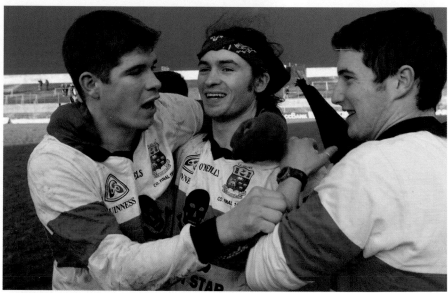

Below: UCC: Éamonn, Seán Sheehy, myself, Dr Con Murphy, Micheál Ó Cróinín, John and Anne Costello. We retired to Costello's bar in Limerick City after winning the Munster Club final against Doonbeg in 1999. John drove the Limerick-based Kerry players to training in Killarney for years.

Above: The six of us: (*L–R*) Willie Dowling, 'Liam MacCarthy', Eddie Brennan, Sean Flaherty, 'Sam Maguire' and Dad at an awards presentation in Lixnaw.

Left: A day out in London Town with my friend Gerry Rochford is one of my favourite things to do. Gerry is from the neighbouring parish of Ballyduff and a loyal supporter of Kerry football.

Below left: Next generation: at my godson Jamie's Communion. He has shown good potential on the field already.

Below right: Enjoying Finuge's intermediate championship win in McCarthy's pub with my father Jimmy and my brother Raymond. Raymond has been central to our club successes in hurling and football.

Left: Up Kerry: Mom and Dad at the 2014 All Ireland semi-final between Kerry and Mayo. I was miles away in Mayo at the time.

Below: With my fiancée, Louise. I never stop laughing when I'm around her. She has great wit.

game because the pitch was much smaller – therefore you got little time to recover. There's also almost a third fewer players on the field than in GAA, where you'll always get more time to recover. I learned to shorten my recovery time quite a bit through soccer training. You can do this if you work to strengthen the core muscles that wrap around your spine. These small muscles share the labour that your intercostal muscles will otherwise have to endure making recovery easier.

When the time came to play for Kerry again I was in the best possible shape. We went on to win the league in 2006 again, beating Galway in Limerick. They played very defensively in the first half and caused us a lot of problems, until Jack changed things at half-time, pushing a man up on the Galway centre-back who had dropped off to play as another full-back, and we got on top. I got 1–2 and Man of the Match. Munster wasn't as straightforward. A laboured display against Waterford and a slightly better display against Tipperary set us up for a Munster final against Cork in Killarney. Snatching late draws against Cork in Killarney became something of a pattern in my time playing: '06, '09 and '10 all went that way. In '06 we pulled back a deficit to get a draw we barely deserved. I played well in the drawn game. That was the game in which Anthony Lynch was sent off for appearing to swing an elbow at Kieran Donaghy, only to have it rescinded on the grounds that he never made contact. We took it on the chin. That game was one of a handful of times when I played near to my best early in the summer. Cork came very close to beating us a number of times in Killarney, only for us to pull it out of the fire for a replay. The replay performance in Páirc Uí Chaoimh in '06 was bad. A promising, thus far successful season, bungeed to a place no one was sure of. I didn't play well in the replay. Only Séamus Moynihan and one or two others did.

It was only our second championship defeat in three years.

The most important game of all was played out in the Hayfield Manor hotel in Cork not an hour after the final whistle.

Páirc Uí Chaoimh is a tough place to go. Hidden in the east side of the city, it's hard to find, hard to get into and harder to get out of. Especially if you lose. The post-mortem couldn't wait. It was good judgement to carry it out there and then in the Hayfield Manor. We had to regroup and look forward as soon as possible. It was all about attitude now. My attitude was simple. I'd have played our next game there and then if I could have. Séamus Moynihan summed it up best for everyone when he spoke. Our pride was wounded, of course, but the real competition only started now. He drew a comparison with the World Cup, which was on at the time. Our World Cup was now beginning. The next game was a qualifier; the tournament proper would start as soon as we hit Croke Park for a quarter-final. Qualifying for that stage was the first goal. We would take the rest as it came. Whether everyone believed him or not at the time, I don't know. I did anyway. We discussed our schedule going forward and set our sights on Sam. Ultimately that was what we judged ourselves on, not Munster final defeats in Páirc Uí Chaoimh. I got a strange kick out of times like this. You have to trawl your reserves of durability and belief. You almost have to cod yourself that an All Ireland is possible. Our search within ourselves told us there was always a way.

The qualifiers would be new to us and would test us in ways we hadn't experienced before. It was important to get that defeat out of our systems quickly. I always enjoyed the qualifiers. League football and qualifiers is how football should be played. Week on week, home and away, something up for grabs every day. We got Longford in Killarney. A dangerous draw in many ways. I couldn't wait for it to come around. Jack felt we needed something new and discovered Kieran Donaghy at full-forward. He was on the panel as a midfielder, really. He gave us something new in the full-forward line, a target to kick long and high to. He was equally good on the floor. Being a basketball player gave him great movement, quick hands and a quick brain. His ball skills were excellent. He ruled the airways that day against Longford, and for the rest of the year, in a way we hadn't seen before. We won well, 4-11 to 1-11. If ever a team took flight it was Kerry in '06.

That win brought us momentum and confidence before a quarter-final draw against Armagh in Croker. For the guys involved in '02 this was a big one, especially for Darragh, having been captain that year. He gave one of the great performances that day. Even more so when you consider he was up against Kieran McGeeney and Paul McGrane, two of the very best around at that time. He was obviously in no mood for a repeat of '02. In the first half he caught a kickout from Diarmuid Murphy and turned in the same movement to land facing Armagh's goal. As he did so he got tackled from the side by Paul McGrane, one of the strongest men you could face on a field. Darragh bowled him over with one arm. Séamus Moynihan came on the burst and Darragh slipped it to him. Seamo carried it on towards the 45 where Eoin Brosnan came on another burst and took a pass from Seamo to stick a goal at the Canal End after maybe 15 minutes. We stuck our flag in the ground. That goal was a declaration of intent. Armagh were hard beaten and full of their own intent. They had the better of the first half: Kieran McGeeney was playing a lot of ball; they played with an extra body in midfield releasing him in space quite a bit. His kick-passing was exceptional in the first half and caused us problems. There was a lot of space left inside by the corner-forward vacating. Ronan Clarke and Stevie Mac were inside two-on-two. Though our inside-backs were the best around, if you have space in Croke Park there is little any back can do with forwards of that quality.

Jack pulled a stroke I haven't seen since by a manager by taking up station behind the Hill 16 goal after 15 minutes or so to see what was happening at the back from the eyes of a defender. He got a sense of the space in and around Mike Mac and Tom. We were conceding scores too easily so he dropped Tommy Griffin from midfield to play centre-back, allowing Seamo to drop into the full-back line to deal with the space around the Armagh forwards. It was up to the rest of us to create a battle zone around the middle so that Seamo's man, Tony McEntee, couldn't influence the game. The half-forwards had to work extra hard to make up for the overloaded Armagh midfield area. I had no problem with that. It was my job to contest on the ground with the opposition midfield. Make it hard for them and easy for Darragh and Tommy Griffin.

I marked Aaron Kernan that day. He was a creative player which is the worst thing if you're a wing-forward. You have to keep an eye on those guys. It's definitely a distraction from your own game. I never minded being man-marked so much because it meant I knew what my man was about. I could move him and lose him. When a wing-back wanted to play it was much trickier because your focus could never be as attack-oriented.

I tackled anything that moved that day. Having been led by 4 points halfway through the first half we kept in touch throughout. Kieran Donaghy was beginning to cause problems inside on Francie Bellew. Mike Frank was dangerous too. It was about as physical as I have been in a game. You could do that against Armagh. They took it like men and gave it back twice as hard. On and off the field they were manly. They were the type of team I liked playing against: McGeeney, Paul McGrane, the O'Rourkes, the McNultys, Francie Bellew – they could all put themselves about. They'd put a hole in you then pick you off the ground. We had to match that physicality to give ourselves a platform to play on around the middle. Tackles and breaks were key back then. After half-time we upped it a few levels as normal. Darragh set the tone from the throw-in, winning it and breaking away through the middle of the Armagh defence. He slipped it to Eoin Brosnan who slipped it to Seán O'Sullivan for a point. Seán had a great year that year. He was more a ball player and runner while I was more of a nuts and bolts type player. The balance between us worked. Early in the second half I managed to dispossess Kieran McKeever coming out of defence. I dived on the loose ball, flicking it to Seán O'Sullivan, who put a high diagonal ball into Star. He caught it under the Hill, lost Francie Bellew and buried a goal to put us on the road. Darran O'Sullivan came on as a sub and stuck a trademark goal to finish. But then my day took another turn.

Armagh had a sub, John Toal, who had been coming on to the pitch all day as a water boy. Tom Sulllivan fouled Stevie Mac near the sideline with less than 15 minutes left. I was nearby and could hear Toal shouting at the linesman to take action. The collision happened so fast that a weaker ref or linesman could have misjudged it and shown a card. Tom was already on a yellow. Between him running out and Darragh running back in, Stevie Mac was sandwiched for a free as they all met together. Toal then came on to the field and started on at the referee, David Coldrick. Then he started on me as he passed by me, shouldering me in the back and knocking me to the ground. I walked over to the ref and told him to get the guy off the field. Toal then approached me after I spoke to the ref and shoved me in the chest. He shoved me a second time. I grabbed him by the shirt and ran him off the field towards the sideline. I forced him back all the way off the field. I left him on the line and found myself standing next to his two water bottles. I picked them up and lobbed them off the field. I didn't mean any harm by it, I was close enough to the sideline to see where they were going to land. There was no great force behind them but I'd had enough of water boys since the Munster final against Limerick in 2004. I was sent off on a second yellow card.

I shouldn't have lobbed the bottles, of course, and David Coldrick was right to send me off. I always found him a good referee. At the time I felt I had to make a stand. I felt the water boy was trying to get either Tom O'Sullivan or Darragh in trouble. I could have been wrong but that was how it appeared to me. I'm sure Armagh understood that I was only standing up for myself and my team. I didn't do anything to instigate what happened, but maybe I went a bit too far in my reaction. Of all counties, Armagh and Joe Kernan know what it is to make a stand for yourself. I sat with Paul McGrane at the All Stars later that year. I got on well with Stevie Mac over the years too. Ronan Clarke was another tough operator. I had my run-ins with Geezer, Kieran McGeeney, but only because I had to. He was their main man. I felt I had to stand up to him for my team's sake. So I did and I took whatever came my way.

I respected Armagh as opponents. They were smart and streetwise. However, I couldn't respect them any more than I did my own teammates. If you want to talk about big players you couldn't look any further than the three Ó Sés on the day. I think the 2002 loss to Armagh hurt them more than anyone after the loss of their father and with Darragh being captain. The three of them were outstanding in 2006. Marc kicked two points from the full-back line, Tomás was indomitable and

Darragh was Man of the Match. If Kerry football has a foundation then these three and their uncle Páidí are the cornerstones upon which it stands. Never was it more apparent than the '06 quarter-final. They were 'The Rocks' that Armagh perished upon.

Cork again in the semi-final. They had beaten us well in Munster. Motivation wouldn't be a problem. We were reaching a peak as a team in '06, physically and tactically. Our mid-summer malaise was a bad memory.

Under Pat Flanagan's methods of periodization we were conditioned to peak in the late summer. Periodization is a systematic planning of physical training so that a group can reach the best possible performance at the most important stage of the year. There are various cycles which must be adhered to in the planning of the year: the macrocycle is the overall yearly plan; the mesocycle represents phases of training that last between two and six weeks; and the microcycle is typically a week's work. Then there are phases within the overall plan: the preparatory phase, the competitive phase and the transition phase. Training techniques are specific to each phase. Pat had us humming nicely by September. We often won games around this time in the 15 or 20 minutes after half-time. We seemed to open up after the break and find another gear without even thinking about it. I always played my best football in the second half in those days. It might take me a while to get through the gears in the first half – I'd feel gassed early on – but the longer the games went on the stronger I felt. Today the levels of prep-aration, strength and conditioning are at full-time professional levels. Techniques, ideas and methods are evolving every year, and teams are getting bigger and more powerful. I was lucky throughout my career in that I never really lost condition to any great degree. It was only after hip surgery in late 2010 that I had to think more about managing my body. That operation took a lot out of me. Before that I could stop gym work for weeks without losing any great muscle mass or strength and regain it all within weeks of starting back. After the surgery I seemed to have to constantly stay on top of things, especially my flexibility and the rehab work required to keep my hip joint loose and healthy. Back in '06 we were ahead of the curve. Nowadays sports science is a prerequisite at the top level – if you fall behind teams in this regard it is difficult to make up the ground. It can take years to catch up because most strength and conditioning coaches who come into a set-up do so with a minimum three-year plan. That's how long the process takes for progressions to manifest themselves on the field and for a group to peak together. Ultimately the right conditioning allows you to play your game at a higher speed, with greater intensity for longer periods of time. No matter how much natural ability a team has, if the opposition is organized and can play at a sustained higher tempo then it will disrupt the gifted side. Ordinary teams with the right sports science methods can do extraordinary things. Extraordinary teams with last year's sports science methods can look very ordinary.

Cork were some way off where we were at physically. That was one of my best displays with Kerry. I was very determined on the day, having played poorly in Páirc Uí Chaoimh. Croker was different. In my mind I had no choice but to play well. We couldn't be dominated, especially in my position around the middle, where the tone was set and the battle lines drawn.

Our physical condition back then was better than anyone else's. We used our physicality because we were expected to. I had to use the power I had built up over the previous three years. Why else were we in the gym? To impose ourselves on teams and give ourselves a platform. Kerry had been bullied off Croke Park a few times over the previous few years.

I worked hard on being strong physically. At 5 foot 11 inches and less than 12 stone I needed every bit of strength I could gain. I was taking on guys who had 3 stone in weight and 4 or 5 inches in height on me.

At one stage in the first half against Cork I won a break and turned Séamus Moynihan upside down with a shoulder in the process. Having been dominated in Páirc Uí Chaoimh earlier in the summer, we were at war. Only because we had to be. If Cork weren't, that was their own lookout.

Our training in the build-up to the final bordered on war too. We reached our third successive final. Mayo provided the opposition. The weekend before, we went to Cork to clear our heads, do our video work and prepare in a focused manner away from the big crowds that were attending our sessions in Killarney. Our final full football session was played in Páirc Uí Chaoimh and would decide the few positions up for grabs on the team and panel. Brian White came down from Wexford to referee it. Brendan Guiney is from Listowel, our rival club in Finuge. They are the town team, we are the country cousins. When he took over Jack identified Guiney, along with myself, Aidan O'Mahony, William Kirby and a few more as the type of players who would put some physicality back in the Kerry jersey. I was physical, Mahony was ultra-physical, Kirby was a combat warrior. I liked playing with him. He was quiet but uncompromising on the field and a good lad off it. Guiney was on another level. He was a sprint athlete at the University of Limerick. For three years Jack had him mark me in training. People thought I was aggressive on the field. I'm only sorry they never got to see Guiney in full blood. He brought the best out of me. I had to be very good physically and smart mentally every night. There were things I could do with Guiney and things I couldn't do. That education served me well later on in my career with Noel O'Leary. After managing Guiney in training I could manage anyone.

At our final trial game in 2006 we marked each other. Jack used our tussles as a barometer to gauge where I was at and where the team was at. A week before an All Ireland final I needed to keep an eye on the barometer myself. The atmospheric pressure was low in an empty Páirc Uí Chaoimh. A week's time in a full Croker was where the high pressure would come in. Getting the balance right was the challenge for me over my career. There were days when we went at it physically. I enjoyed those battles. Other days I'd try to stay out of Guiney's line of vision if I could. If he could see me he was hard to shake off. At one stage in the first half Tomás got a ball on the terrace side of Páirc Uí Chaoimh, playing towards the Blackrock End. I showed in front of Guiney then rolled in behind his back at the last minute. Tomás read it and put the ball over the top. Guiney turned his back on the kick. As I went to catch it he jumped to try to deflect it away. Just as I caught it he landed on me. We fell to the ground. A week before an All Ireland final I was conscious of not getting injured. I tried to push him off me. Next thing we were wrestling on the ground. He grabbed a hold of me, I grabbed a hold of him, until we were separated. Brian White came running. His accent rang out around the empty ground: 'Laaads, laaads, will ye stop. Ye'll be sent off above in Croke Park for that!!' I didn't care. Guiney didn't care. Jack, as it turned out, didn't care either. He said afterwards it was the perfect storm. He and Darragh were laughing as it happened. Whatever streak was in me I enjoyed those battles. It often made me play better. Fighting came a little too easily to me at times, though I'm aware of that. My first instinct when challenged is to fight. I have worked to change that. Guiney and I always got on very well. He came on in the '04 final towards the end, and deserved to for everything he had put into the year. He was unlucky in that he came along at a time when we had excellent defenders who could man-mark, kick well, field well, carry the ball well, set up play from the back and score too. Brendan was an excellent man-marker but our other man-markers were also some of our best footballers: Marc, Tom Sullivan, Mike Mac, Aidan O'Mahony, they could have played in any position on the field, yet they also marked the best forwards in the game out of it. That left Éamonn Fitz, Tomás, Seamo and Tommy Griffin for him to dislodge, who were also supreme footballers. It goes to show you need luck and more besides to make it in Kerry.

The '06 final was memorable for us. Nearly four years of work came to a head. We synced. The result was final. That was a complete team, really, from Murph in goal to Tom and Mike Mac and Marc, Tomás, Seamo, and Mahony, Darragh and Tommy G, Declan, Sean Bawn, Mike Frank, Gooch and Star. Nearly everyone could play in a number of positions. Again, that final threw up surprises. By half-time we had scored three goals and conceded three. 3–08 to 3–02. Conceding three goals in the first half of an All Ireland final would normally be fatal. We had a lot of firepower in that side, though. Star, Declan and Gooch got our goals. Mayo were more physical and more clued-in tactically this time. They had dangerous forwards who could win a game, so we had to be ready. They always had goals in them. Ciaran McDonald was their star man, and when we managed to pin him down they struggled. Aidan O'Mahony tracked him down and won Man of the Match. Ciaran Mac is his own man. When everyone tipped Dublin in the 2012 semi-final he went for his own Mayo to win. They did. He did his own thing. Alan Dillon was the other danger man for Mayo.

Marc usually picked him up. I roomed with Alan on Ireland duty too. He is a good lad. Conor Mortimer was another dangerous player who could hurt us – but we had Tom Sullivan, who marked him out of it. We were lucky to have the calibre of defender we had at the time.

Later that night – very late, in fact, around 5 a.m. – I found myself in the car park of the Burlington Hotel with my cousin Séamus O'Sullivan. We were shooting the breeze about the game. For some reason I had already forgotten about it. All I could think about was the following year and how we would get back to where we were right then. All I could think about was All Irelands. We bounced back from the '05 defeat like we said we would. The challenge now was to stay high. Back-to-back All Irelands beckoned.

Later that year, in October 2006, Australia came back to town for the Compromise Rules series. I played two tests against them in 2004, when we won the series. It was good craic back then. It wasn't such good craic two years later. The Aussies hadn't seemed to take defeat in 2004 too well. We beat them comprehensively. Historically the tests were characterized by violent outbursts of fighting. This series compounded that history.

The '06 version of events found infamy on the internet, and not without reason. The second test, in particular, did no one any favours. It all started in Galway. We won the first test. Graham Geraghty was subsequently cited for appearing to put a knee in an Aussie player's head after he fell in front of him. However, he was cleared of any wrongdoing by a disciplinary tribunal which meant that he was available for the second test. By the time the second test came round the Aussies were mad. They started on to him in the parade. We were walking down the Hogan Stand sideline towards the Canal goal. I was number 12. Geraghty was behind me wearing number 13. The band played, we marched and the Aussies threatened. 'You're gonna get it today, Girighty. You're facked, mate.' Several players were shouting. I made up my mind: if anyone tried it on with Geraghty I would back him up. I didn't know him very well, but that's not a nice place to be, and in my experience the Aussies were full of hot air anyway. The parade finished and we went to the Canal goal to kick around. The Aussies took Hill 16. As luck would have it we had to swap ends for the first half. That's when the entertainment started. A pod of four or five Aussies lined up Geraghty on the way down. Barry Hall led the charge. I knew it was coming from the parade, so I stuck by him. The boys bumped him and barged him on the way past. I hopped off Barry Hall in a moment of pure insanity. He turned and looked down his nose at me with a sneer. Don't ask me what I was thinking. Benny Coulter stuck around and stood his ground too, in fairness to him. As the ball was thrown in, Tadhg clashed with Barry Hall, his Sydney teammate. It was that kind of day. By half-time Geraghty had been knocked unconscious and removed from the field to hospital by stretcher. There was some chaos at half-time. The President of the GAA entered the dressing room and made a speech. It was suggested that we not take the field for the second half. No one took any notice of that, obviously. We did take the field and were well-beaten, giving the Aussies series victory. That was my last time playing for Ireland. A glorious career that will live long on YouTube.

11

A Life Less Ordinary

It's ironic that Australia was part of my story in late 2006 because I couldn't get the place out of my head for months. Australia: the people, the lifestyle, the weather, the beaches. The world in general was occupying my thoughts. Travel. Opportunity. New experiences. I wanted to see some more of the world. I like to be on the move. By the end of 2006 I had grown restless. Nine years in Cork, studying and working, had me thinking about life away from where I was. My pal Scruff had taken off travelling a few years earlier in search of what he called 'a life less ordinary'. I wanted to live a little less ordinarily too. He would email me every so often from some far-flung destination. I wanted to get away. Away from the routine, the convention, the here and now. It was around this time that I realized the rat race wasn't for me. No one ever really won that race as far as I could see. It was neck and neck all the way until someone fell down or gave up. Then someone else took their place. There were no prizes for first place. All I had known was the safety net of work, rest and play. The thoughts of travelling and experiencing a different way of life wouldn't leave me.

As it happened Kerry were heading on the team holiday to

Australia at the end of December. I decided to stay there for a while after the holiday. I appreciated Tomás Ó'Caoimh's understanding. 'You only have one life, you must do what makes you happy,' he told me. I thought about it for a while and decided that was my lot in Cork. It was just about moving on to the next phase of my life. If and when I went back to teaching it would be in Kerry. For now I had to scratch the itch that had been at me for months. Australia was calling.

We were off on what felt at this stage like an annual team holiday. Australia via Kuala Lumpur. We rang in the New Year in Kuala Lumpur. An unremarkable place. I loved Australia though. Sydney is a beautiful place and the lifestyle is hard to beat. The team stayed in the Grace Hotel and we took in the city at every opportunity. I roomed with Diarmuid Murphy. Murph is a leisurely man, takes everything as it comes. I'm the opposite of that. When the team left, Tommy Griffin, Declan O'Sullivan and I stayed on. The three of us booked into a hostel on Carrington Road in Coogee straight away. We dropped our bags in a room and lay on our bunk beds to take in the new arrangement for a minute. After not very long at all I was off the top bunk looking for my suitcase, and so was Tommy. We checked right back out again and moved down the road to the Coogee Bay Hotel for a few nights. From there we moved into an apartment in Pyrmont for a week or so before Tommy left for home. By then a former minor teammate of mine, Kevin Lynch from Castleisland, sorted me out with a beautiful apartment on the corner of Carrington Road and Coogee Bay Road with a balcony that looked right to the sea. Kevin is a good guy and someone I consider a friend for all he did for me Down Under. Declan and I became good mates with a gang of lads from Kildare. Terry Rossiter, Johnny Brereton, Ross Sullivan and Niall O'Loughlin from Galway. I rented a car from a Dublin man called 'Mick the Car'. It was a red Volvo estate and cost me a few hundred dollars – and many more hundreds of dollars in fuel. Very heavy on petrol. It ran out of fuel on George's Street one day. Stalled. I got out, locked it and walked away. They have bays in Sydney city centre where cars get dropped if they get towed away for illegal parking. I knew it would show up in one of those. I found it about a week later. I went to Melbourne for ten days to visit a friend. When I came back the boys had crashed my car – coming out of a petrol station, ironically enough. I didn't spot the considerable damage for ages, which tells you something about the condition of the car in the first place. No one ever owned up.

For something to do I worked for about three weeks for a Kerryman called Mick Daly, who had a construction company. He gave me the keys to a van, and every day I'd leave Carrington Road at 6 a.m. and collect men for the drive to Bankstown, out past the airport. The motorway has about six lanes on either side and on the way out you pass underneath a runway. Some mornings I'd drive under the tunnel as a plane would land or take off just over my head. Mick was a character. I was like a trophy he had won. He'd bring me around to meet friends of his in the industry and get me to tell the lads stories about the Kerry set-up and answer questions about football and other county teams. I'd fire out a few clichés and a few yarns. It was no burden to me to be meeting people and shooting the breeze. It beat being down a hole. Driving the motorways and navigating my way to and from the site in rush-hour traffic was a great experience. I discovered skinny jeans in Australia too, in a shop called General Pants Company. No one batted an eyelid at them in Australia, funnily enough. Then again, Australia is a big country.

Leaving Críost Rí and going to Australia was a risk in some

ways, a leap of faith. I figured I had to leap to find out more about life. People say you should look before you leap. That sounds boring. I'd rather leap and then have a look around. I came back to Ireland refreshed and ready for a new challenge.

By then it was all change in Kerry. Jack had gone in October 2006. We were all surprised. With him you were guaranteed success. You could nearly take it for granted. Maybe we did in the end. Pat O'Shea had taken over as manager. I knew Pat through coaching, from when I was younger. At the beginning of his tenure I told him I would be spending some time in Australia – not ideal from his point of view; I doubt he was too happy about it. For me it was a straightforward decision. I would miss the start of the league anyway after surgery on my nose. I couldn't breathe through it after breaking it years earlier. It was affecting my recovery in games and my sleep. I had it fixed in late December 2006. The surgeon's advice was not to play for three months. I was back by late March 2007, having trained every second day Down Under. I was in good shape when I returned, but I negated the work I did in Oz with my next move.

Twenty-four hours after getting off a twenty-four-hour flight from Sydney I was back in training with Kerry. Crazy. Ten days later I played 40 minutes of a league game in Ballyshannon, against Donegal, and damaged a hamstring tendon in my left leg. Declan Quill hit a short free to me and as I bent down to collect it I felt a snap up high in my hamstring near my sitting bone. It was sore but not debilitating. I carried on for the game. And for the rest of the year. I played all through 2007 with it. The significance of this moment didn't register with me at the time, but it would have ramifications twelve months down the line. I didn't know it at the time but I had torn some of the tendon from my sitting bone on my backside. I was walking off the field when I spotted Mick Daly near the tunnel. He was home to see family in Knocknagoshel and Abbeyfeale. I took off my jersey and gave it to him. He'd looked after me well in Oz. Vince Linnane, our kitman, wasn't too pleased, but we are great friends – Vince and my late uncle Jack were friends too – so he found a replacement jersey. He always looked after me for gear. Vince is a Mayoman and is very popular amongst the players.

Kerry in '07 were the same machine as in '06 in many ways, minus some notable names. Pat arrived and Jack left. Then Seamo left. And Mike Mac too. Things changed quickly. That is the nature of sport. Ebbs and flows, comings and goings, highs and lows.

It was hard to quantify what losing the lads meant, impossible to know what we'd gain through Pat and his new ideas. In between lay the same old challenge, the grind, and the plans to stay ahead.

Séamus Moynihan was something else. Darragh has an interesting take on him. He says he never saw Seamo use his left leg in all his thirteen years playing with him. 'That's how good he was, he never had to.' Darragh's point was he could never get away himself without using his left leg now and then. I was the same. I used my left as much as my right. Sometimes because I wanted to, more times because I had to. Seamo's balance and vision and ball control meant he never had to. He was driven too. People call it desire. Want is a better word. Séamus Moynihan wanted it all his career. Wanted to win, to get stronger, fitter, faster; wanted success and medals, wanted men around him who wanted the same thing.

By the end of '06 he had everything he wanted. Including a redemption of sorts after Tyrone had broken us in '05. It was a long road back for everyone, but especially for Seamo, with the condition of his body at the time. For the '05 final he was struggling badly with his back, couldn't bend down, couldn't turn or twist, couldn't sprint. The winter of '05 into '06 was a long purgatory for all of us, but was longer for him. He rehabilitated with the help of Ger Hartmann – boxed day in, day out, in a garage at the back of his house when retiring was the easy thing to do. For some giving up is harder than trying. Back he came. Now he had Sam Maguire in one hand and his new son Jamie in the other on the steps of the Hogan Stand. When the battle lines were drawn in the hungry bowels of Croke Park the warrior in him came out. This mask would come down over his face and he'd go pale white. His blue eyes would seem even bluer, like something had lit behind them. They'd be out on stalks. This want had taken hold and had to be satisfied. Again.

Mike Mac was another exceptional player. Quiet but no less driven. Sometimes the quieter guys are the ones you listen to most. They're the most driven, the most passionate, the most important. Mac had his own ways. He could play anywhere on the field with his football ability; he had soft hands and a hard edge. He was barely 30 years old when he retired. So they went with Jack and we took stock.

The stock take revealed that we were still out ahead of the pack, as far as I could see. Still that bit better than the rest. Still had Darragh, Gooch, Declan, Tomás, Marc, Star, Tom Sull, Éamonn Fitz, Murph, Tommy G. With Darran, Killian Young and Tommy Walsh coming through we still had enough. I was sure we'd win the 2007 All Ireland.

As a team we had to adapt to the changes in personnel, the change in management and the obvious changes in methodology that came with a new management team. The physical conditioning work we were used to under Pat Flanagan changed a bit under the new physical trainer John Sugrue, and the style of play changed slightly too. I played minor football with John in 1997. His methods were based more on fitness than power. Our style of play changed accordingly. We tended to run the ball more under Pat O'Shea. We went through the gears in the same way until the summer when we beat Cork in the Munster final in Killarney, setting up an All Ireland quarter-final against Monaghan. This was always going to be a tough draw against a strong, physical side. On a wet day in Croke Park we struggled with them right to the end until Tomás fisted a point to get us over the line by one. Our experience told. We scraped through to a semi-final against Dublin. They would have fancied themselves after watching us play, I'm sure. We had been well tested by Monaghan. This would be a few levels up in terms of quality.

By the weekend of the semi I had started back teaching Irish and geography in St Brendan's College in Killarney and was happy to be back closer to home. I found the Sem quite different to Críost Rí. It's hard to put my finger on what the difference was. It was something more of a serious place. Perhaps the kids were a little more affluent too.

Dublin was my best performance of the year, which didn't take much doing considering how I had played up to that point. I kicked two points and created a few more. The final against Cork was probably the easiest All Ireland we won simply because we were a good bit ahead of most teams at that stage. Along with that, Cork didn't play very well on the day. In the course of the 2007 All Ireland final I learned a lesson that changed the way I trained and prepared my body for the next few years. It happened towards the Cusack Stand side of the field as Cork attacked the Hill, just beyond halfway. A Cork defender took a ball forward towards our goal. I chased him.

The harder I chased him the slower I seemed to get. It was as if something were pulling me backwards. I didn't get to him. The play broke down. Just then the half-time whistle went. I walked to the dressing room thinking I'd have to box clever for the rest of the game. Afterwards, when I was taking stock, it became clear that physically I wasn't in great shape any more. Strong, yes; powerful, maybe – but my flexibility, agility and speed had suffered. I wasn't able to run freely. I was too muscular, if anything. The quick-fire way I started the year had set me back in the long term. I hadn't allowed my body any time to reacclimatize after being in Australia for three months. I threw myself back into training and never really got going until the last two games. As it was, by the end of 2007 I had my third All Ireland in four years. I only played anywhere near my best for the semifinal and final. It was an important win. The first time Kerry played Cork in an All Ireland final. I felt that in the build-up. One hundred-plus years of tradition was riding on the result.

Gooch was outstanding that day. His All Ireland final record puts every player in the game in the shade. We roomed together for a few years and he was always very easy company. How easy? The morning of the '07 final we got up for breakfast, and then had lunch as the day moved on. After lunch was the time you began to organize yourself – players might quieten, get lost in their thoughts, think about the afternoon ahead, start to think about their particular jobs, get strappings or any other physio work they needed done. Others would be a bundle of nervous energy, giddy on the move, restless, walking, talking. I liked to be relaxed and laughing a lot in the build-up to games. It helped me. This particular day I did my business and went back to my room to get my gear bag before our team meeting.

It was about ten to two. We had our final team meeting at two. There had been no sign of Gooch all afternoon. I opened the room door and saw a Gooch-shaped lump under the duvet and a tuft of his red hair sticking out from under it. He was sound asleep. I was worried that he may be sick, or something. There was no sign of life. Without stirring from under the duvet he finally woke. 'What time is it?' It wasn't so much what he asked me but the inconvenienced way he asked me. Like a teenager who has been woken from his lie-in on a Saturday morning. It seemed he was more concerned with how long more he could knock out of the scratcher than the game. It's good to be around guys like that. Relaxed, unconcerned, bigger than any occasion. 'It's now ten minutes to two, Gooch. We have a game there in a bit. You might join us for it?' No reply from Gooch. The very air of a man on holidays who had just woken and was taking a few moments in bed to plan his day. For all we know he could actually have been planning his day. I can imagine him thinking to himself, 'Right, what did I score in '04? 1–5 – not bad. '05? 0–5 – not great. '06? 1–4? Not bad, I suppose. I'll beat that today. Right, I better get up.' You wouldn't know with Gooch. He scored 1–07 and won Man of the Match – he was dead to the world at ten to two.

The aftermath of the '07 final is memorable for something that happened in the warm-up room, away from the eyes of the audience. Dr Dave Geaney was someone I got on well with during my time with Kerry. I enjoyed his wit and his way. We both were schooled, albeit in different generations, in North Kerry football. He with Castleisland Desmonds, me with Finuge. A GP by profession, Dave managed his Desmonds to the All Ireland club title in 1985. He played with Kerry for years, winning All Irelands, and served as selector and team doctor for many more years. In 2007 he was part of the management team under Pat O'Shea. A memory from that year's All Ireland final has stayed with me since. It involves

Dave and the Cork manager Billy Morgan. On the pitch at the final whistle Dave asked Billy to come into our dressing room after the game. He had some convincing to do, I'm sure. Billy was Cork. A rebel in every sense of the word. I had listened to stories about him for years around Cork. I found it hard not to enjoy them. His record in the game stood for itself as a player and a manager. Dr Dave and himself were lifelong friends from their UCC days. It must have been hard for him to come into our dressing room and speak. I'm sure he only did it for Dave. We were gathered in the warm-up room when he appeared. The warm-up room in Croke Park before a game is about as real as it gets. You're there. You can smell it. You can taste it in your mouth. You can hear the distant rumble of the crowd. You know that once you go out there's no going back. It's different after-wards. It's not about what is about to happen any more, but what has happened and what is happening right in front of us. Billy is speaking in that soft, melodic lilt of his. And what he has to say couldn't be further removed from what he had to say in the same room just down the corridor two or so hours earlier, I'm sure. He spoke of his pride as a Corkman, his passion as a competitor and his friendship with Dr Dave that stretched back nearly forty years. No man had more battles with Kerry and no man wanted to beat Kerry more. He was disappointed, but he put his disappointment aside out of respect for his friend.

As Billy spoke I caught a glance of Dr Dave. Tears rolled down his cheeks as he listened. I don't know what he was feel-ing but I imagine it was part joy for Kerry, maybe part sorrow for his friend Billy, but mostly pride at what he was witnessing. Whatever he was feeling was his own. You don't judge a man on his emotions. You judge him on his actions. Billy's action spoke for itself. It was one of those rare moments in sport where you let your guard down and think maybe there is something more important than winning.

That thought lasted about as long as the moment itself. There was *nothing* more important than winning.

2007 was a year of change. I was glad to be back living in Kerry after years in Cork, teaching Irish and geography in St Brendan's College. I was also involved in a sports bar in Ballybunion, which had been going very well for nearly two years. We opened in the summer of 2006, and I was involved right up to the end of 2008. The night it opened we had a huge crowd and a lot of the Kerry lads were there. We had Sam down twice. I bought a house in Tralee and settled into grown-up life down the road from my sister and Éamonn Fitz, who married in late 2007.

In the course of the year Éamonn retired from inter-county football. He wasn't getting the game time he expected and deserved. He made his decision after a league game in Parnell Park against Dublin and retired the following day. He'd expected to play, and wasn't prepared to be a sub. We could have done with him over the next year or two as it turned out. With Seamo and Mike Mac retiring, Fitz's experience and defensive know-how would have served us well. I was disappointed he was gone on a few counts. I couldn't see us not winning the All Ireland that year and I tried to talk him around, but that didn't matter to Éamonn. He wanted to play – or nothing. An All Ireland as a sub would have meant nothing to him. I admired his ability to make such a clear decision. It was one that would have an impact on my career in a very short space of time.

The early damage to my hamstring tendon in Donegal had become a source of constant pain in my daily life. Sitting down was very painful, which made simple things, like driving, a problem because the injury was high up on my hamstring where the tendon inserts on to the ischium – your backside bone. I was taking two anti-inflammatory tablets every day for months. One evening in the summer of 2007, just before going out for training in Fossa, I wasn't feeling well. Months of anti-inflamms had taken their toll. I puked blood in the sink, then passed blood in the toilet, then went out to train. I told the doctor later, and he told me to stop taking the Difene. Overuse had damaged the lining of my stomach. The thing was, I needed them to get by. Without them the inflammation in my hamstring was debilitating. Dr Mike Finnerty prescribed some alternative options to get me through the summer. I got away with it to an extent, but I knew I would have to do something about this lack of flexibility if I was to compete at the top level much longer.

But deep in 2007 there was another medal to be won: the Kerry County Championship. I had won two hurling championships, a Cork football championship, but no Kerry football championship.

Feale Rangers is an amalgamation of five clubs in North Kerry – Finuge, Listowel, St Senans, Duagh and Moyvane – all junior or intermediate clubs spread throughout the five divisions of the county league. While we won county championships in the '80s during the time of Jimmy Deenihan and Tim Kennelly, success was sporadic, far from sustained. We would come strong for a year or two then disappear. We were notoriously disorganized, as most divisional teams in Kerry were. In 2007 we got our act together and took on the challenge. We'd always had good players, but to harness the talent we needed a strong leader. Jerome Stack from Listowel was that. He took over and took charge. I had played with Jerome for

Feale Rangers myself, and he was a tough, honest competitor. As a manager he was just what we needed. The other big factor in us getting it together was Éamonn's retirement. He rowed in behind Jerome, which meant other players got the message. Everyone bought in. Noel Kennelly and Éamonn were friends and former teammates, so between the three of them and selectors Johnny Mulvihill and Christy Killeen, my club-mate, we were in good hands. Training went on while I was with Kerry. I got there as much as I could. Éamonn was captain. He had his plans made. Feale Rangers would win the county championship. His motivation was two-fold as far as I could see. Firstly he wanted to show the county selectors what he was still capable of. The second motivation was he wanted to see me captain Kerry. If Feale Rangers could win a county champion-ship I would most likely be captain, tradition dictating in Kerry that the county champions nominate a captain.

Feale Rangers reached the '07 county final (against South Kerry) by beating some good sides along the way, including An Ghaeltacht in the quarter-final. That gave us the confidence to believe we could do something. I found it tricky playing against them as I was so close to the Ó Sés. There has always been a strong bond between the North Kerry players and the West Kerry players for some reason. South Kerry were the dominant team in Kerry at the time and going for four wins in a row. It was a low-scoring, physical game. We were that kind of team: physical, very strong defensively, with enough quality up front to get by. With almost the last kick of the game in the final, and the score tied at 7 points each, Éamonn kicked the winning point from distance. The following day he was named Man of the Match at the banquet.

He was true to his word. He had achieved what he set out to do when he retired from Kerry. It was typical of him, finding a silver lining in the cloud of his retirement. It was equally typical of him to do what he said he would do. That story tells you all you need to know about Éamonn and why he is so highly regarded by people. When he sets his mind to something there is usually only one result. He gets there and brings others with him. There were other guys who had been great club men for years around the paddocks of North Kerry who deserved it too: my club-mates, the Corridans, Jack, Maurice and Pat; Noel Kennelly, who drove the effort too; my second cousin, Breandán Whelan, from our neighbouring club St Senans; John Somers, our goalkeeper of the same parish; Kieran Quirke from Duagh; John Mulvihill from Moyvane; and my old sparring partner Brendan Guiney from Listowel. The whole squad deserved all the credit. 2007 was a year of change all right. It began with a desire for travel, new experiences and a life less ordinary. By the end of it I was named as captain of Kerry. Life was about to get a lot less ordinary.

12

#JOSTLING

I was driving. It was a dreary, drenched evening in December. One of those ordinary days that makes your mind wander. I was in the car on my way to Limerick. It was 5 December 2007, to be exact, and I was beginning my preparations for the 2008 championship. I left the Sem in Killarney straight after work to make my appointment time. I was on my way to the Hartmann International Sports Injury Clinic at the University of Limerick. The hamstring problem I'd carried through the '07 championship had gotten worse. Because of Feale Rangers' run in the county championship I hadn't been able to see to it. Doing regular things was just becoming more of an issue. I had pain when sitting down. Taking off my shoes and socks was tricky. From a playing point of view I felt I had lost some pace and power off the mark. The county final was a case of gritting my teeth and contributing somehow. A block down on Bryan Sheehan as he was about to kick a point to put South Kerry ahead late on was my biggest contribution. It was enough. I used that moment as a reference point later on. It told me that no matter how a game is going you can always do something to affect the outcome.

I remember the journey to Limerick clearly: it was lashing rain all evening and I was rushing to be on time for my appointment. The Killarney to Limerick road is notoriously slow. Killarney, Farranfore, Currow, Castleisland, Abbeyfeale, Newcastle West, Adare. Bottleneck after bottleneck. The torn tendon was right on my sitting bone. Clutching the car was causing me difficulty too. I had to get out of the car twice en route to relieve the pain when driving. You remember such moments. Standing on the hard shoulder of a motorway outside Limerick in the pissing rain, cars whizzing by, my hazard lights flashing. If any metaphor would sum up my 2008 it would be that. Hazard lights. Danger up ahead. Beware.

After a three-hour session in the Hartmann clinic that consisted of assessment, hands-on manipulation, massage and painful joint loosening, followed by a full run-through of the stretching programme and a core-stability programme, I sat back into my car. The time was somewhere around 9.30 p.m. Nearly six hours had passed since I'd left St Brendan's. It would be 11 o'clock before I got home to Tralee. The 2008 campaign had begun. Captain of Kerry. I faced the car for home sitting up on one side of my backside so as not to aggravate the tendon. It was still pissing rain.

I had heard about the quality of Ger Hartmann's work in rehabbing and pre-habbing athletes in the recovery from, and, more importantly, the prevention of, injury. While I was injured I knew if I didn't do something about my flexibility I would continue to get injured. I needed rehab and pre-hab. The aim was to break down my body and reassemble it. Ger saw me, treated me and put me on his ten-step rope-stretching programme. This programme and my diligence in doing it helped my career, no doubt, and improved me physically. Ger Hartmann is a larger than life character with a devil-may-care attitude. His work-partner at the time, a Kerryman called Ger Keane, took me on from there, and I went about the ten-step programme to free my body up. The hands-on work that went into loosening my muscles and freeing my joints was painful but necessary. Ger Keane and I are still great friends today. He is an integral part of the Kerry back-room team. Whilst their programme helped and took pressure off my pelvis and back, it didn't cure my hamstring trouble. The damage was done there. I couldn't dwell on that. I wanted to get to work on the year ahead, so I had to let it heal as best I could. At the time I was keeping training diaries. Pat Flanagan had encouraged the practice when he joined us in 2004. I found it a useful thing to do. I kept a diary for 2008 mainly because I was captain. Captaincy was never an ambition of mine but it showed up on my door. It was a very brief diary.

My flexibility was improving so I reckoned the hamstring would improve too. I was getting physio on it but the pain wasn't subsiding much. I could run pretty well but my acceleration wasn't quite there. Bending down was my only difficulty on the field. In those days we trained at the back of the stadium in Killarney on the small pitch. It was heavy and wet, especially in January, and not really suited for inter-county pre-season training. I went about my work and kept my head down. For around four weeks I worked – gym and field – hoping the hamstring would improve day by day, managing it before and after training as best I could, right up to the week of our first league game against Donegal. I was able for the pitch work, but lower-body weight work was causing stiffness and inflammation in the joint. Every day I was icing, taking anti-inflammatories, trying to stretch, then training again. Things eventually came to a head. We were training in Austin Stack Park on the Tuesday night before that game. I was going through some warm-up drills with the rest of the lads. By this stage, although I was trying to do some strengthening work, I was sure my pace had been reduced. That was a worry. It felt like something was pulling me back as I ran. When I needed to up through the gears I couldn't. I called the session to a halt. In the dressing room, the medics were perplexed as I had been training pretty well and hadn't visibly pulled up injured. The management appeared sceptical and seemed to think that I was being overly sensitive about the hamstring, which was surprising. I explained how I was feeling and asked for a scan on the injury. Back then, MRI scans weren't as frequently used as they are today. I insisted and they agreed. I had my scan later that week with Kerry due to play Donegal in the first league game of 2008 the following Sunday. Mike Finnerty rang me with the results a few days later. The news wasn't good. Mike sent me to see a specialist in Cork for a further examination. The results showed that the tendon connecting one of my hamstring muscles to my backside, the ischial tuberosity, was almost ruptured. A bad, grade-2 tear was the diagnosis; a grade-3 is a complete rupture. The surgeon in Cork University Hospital, Declan Bowler, a Kerryman, had trained in Australia with AFL teams. He said the injury was serious and rare. He asked me to slip my foot out of my shoe on the injured leg, using the other leg. I couldn't. He advised surgery to repair the damage. We were standing in a corridor deep in the bowels of CUH. 'Surgery?' I said, surprised. 'How long will I be out for?' I was hoping for good news. A month, two months max. His answer surprised me even more. 'Minimum six months, but more likely nine months.' My season as captain was over before it had begun. 'That's not an option,' I told him. 'I have to play this year. I'm captain. There must be something else I can do.' Declan gave me a glimmer of hope. He felt surgery was the best option but, given my position, he offered an alternative. Flimsy as it may have been, I was glad to hear it. My only hope would be to try rehabbing it, to loosen the pelvic joint and my back and to strengthen the tendon through eccentric loading exercises. I would be ruled out for five months but at least I'd still have a chance of playing in the championship.

I carried the news back to Kerry. I think everyone was quite surprised at the severity of the injury. A rehab plan was put in place. John Sugrue, who was our physical trainer at the time, took over the physio and rehab. He did brilliant work on me – from the physio work itself to overseeing the daily rehab work to eventually overseeing my return to the pitch. The initial field work was basic, graduating from gentle straight-line running, to bounding, to more intense running, then twisting and turning drills for a few weeks, until we eventually began to replicate match-like conditions. This one-on-one work was some of the hardest training I ever did. Between classes I would go down to an empty Fitzgerald Stadium and meet John. We would play in tackle boxes, play possession games, one-on-ones, then break into longer endurance runs. When I had strengthened the hamstring and done the various stages of gradual rehab I began to run and eventually sprint again. There were a few setbacks at this stage, but I was almost there. I was grateful to John for his help in getting me back. By now we were into April and Kerry had been going well in the league. We reached the league final that year, against Derry. I'd had a few weeks' training by now and was hoping for game time. It didn't come and we lost to Derry in Parnell Park. I hadn't gotten any game time in the semi-final either. I was getting frustrated. I would be five months out of the game before I would play for Kerry in 2008. My first championship game as captain was against Clare on 15 June 2008. It would also be my last.

*

Context. It is easy to overlook and ignore context in any story. Context is malleable of course, which makes it dangerous too. It is important for me to add some to this story. For the previous four months I had staved off the advised surgery on my hamstring tendon. By the time the Clare game came around there was a lot of water under the bridge from 5 December 2007, but no football played. The physio and flexibility work as well as the eccentric loading, fitness and core-stability work had paid off. The morning of 15 June 2008, Paddy Russell and his officials got on their way to Killarney to officiate our opening championship game against Clare.

The game is stuck in my memory for obvious reasons. Clare are a difficult team to play against any day, at club or inter-county level. I've had many battles with them through the years, going back to my University College Cork days. This day in Killarney was no different. It was physical from the off. We never minded that. We could be physical ourselves. You have to be. I was probably our most physical player. Physicality on a given day is fine once it's backed up with football; when it's physicality followed by physicality for the sake of it you can get a bit pissed off with it. That's where good referees and officials come in. After only a few minutes Declan went through on goal on a solo run towards the scoreboard goals, and the tackle that came in burst his nose and left him on the ground. No free. Paddy Russell ran past me as play continued while Declan was laid out on the ground. 'Are you leaving that go, Paddy?' I wasn't aggressive towards him but as captain I had a right to ask him, and I was entitled to some degree of communication in return. He didn't reply. Not communicating with players appeared to be standard practice back then. It seemed to be regarded as an insult by some referees if you asked any kind of question of them regarding a decision made, and a sign of weakness if they answered you. I played OK in the first half. I was busy and getting around the field, reacclimatizing to football at that altitude. My handling was a bit off, as you might expect having not played for a few months, although that is no excuse for poor handling of a size 5 football. The game was competitive, although I felt this came as a surprise to the officials. The first half, particularly the first 15 minutes, were frantic. I felt Paddy Russell's decision-making was erratic: eight frees in the first 5 minutes – some were fouls, some weren't. In my view he was blowing for small things and then not taking any action when he should have. As the half wore on I was finding my feet more and more.

By the second half I was right where I wanted to be. I was playing well after half-time. That is a point of context also. As I run back out to my position, having just scored a point, one of the Russell brothers lays into my direct opponent to get tight.

Not long after that I receive another ball, and he decides to try to get tight at last. Darragh had won a ball at midfield and slipped it to me. I spin and look inside. A give and go is on. I give the ball inside to Gooch and look to attack the space behind their half-back line which has been sucked out under the kick-out. I try to go by my man, but now he has taken the advice of his teammate to heart. He gets tight. Very tight. He grabs me, preventing my run for the return pass, pinning my arms down. I'm stood up and taken out of the play as it develops. When I am released, after two or three seconds, I turn to the linesman with my arms outstretched to bring his attention to it. (Was drawing the linesman's attention the right thing to do? I don't know. It wasn't a habit of mine to look to officials. I dealt with things myself.) The linesman calls the ref. I don't hear what is being said. Paddy books my man and turns towards me. A hum rises from the terrace. I'm about to be sent off. I want to know what exactly it is I'm being booked for. Paddy, having booked me already, doesn't ask my name. He just writes in his little book. 'You can't be serious, Paddy?' No response. 'What are you booking me for, Paddy?' No response. 'What did I do, Paddy?' No response. As he reaches for the card I impulsively slap the book from his hand.

It was basic instinct, an impulsive reaction born out of frustration. Frustration at not finishing my first game as captain just as I was getting into my stride. Frustration at the seven or eight other games I didn't get to start or finish as captain. Frustration at missing the whole year up to this point through injury. Frustration at the long hours of painful physio and rehab work to avoid surgery. Frustration at training on my own. Frustration at having played all through 2007 with the help of painkillers for the same injury. Frustration at the doubts about whether I was even injured in the first place because, in my desperation to play for Kerry, to captain Kerry, I continued to train and play on the injury. Frustration at watching us win a league semi-final. Frustration at watching us lose a league final. Frustration at being on the receiving end of a bad decision. Frustration at Paddy Russell's omertà. Pure frustration. None of that offers any excuse, just a little context.

Because I'm getting no answers from him I turn my attention to the linesman. I ask him what I've done to be booked. 'G'wan away now, boy,' is his reply. I turn to walk off the field. I want to get off the pitch as quickly as I can. As I do so someone grabs me from behind by the end of my jersey and pulls me back. It's Tomás, one of my good friends and probably the guy I grew closest to in the group as a room-mate. He is trying to calm me down. I break his grip and walk away. I'm gone.

*

I was suspended for six months. The county board contacted Croke Park to check out the situation regarding training with the team. Word came through from Paraic Duffy, the Director General of the GAA, who told the county board that he had no issue with me training with the group. I could return to training at any point. It was a Tuesday morning, if I recall rightly. I packed my gear bag for training later that evening. By lunchtime Paraic Duffy had called the county board back and changed his mind for some reason. I was banned from training with the group as well. The GPA were first on the phone offering help and support. Eamon O'Sullivan, the county board secretary, handled the case. A defence lawyer called Donagh McDonagh took on the case when it reached the DRA (Disputes Resolution Authority) stage. There was uproar in the media. I kept a low profile as the case was heard. Paddy Russell's match report was fair. I was reported by the linesman for jostling, which earned me, Paddy Russell wrote in his report, a second yellow card. What Paddy didn't say in the report was that I had knocked the notebook out of his hand intentionally. That and the fact that the Central Hearings Committee neglected to introduce video evidence in support of their case meant there were possibilities and reasonable grounds for appealing the case. There was ambiguity. How did the Central Hearings Committee or Central Competitions Control Committee know that I didn't knock the book by accident when they didn't introduce video evidence? The members of the board were in danger of prejudicing their own case by talking about the incident like they had seen it happen, when in the strictest sense and going by the only admissible evidence submitted to them – the referees' report – they couldn't really know whether I had done it on purpose or not. They also had the opportunity to go back to Paddy Russell for a clarification, which they didn't do in their haste to be seen to be acting. On top of this there was an issue with the proposed six-month ban by the CHC. It was being reported by the media as a fait accompli though it had yet to be imposed by the CCCC. This disclosure also gave rise to potential prejudice. It was getting messy.

After going through the various stages of the disciplinary system in the GAA, each one taking weeks to come around, the case was handed on to the final Disputes Resolution Authority stage. My uncle, Pat Smyth from County Meath, picked me up from Dublin airport one evening and dropped me to the Dunboyne Castle Hotel in Meath for the DRA hearing. Pat is a straight shooter and a man with good opinions on football, having been immersed in it with his club Navan O'Mahonys for years. He told me I was out of line, but that six months was draconian. At this stage I didn't know what to think. Six months meant up to thirty games, potentially, considering all competitions, club and county, hurling and football. It would be eight months by the time Kerry played again, the following February. From that point of view it was hard to get my head around it. The density of the disciplinary process was hard to fathom too. The different bodies required to deal with the offence didn't make sense to me from either a decision-making or a practical point of view. The DRA had to accept that we had a strong case for the sentence to be overthrown, and so put the case back in the hands of the CCCC, who reduced the ban from six months to three months. By now Gerald McKenna was on the case. His input was invaluable in ensuring my appeal was successful.

Going before the various layers of the GAA's disciplinary bodies was worse than the actual punishment itself. The reduction to three months meant I had the chance to play in an All Ireland final. It did occur to me to not pursue the appeal. Why didn't I? Fear. Hope. Defiance.

Paddy Russell struck me as a decent man. I shouldn't have reacted the way I did. It was an impulsive thing to do. At least Paddy handled himself with some dignity afterwards. He issued a report which was fair and then kept his counsel, unlike his linesman, on whose advice he was acting. In his report, the match assessor, Eddie Cunningham, maintained that my second yellow card was harsh and that Paddy's performance hadn't been up to his usual standard[1]. I would have to agree with that. In fact, the first yellow card I got was equally harsh in my opinion. Footage of this never came to light. Context? The whole day was a farce in my opinion. This was encapsulated in Paddy's failure to send off my direct opponent later on, having given him a second yellow card in the second half. He had to be informed by his fellow officials. The reason? In booking him for the incident with me he noted him as number 10 (that was me) even though he was number 7[2]. As for the linesman, the last place I saw him was the same place I first saw him. On a sideline waving a flag. Not in Killarney but in the new John Mitchels field in Tralee for a McGrath Cup game in January 2014 between Kerry and Cork Institute of Technology. He'd had a lot to say in the aftermath, about the incident and about me personally. He publicly referred to my 'stupidity' and a lot more besides[3]. His need to explain himself, though that didn't appear to me to be standard practice, was telling; as the saying goes, when you're explaining you're losing. His decision to report me for jostling was incorrect in my opinion. My reaction made that irrelevant. Nonetheless I didn't appreciate him talking about me so publicly. It was pretty small stuff. There's a lot I could say in return but I don't need to. Of course officials have a tough job. They get assessed. The linesman has been quoted as saying that, for officials, 'there's no such thing as common sense – only the rules'.[4] For me, the game has to mean more than that.

It would be eighteen months before I spoke about it publicly. And I never spoke about it again. I wasn't interested in speaking to anyone. My inner dialogue was more important than anything I said publicly and would decide my reaction. I listened carefully to that. I am now happy to address this issue from my point of view, so as to contextualize the story and leave it at that. In what was one of the most talked about GAA incidents of recent times there was the least amount of context offered around what actually happened. In fact there was no context at all. Maybe none of that matters when you take my reaction in isolation. Maybe it does. Make up your own minds. I made up my mind on it pretty quickly. I won't underplay what I did. It was a moment of impulse. I can't say it was blown out of proportion either. The problem for me was my reaction blew context out of the water. Something struck me early on which helped me to rationalize the whole situation. From the linesman to the referee, to myself, to the CHC, to the CCCC, to the CAC, to the DRA, and back to the CCCC again, the whole thing was unprofessional. Then again, aren't we all amateurs? I'm not sure if it was the sadist or the survivor in me that eventually looked for levity in the situation. Paddy Russell provided it. I have to give him credit for the line he threw at Darragh on the field that day after Darragh told him he was having a stinker. Paddy stumped him by giving him some lip back. 'You're having a stinker yourself,' he told him. Darragh told me the story on the phone one day. I had to laugh.

In the aftermath, a question kept popping into my head. I wanted to ask someone what the hell 'jostling' even was? Forcing your way by pushing is the actual definition of jostling. If that is the case then I should have got a yellow card every time I went for a breaking ball. And so should every other player on the field. My next question is how the hell is jostling a yellow-card offence in the game when more sinister tactics like 'instigation' or 'provocation' aren't even recognized as offences in the rule book? Jostling? In the All Ireland final that year I saw more jostling in the first half than I had seen in any game all year. The jostling continued down the tunnel at half-time when our vice chairman was turned upside down and left on the flat of his back by a shoulder from one of the Tyrone players. I have no problem with that. Tyrone turned us over on the field too. They 'jostled' us out of it when they had to but for the most part they were just better. Mickey Harte pulled a few strokes with his selection: Sean Cavanagh went to full-forward from midfield; Joe McMahon went to full-back from the half-forward line alongside Justin, his brother, to negate our two big men, Kieran Donaghy and Tommy Walsh. They seemed to be a second ahead of us all through.

I came on in the second half, won a few breaks and got on a few balls. Tyrone seemed to up it a few gears from there. With the last play we won a frec in to the Hill goal. Gooch held the ball and surveyed his options. We needed a goal. He played it short to me across the 21-yard line. I stepped past Brian Dooher and blasted a shot for goal. Someone got a hand to it and the ball flew past the angle of the crossbar and post. A few Tyrone tackles landed as I got my shot away. I was on my knees when the final whistle went a few seconds later. I wanted to dig a hole and crawl into it. Instead, I stood up and walked for the tunnel. The field was overtaken by hyperactive Tyrone supporters, rushing and racing, pushing and chasing, forcing their way through to get to the players. Victory and pitch invasions. The only #jostling that ever counted.

That night at the players' function, I made a silent pledge. Upon my soul, I'd make this up to my teammates.

13

Redemption?

Changes were afoot in the weeks and months that followed the 2008 final. Within Kerry Pat O'Shea stepped down as manager. He probably needed a long holiday after the year he'd had. He did an excellent job in what were difficult circumstances. Primarily because of my suspension. We had a lot of strong minds in the group, but Pat handled us well. His record speaks for itself: two years, two All Ireland finals, one win.

Some few weeks after Pat resigned Jack O'Connor was reappointed. He had been at the '08 final. He still had his finger on the pulse. He went about his second term in charge, reinstalling his ideas and reprogramming the team to his way of doing things. Alan O'Sullivan from Tralee worked alongside him as our strength and conditioning coach. His background was in rugby. He brought with him some very good ideas and energy. The changeover from Pat Flanagan to John Sugrue to Alan inside three years was a challenge for me. People can underestimate the effects of that change. The public focus only on the manager. Ultimately, on match day, players are the products of the weeks and months of work they do under their physical trainers in the build-up. You could catch on to the new manager's ways and ideas easily. Adapting to new physical trainers wasn't as easy. For me, anyway. They each had their own ideas and approaches, which placed different demands on your body. The way my body was, certain specific work suited me. Once I was doing these things I was sure of my performances. As the trainers and training methods changed, my preparations changed and my performances could change as a result. My job was more dependent on my physicality than most other players. Pat Flanagan's approach suited my body best. It was a power-based approach based on the principles of periodization. John's was more of a running and fitness-based approach; Alan's was somewhere in between. Alan and John were great guys to work with. They were diligent and worked all hours with players one-on-one when rehabbing from injury. They were enthusiastic and had massive energy, which is half the battle when driving a group of thirty or so players.

Ger O'Keeffe was back also, and he brought his own unique skill set. Only Johnny Culloty didn't return from the 2004 management team. For his third lieutenant Jack went left-field and called on Éamonn Fitzmaurice. Éamonn was apprehensive at first, I think. He was playing good football with the club and was writing a well-read column in the *Irish Examiner* for the summer. With Éamonn and me being close he wondered if I had any issues about him being on the management team. I had none. The opposite was the case. I was excited. My position on the team was my responsibility, and if I was dropped or not playing well it wouldn't be his fault. It would have been a poor sign of me if I had any issues with his involvement. A sign of weakness. It was a great opportunity for him. The chance for us to win an All Ireland together was an added incentive. Éamonn's playing career finished abruptly, so to be back involved together within eighteen months was great.

I went back training with the lads in early January and kept my head down. I knew what lay ahead and what I wanted to achieve. Tadhg Kennelly had returned home from Australia to play for Kerry. He rang me for a lift to our first session in Killarney. I was delighted he was back. It was exciting to have him involved, for his ability, experience and his personality. He is a great guy to have in any team. He was nervous that morning and wanted to get into the stadium to get that first session under his belt. He was conscious also of keeping his head down and just being one of the lads. It is in his nature to lead and be vocal, so he reined himself in initially. Before long he was a big part of the group. His presence suited us, me in particular. Amongst the media and the public generally the interest in Tadhg was huge. His story, his history, his move to Australia, his move back home and the constant surveillance of his progress as a GAA player meant he was the main focus of everyone's attention. That suited me fine. I'd fly under the radar for the year.

Our league campaign started in Tralee with a win over Donegal. I kicked 3 points. It was my first full game since sometime in 2007. There was a talking point from the league game against Tyrone in Omagh. We changed our formation and played with only four forwards. We tore Tyrone up and led at half-time by 10–12 points. They roared back and made it a game in the second half. When they raged they really raged. I admired that about them. We won by a point or two in the end. We took points in the scuffle that happened as the players were leaving the field too. Ryan McMenamin and Marc Ó Sé clashed, then Jack got stuck in after one of the Tyrone lads threw some verbals his way. We enjoyed Jack's reaction, getting stuck in like that. Personally I was enjoying the fact that other people were getting into scrapes besides me. Marc and Jack. Our calmest player and our manager. Lovely. I knocked some mileage out of that.

The best part was seeing Marc stuck in a ruck. He was usually too cool to fight. Tomás and I tried to get to the bottom of what made him lose his cool but he wouldn't tell us. We knew that even asking him would annoy him. Marc is the most stubborn man I ever met. He wouldn't even give it to say that he'd lost his cool. He says I am the most stubborn man he has ever met. We argue about it for a few minutes, each giving examples of the other's stubbornness, then we laugh and decide it's actually Declan who is the most stubborn of all.

For me the aftermath was a bit different. There was always something. I was scratching my head after this one: I couldn't help but wonder where I stood in the eyes of match officials, both referees and linesmen. In the first half I chased a ball which went out over the line on the stand side of Healy Park. I dropped the ball where I was. As I walked away I got a punch in the balls from one of the Tyrone players. It happened right beside the linesman, who called the referee, Jimmy White from Donegal. Jimmy, on his linesman's advice, gave me a yellow card. He never spoke to the Tyrone player. I asked him what it was for, but he didn't tell me. That seemed to be how it was back then. Communication was seen as weakness, I think. I didn't dwell on it at the time. It would only distract you. I put it out of my head. When I thought about it after the game I was philosophical. It was clear that I had a certain reputation amongst match officials. I would say that's been the case since the 2008 incident with Paddy Russell, but more likely it went back to tossing the water bottles in 2006. In 2007 there was an incident in Killarney when a Cork player kicked me on the ground a few feet from a linesman. That linesman called the referee too. The referee gave me a yellow card. *The Sunday Game* highlighted the incident later that night. Nothing happened. I still don't know what that yellow card was for. I don't know what the card was for in Omagh either.

Jimmy White called me a few days later to explain the decision. He apologized. I accepted it. Why wouldn't I? It wasn't his doing. Jimmy hadn't seen the incident, he was only going on his linesman's advice. What that advice was I don't know. Linesmen were a breed I couldn't relate to at all. I wondered a few times what their role actually was outside of deciding which way line balls went. Were they agents for protection or agents for punishment? Were they there to pre-empt trouble and protect players, or react to trouble? For me they could do so much more to pre-empt trouble if they were looking for it. Then again, if there is no provision made for offences like 'instigation' or 'provocation' it's hard for linesmen to legislate for or against.

At that stage I was too focused on other things to get bogged down in it. I'd be no use to Kerry stuck in the mud. We won the league final against Derry in Croke Park on the May Bank Holiday weekend. That was all the assurance I needed to know we'd be heard in Fitzgerald Stadium in the late summer again. My balls were still intact too. Lucky that. I'd need them later on.

The summer brought the hard ground. No bogging. It did however take on a roguish shape that was becoming almost familiar to us. Codding us. Promising one thing and delivering another. Even in those years we won Munster we often laboured, dragging ourselves through games, shadows of ourselves, deflecting the doubts and questions that followed, before rising again in August and September. How many times can you do that was the question? Some of it was down to our conditioning, surely. We had to trust in our methods. 2009 started in earnest in Killarney against Cork. I had this day in my head for a long time. My man Ger Spillane was replaced before half-time. Noel O'Leary came on and did a man-marking job on me for the rest of the day. It was my first full championship game in two years. I tired a bit after half-time, when usually I would be at my best. We got a late draw on the day from a massive Bryan Sheehan free in injury time. Sheehan was one of the best all round footballers I played with.

The replay was a more straightforward affair. They caught fire as they sometimes could and beat us well in Páirc Uí Chaoimh. O'Leary had been following me around from the start this time. It was bizarre. During a break in play, he was getting in my face again. Off the field I have a thing about people invading my personal space. I'm sure everyone is the same. It agitates me if people get too close. O'Leary was right in my face. I threw a hand back at him to get him out of my face. Pat McEneaney only spotted O'Leary's reaction and sent him off. It was only on the linesman's advice that Pat sent me off too. That was a blow to me following the previous summer. I decided the best thing to do at that point was quit. I was quite happy with the decision. Relieved, in fact. I felt it was the best course of action. To be suspended again was unacceptable. I was sick of the game and what came with it. I dealt with 2008. I was disappointed with myself for allowing this to happen.

Jack was in Kenmare for a few days after the game. I went to meet him and told him. He talked me around over a rare steak. He told me about some shenanigans on the sideline as I was sent off in Cork. There was some loose talk flying around and some congratulations being meted out. Twenty minutes into a Munster final is no place to be letting your guard down, especially within earshot of the opposition manager. That changed my mind. I forgot the past and thought of the future instead.

It was after this I felt I had to cut the emotion out of my game. Or at least manage it better. It was getting me into trouble. There was no point in codding myself. My ways would have to change, to an extent. I couldn't do anything about opponents testing me out, but I could manage myself better. To improve as a player and to protect myself from falling into any traps that might be set in the future it had to be done. The way I played was fuelled largely by emotion. When you play like that you are susceptible to overstepping the mark from time to time. After six or seven years of playing that way at inter-county level I was close to burn-out. By June 2009 I felt completely burned out. Physically it wasn't such a problem. Even so, once you hit your thirties it's hard to play that kind of all-action, physical game effectively. Mentally it was even trickier. The physical nature of the job brought conflict. I don't think people were used to seeing Kerry footballers play as physically as I did. There seemed to be more scrutiny. I was being watched by opponents, officials, TV cameras and certain opposition managers.

Ultimately I felt I needed to get better as a footballer. I wasn't fulfilling my potential. I had hit the limit of what you can achieve as a heart-on-your-sleeve-passionate type of player. There was a certain shelf-life for that kind of performer, and you only ever got a certain type of performance. Often a blind one – with an inhibited awareness of what was going on around you – committed, aggressive, physical, and with a little football thrown in. You need that kind of player in a team and I always played with those qualities, but there had to be more. When you reach thirty you won't get much better at the disruptive side of the game. It's a young man's game, anyway. I could have done with a young pup coming along and picking up the slack. A change of direction was needed. Some balance too. I wanted to play more with my head than my heart.

It took the sending off in '09 for me to address that. Emotion was the key. As long as I continued to play on emotion I was liable to react on the field or get involved with an opponent. For years it was what made me. Now it was undoing me. Outside of the danger of being seen as a liability, outbursts on the field in front of people are just not cool. I was better than that. I had to improve. The question was, at nearly 30 years old, could I change for the better?

To find out I called on Enda McNulty, a performance coach and sports psychologist. I explained to Enda where I was coming from and, more importantly, where I wanted to go. I wasn't fulfilling my potential. If anything, I was inhibiting it. Enda had won an All Ireland himself as a player with Armagh. He listened to what I had to say and asked me some questions, noting my answers and asking some more questions. I asked him what the key to peak performance was. He said the ability to relax and stay relaxed before and during competition. He asked me in return how I relaxed before and during competition, what I did to forget about the game in the build-up. I had nothing. Why would you want to switch off from the game? The game was all I thought about. According to Enda this wasn't a good thing. He asked me what I did to stay relaxed during games. I told him I had no problem staying relaxed during games once I was left alone.

Finding distraction from the game became my focus, especially in the days leading up to games. Less was more. I managed to switch off from the game quite easily by identifying the things that relaxed me. I discovered, through talking to

Enda, that I had no real hobbies in life, nothing that occupied me for periods of time. Work was just work. Golf was something all my friends did. I never got into it – it didn't give me a buzz. Football and competing and winning was all I thought about. There were things I had an interest in – fashion, music, magazines – but that was it. I never pursued anything enough to say it was a hobby. I thought more about developing my interests into hobbies and activities that would occupy me for long periods. Music became part of my preparation on match days. I'd read blogs, magazines and books, more so in the days leading up to matches. Fashion was a real interest of mine too: from looking at how magazines were edited to studying how brands were positioned; from examining ad campaigns to watching shows online, studying designers and shopping. I had never taken the time to look at these things before. I was too focused on one thing: football.

This more laid-back approach suited me. On and off the field, I found a way to change my approach and improve as a footballer. When you play with emotion, or your heart, you have no vision, no awareness of outcomes or consequences. You play blind, almost – or at least with a very narrow focus. When you play with your head, you play with vision, all you think of is the outcome and consequences. You see things before they happen. You are aware of your position and your movement, and the consequences of both, to a greater extent. It was just a pity it took a sending off for me to really address my whole approach to the game. Had I not done so I wouldn't have won Footballer of the Year in 2009 or improved from there on.

Having missed the qualifier against Longford, my first game back was against Sligo in Tralee. I was at home all that day listening to music on the floor of my sitting room. My house is only minutes from Austin Stack Park. I drove down around 90 minutes before throw-in. I sat in my car for a few minutes before going into the pavilion. My conditioning was good back then. I would lift weights maybe two hours before a game, some light squats and some dumbbell lunges. It was a great way to recruit power before going out. I often found that power would dissipate during the warm-up so I'd get one of our bigger players to jump on my back before throw-in and I'd do some squats. It may have looked funny but that put the explosiveness back into my legs.

We got a right game off Sligo. It took a late penalty save from Murph to keep us in it. Tadhg was out with a broken hand. He was laughing after the game telling me he watched the last few minutes from behind his cast thinking, 'What have I done?' He had come home from Australia to win an All Ireland. Now he was watching on with a broken hand as Sligo had a penalty to win the game and dump us out in the qualifiers. It was no laughing matter at the time. I dealt with the disappointment of the sending-off in Cork the only way you can. On the field. I kicked 3 points from play and won Man of the Match. In the first half we scored 8 points. I scored 2 points and had 5 assists. My work with Enda McNulty was paying off already. I was seeing the game more clearly. The fact that the game was tight and we struggled was great. It gave me even more of an opportunity to prove myself to my teammates. I enjoyed the fact that the team was struggling a bit. The longer the poor form went on, the more opportunity I had to lead through it.

If beating Sligo was tough, things were about to get even tougher. Antrim came to Tullamore full of hope having watched us struggle against Sligo. They played like they expected to win. With ten minutes gone in the second half they led by 2 points, playing with a gale of wind. Our backs were to the wall. The only thing you could do was come out fighting. You'd scrap for anything that was going. It only takes a moment to take momentum. You turn on your opponents, the officials, and your teammates if you have to – the offence you feel as the thought of losing takes over and you find a new gear. Mike McCarthy did. He didn't come out of retirement to lose on his first start. He played at centre-back for the first time in his career. You had to play with Mac, or maybe directly against him, to appreciate how good he was. Though a quiet, shy guy, he had a lot of pride and character. He had a streak in him when he needed it and he was capable of inspiring on the field. Days like Tullamore were my favourite. I enjoyed it most when the going was tough. We won by 8 points in the end, which people seemed to forget.

Kerry people told me afterwards that the reason there was such a big crowd there on the day was they felt it might be the last time they would see us play. Maybe they felt we had nothing left to give. Nothing left to prove. There was evidence to that end. We were staggering through games. Antrim had us on the ropes. They led by 1–4 to 1–3 at the break. The dressing room at half-time was a tough station. I got some kind of perverse enjoyment at times like this. I was on my own crusade. I had more to prove than anyone. Losing would have compounded 2008 in the worst way possible for me. We roused ourselves again. I scored a goal that day against Antrim. I remember the move. I think I won a break and slipped a pass to Tomás on the run. Tomás knocked it on to Gooch, who slipped it to Tommy Walsh, who gave it to me on the run through the middle. I picked it up again on the 21 and slipped it inside to Donnchadh Walsh, whose shot for goal was saved. The rebound fell to me. I slid the ball home from all of 6 inches. As I made my way back out the field I pointed to Star on the sideline. He was injured and would miss most of the year. He was a great teammate. My goals were so rare that when Tommy Walsh chased me out the field after it I could hear him laughing. I think that says everything for my goal-scoring prowess. In my minor and under-21 days I got lots of goals. When I started out with the club I was a high-scoring corner-forward. As a senior I didn't get too many. We went on to win by a few points. The Kerry supporters played their part that day. We could feel them. I met my friend Gerry Rochford on the field afterwards. He was proud as punch. If he were a footballer he would take some stopping. The performance was full of spirit and character. We still had a lot to do in terms of performance – in the first half we'd been stuck in gear – but in the second half we had found something like our old form. The signs were there.

Facing Dublin next in the quarter-final was perfect in a way. We were written off. Clapped out. Our backs were up going in. I know mine was anyway. The more I thought about it, I couldn't understand how anyone was writing us off. Of course people had every reason to. Performances pointed towards something final. It pays to delude yourself sometimes in sport. I couldn't accept why anyone was writing us off. I was defiant. We all were. Our preparation the week of the quarter-final was spot on. We only trained on the Tuesday. For the Thursday session we checked in at the Europe in Killarney, had a swim, dinner and did our video work. Relaxation and preparation. No need for any big talk. That was taken care of. Around the Crowne Plaza in Santry, where we stayed that weekend, was good craic. There was always a lot of messing going on with our fellas. Any kind of mischief that would cause annoyance or dis-comfort to the next fella was seen as fair game.

My thing was swapping the numbers on the room doors. Sometimes I'd swap my own too so no one could find my room.

If someone asked my room number I'd sometimes give it to them then switch my door number. It depended where we stayed. On some doors you couldn't replace the numbers. I always did it directly across from my room too, so I could watch others get locked out and have to go back down to reception and have their cards validated again. A right pain in the hole that is. All you want is a cup of tea and a biscuit while watching *Match of the Day*. The night before the Dublin game Tadhg and I swapped numbers on the doors opposite us. They screwed off easily so that room 133 would be 135 and vice versa. Our team doctor Dave Geaney was in one of the rooms. We were watching out of the peephole as he tried to get into someone else's room thinking it was his own. He'd stand back and check the room number, then check his key card, then continue sliding the card in and out. He returned to reception and tried a second time before disappearing again. Tadhg and myself were lying back down on our beds watching TV maybe twenty minutes later when we heard a familiar voice erupt outside. 'Jeeeesus Christ allmiiiighty!! What kind of a hotel is this?? I just want to get into my roooooom!! Rooooooom 1–3–3!!' We looked out of our peephole. Dr Dave had a stressed member of staff at the door of 133, which was actually room 135, sticking a key card in and out of it. I slid down the back of the door laughing.

Another evening I was unscrewing the numbers off another door when a woman opened it. I thought we had the floor to ourselves, as usual. I stood there with the room number in my hand looking like a maintenance guy.

'Can I help you?' she enquired.

'I found this on the ground. I was just screwing it back on,' I told her, as I handed it to her and walked off.

I found a good laugh the best way to stay relaxed before games. There was no shortage of laughs with Tadhg around.

The morning of the game we were a bit more serious. Our thoughts turned to Dublin. They tore through Leinster as usual. We tore through them from the throw-in. A goal into the Hill after one minute sent us on our way. Tomás started it and Gooch finished it. Tomás knocked a free to me from the half-back line. I had left my spot at right half-forward to pick it up around centre-forward. I spun away from Bryan Cullen and slipped a ball to Darragh on the run. He switched play to Darran, who had moved into a pocket around the top of the D. Mike Mac had left centre-back when Tomás took the free. Darran slipped it to him on the D. Gooch just stood to the right of the goal between the 14- and 21-yard lines and waited. When Mac took the pass Gooch came alive. He was behind his man's back. Instead of running out in front of him he pedalled backwards towards the goal. Mac slipped it to him. He still had his back to goal when he received it. Without looking he spun and rolled it past Stephen Cluxton. Beauty.

We played some great football for the rest of the day. The Dubs were starting out under Pat Gilroy. It was a tough day out for them. Often they can be the days that make you. By half-time we were up 12 points. By the end we were up 17. Tadhg had still been out with the hand injury and was a bit disappointed not to start. He came on for Tommy Walsh in the first half and played well. He's a very unselfish player. It was a day when everyone played well. Darran as captain was flying and deservedly got Man of the Match. Meath were up next in the semi-final. The last time Kerry met them in an All Ireland semi-final they'd hockeyed us in 2001. They never feared Kerry or anyone else. I have family there. My aunt Nuala Smyth and her husband Pat are big football fans, so that added some excitement to the build-up. We won the semi-final on a wet day in a low-scoring game. Meath were physical and dangerous up front, but we dominated around the middle. We won without playing well. A great way to win a semi-final. At the final whistle I sprinted for the dressing room. All I could think about was the final. Against some odds we were right where we wanted to be.

The previous Sunday Cork had beaten Tyrone in the other semi with a great display. They were intense and aggressive. They were so impressive on the day, and their physicality was such that I was happy watching them. It was going to be very hard for them to repeat the intensity levels they showed. We would meet them in the final.

2009 was our sixth consecutive final. All I thought about every year was another final and the chance of another medal. I came to expect to be there. The build-up was always enjoyable. I spent days in the relaxation rooms of Ballygarry House, outside Tralee. The staff looked after me very well. They would bring bowls of fruit and smoothies. I'd read magazines and take in the views of the Tralee mountains. Even though Cork were strong favourites we were rising again at just the right time. It was nicely set up for us as far as I could see.

We stayed in the Radisson in Stillorgan the night before, one of my favourite hotels. I was always particular about where we stayed – the Crowne Plaza in Santry was another favourite. We had our team meeting out on the back lawn in the dusk. Somehow it added to the sense of ambush that we'd carried with us since Tullamore. We were insurgents. We stood in a circle and spoke in the dusk about our plans and our preparation and the importance of execution. By the morning of the final I was light on my feet. Relaxed.

Cork started well, like we expected. By now they were a match for us physically. They weren't just fit but were powerful and capable of playing at high intensity. Stopping them was hard work. They were so big and strong that once they had possession they were difficult to stop. We knew what to expect. What we didn't expect was the team they picked. We knew of an injury to Ray Carey in the lead-up to the game. We expected Eoin Cadogan would be picked to mark Tommy Walsh. His non-selection was surprising. We copped the change during the warm-up out on the field when their team was called out. The Cork manager had gone for his club-mate Kieran O'Connor. The resulting match-ups suited us perfectly. Declan, Tommy and Tadhg did a lot of damage as a direct result. This was a big game for us. For me especially.

All three were flying, particularly in the first half. From the throw-in Tadhg caught Nicholas Murphy with a high tackle. Murphy went down, Tadhg was booked. I thought nothing of it at the time. I didn't think there would be the furore that ensued. Cork went ahead early on. When they scored a goal by the 15th minute or so we were 5 points down.

I felt a shudder as it hit the net. The game was theirs for the taking. We'd started a few finals like that ourselves and weren't caught. It was time to act. We ramped it up and started scrapping for everything. I got into the game in the middle; Tommy Griffin and Tom Sullivan shut up shop at the back. They had their hands full in the first half. Mike Mac dominated. Tomás dominated. Darragh and Séamus Scanlon dominated the middle of the field. Tommy, Gooch and Tadhg, with two great scores, put us 3 ahead at half-time. All our forwards were good, but Tommy Walsh, Tadhg and Declan were excellent in the first half.

Cork had chances in the second half and had momentum for long periods. Murph made a great save from Daniel Goulding after he broke in along the end line. They pushed and pushed. We got numbers back and countered. Darran got an early second-half score after tearing down the Cusack Stand sideline. He took on Anthony Lynch and a few others and scored an important point. We'd had a pow-wow just before that. I asked him if he was going to do something today. He told me where to go. I enjoyed that. You always get a reaction from him.

A decisive moment came with 15 minutes to go. Donncha O'Connor had a chance for a point. I was close enough to him. I went to cover the path to goal in case he took Marc on. He didn't. He shot for a point. Marc got a block down. Darragh picked up the break and worked it towards the Hogan side. Tom Sullivan took it on the burst down the middle and gave it to Séamus Scanlon, who found Gooch out wide down the Cusack sideline. He worked his way in along the end line and hand-passed across the goal to Donnchadh Walsh. Tommy Walsh had peeled away from the goal outside him. Donnchadh slipped him the ball, Tommy landed a point with his left. That was a crucial score. We worked another one down the Hogan sideline. Séamus Scanlon won a free. I released Tomás. He found Tommy near the corner of the Hogan and the Canal End. Tommy played a one-two with Donnchadh Walsh and landed a similar point from the opposite side. There was no score for the final 12 minutes.

The last few minutes were intense. We played the game out protecting our lead. The last kickout came from our end. I was on the opposite side of the field. I went early and ran across the field to get as close to the breakdown as I could. Even if I didn't get to it I would be an extra body in the road. Darragh and Tadhg were gone off by now. The ball travelled from Diarmuid Murphy to the middle of the field towards the Hogan Stand side. Heads, shoulders and hands reached for it. I caught a glimpse of Tomás underneath it. The break count was important to both of us. We fought between us for any break that fell anywhere near us. I'd knock him over if I had to and he would me. I'd be pissed off if he got there before me. Breaks were like scores to me. As I raced to get there the whistle went. Marty Duffy called time. Suddenly all that desperation for the ball evaporated. No one wanted it. If I had got it I'd lamp it out over the roof of the Hogan Stand. Out of the corner of my eye I saw Tomás fall to his knees, two fists clenched, teeth gritted, a snarl carved on to his face. I couldn't tell you exactly what the look on his face said or what this meant to him. I couldn't tell you exactly what it meant to me. I just knew that this was an important one. It had to be done.

It was unusual to win an All Ireland without scoring a goal in the final, but that was what we did. We won 0–16 to 1–09. The final whistle brought me a feeling I hadn't experienced for a while on a pitch. It washed over me for maybe ten seconds and washed away again like a wave breaking on a shore. I couldn't put a finger on what it was at the time. It was only after it had washed away that I recognized it. It was pride. In Kerry. In my teammates. In myself. Mike Quirke, Killian Young and Aidan O'Mahony ran to me. Quirkey bent down to lift me off the ground and as he did so Mahony jumped on my back. Quirkey couldn't move us. The four of us were just there in a small huddle, bouncing and laughing at our attempted celebration. Éamonn came bounding in. All the way from Ballinclogher. I wanted to tell him I was sorry I didn't live up to the captaincy a year earlier. The words wouldn't come to me, though. Instead we embraced and my laughing turned to tears. I quickly quelled them. Tadhg came running at me, his eyes full. We all have our journeys. His was longer than most but he got there, like he knew he would. His father, the Horse, was a hero. Kerry lost when he passed away. Jimmy Deenihan's oration by his grave-side told me more about the man than any game he played. It said more about Kerry football than any game Kerry ever played. My respect for the men who went before me in Green and Gold goes deep. Without them we could never defy odds and win when we're not supposed to. We weren't supposed to win this one.

Tommy Walsh ran over and lifted me off my feet. If anyone had won us the game he had. I was under the stand by the time I met Gooch. He grabbed the back of my head and clenched one fist and looked at me dead on. We roomed together, won together, lost together and grew up together in Kerry jerseys. We needed this one. I told him how much respect I had for him. Then I just stood there motionless looking up at Darran climbing the steps. He led us well. I met my mother as I climbed the steps myself. 2008 was hard on her and my family. They have always been there for me and supported me. I felt that I had let them down badly in 2008; 2009 was the only way I could try to put right what I had done.

I didn't meet Darragh or Marc until the dressing room. Darragh was quiet. Relieved like myself. We shook hands. Darragh wasn't a man for hugs. If I had known that was the last time we would tog out together for Kerry I'd have spent a minute with him. Mind you, I'd have done well to get a minute with him. He never stops. I didn't anyway. Why? Because when you're winning you think it will never end. You feel invincible. I thought Darragh was invincible and would play for ever. I didn't know it at the time but that was the end for him. The end of the invincibility. It was the beginning of a few days of right craic though. Marc was livelier. As soon as we spotted each other we started laughing. We couldn't talk for laughing. He was trying to say something to me but he couldn't. I was trying to ask him what he was laughing about but I couldn't. I am always laughing around the Ó Sés. We share a kind of dark sense of humour. We find humour in hardship for some reason. Each other's hardships more so than anyone else's. There was no hardship in this though. We both knew the next few days would be mighty fun. Jack shook my hand. He made allowances for my rough edges up to a point. I delivered for him on the field.

I remember all those moments because that was what I played for. Those short, sweet moments of victory. They mean more than medals, they just don't last as long. 2009 was the best All Ireland we ever won.

The madness that follows an All Ireland win can be hard to handle. It can intoxicate. You need a sound head on your shoulders. I could be a bit wild at times, but I grew out of that. Insouciance suited me. Whatever way I rewired myself I now find it takes quite a bit to turn me on either way, in victory or defeat.

In the first six years of my career we played in six finals, winning four. We lost only five championship games in that time. None in '04, one in '05, one in '06, none in '07, two in '08 and one in '09. On top of that we only lost a handful of league games. We were sure of ourselves. After 2009 that surety seemed to desert us. I didn't think that would be the last All Ireland I would win, but it was.

We stayed at the Berkeley Court afterwards. One of the first people I met in the lobby was the great Jack O'Shea. Every young fella in Kerry felt they knew Jacko growing up because of the Golden Years. 'Jacko Shea to Páidí Ó Sé, Páidí Ó Sé back to Jacko Shea, they're not brothers they're not related.' That was the line. Even young fellas with no interest in football knew it. I got to know Jacko when I did eventually grow up. We spoke on the phone a lot in 2008. He didn't need to give me his time but he did. It was great to meet him that night in 2009. If I ever wanted to show Kerry football off to a stranger I'd show them footage of Jacko playing. The best advertisement you could ask for.

Late that night, or early the following morning, to find some peace Tadhg and I escaped outside. Inside was heavy going. Outside gave us a chance to have a laugh. Tadhg's attitude was good to be around. Even outside there were people milling around. There was a tree between the hotels. We climbed it with two bottles of beer and spoke about the game and games we'd played when we were younger, both with and against each other. We laughed at pranks we had pulled along the way in hotels around the country, and the pranks we would pull the next day on the train to Kerry. People passed underneath us and couldn't see us. It was a nice release. When our beers were finished we jumped down and went back inside.

Back then we had a tradition of visiting the Boar's Head on Capel Street the morning after a final. Páidí started it off and before long Darragh, Tomás and Marc were joining him. Then Éamonn Fitz joined them. Then I joined them. 2006 was my first trip. I got a call from Éamonn telling me to call down. He was delighted. He had just been fitted for a new suit. Louis Copeland has a shop on Capel Street. Páidí rang him. Louis went down and measured Páidí, Darragh, Tomás, Marc and Éamonn for suits upstairs in the Boar's. They were beaming when I got there. Páidí was a man who actually appreciated fashion. He loved fine suits and ties, he just never used the word 'fashion'. Irish men don't like to use the word 'fashion', some find it emasculating.

Nowadays every team who wins the All Ireland goes to the Boar's Head the morning after. Hugh Hourican, the proprietor, is a great GAA man. He's waiting patiently for the day Cavan join him the Monday morning after an All Ireland win. The morning after the '09 final we all jumped in a cab from the Boar's to the Sunnybank in Glasnevin. Upon arrival Darragh informed us that Billy Morgan and Jimmy Keaveney were inside. I was looking forward to meeting Jimmy. I wasn't sure how to take Billy or how Billy would take me, so I just went straight up to him and said hello. We ended up having a good chat that day.

In his autobiography, later on, Billy said he had made a new friend that day. I did too. We left the Sunnybank and faced into the best part of any All Ireland win. The train journey home.

Redemption is a dangerous word. It doesn't sit easily with me. What happens if you slip again? What is that called? Disaster? Doom? Tragedy? No redemption is too deep, too dense. Things are what they are. I did what I did in 2008. I did what I had to do in 2009. It was a journey. I got there. It was easy to come back from it in some ways. Sure, if I made any shape at all in 2009 it was an improvement. I didn't try to redeem myself, I just tried to be better. In October '09 I was named Footballer of the Year. The names on that list humbled me. I was honoured and grateful to those who picked me. I never got the chance to thank them. I will do so now. I had my eye on winning it all the same. Not just in 2009. In 2010 too.

Tommy, who the f**k threw that?

It's just after New Year's in 2010. It's dark and I'm very far from home. I'm with about thirty of the strongest, fittest men in Ireland, and somehow I don't feel safe. We're walking through what looks like a massive car park late at night, so it's hard to know exactly where we are. Either side of us are small, wooden shacks, some empty, some occupied. Outside these shacks are groups of local men. Bahamians, dark-skinned, white-eyed, vested and barefoot. They observe us as we pass through. We stare straight ahead acting like we belong. We don't belong. Eventually we find our destination. A bar. We are the Kerry football team on our annual team holiday. We're staying at the Atlantis resort nearby, which has everything we need to enjoy a nice holiday. We're not supposed to wander too far away from it for safety reasons. But we do anyway. As soon as we pile into this little rum shack a crowd gathers outside. The locals. They're drinking bottles of beer and smoking. We're not sure if we're surrounded by dangerous locals or just curious locals. We're giddy with nerves. I look through the cocktail menu. A Bahama Mama? Yes ma'am. Another? OK ma'am. Before long the Bahama Mamas are flying and we have forgotten about the prying eyes outside. There is a jukebox somewhere. The tunes are flying. I love a dance when I'm out if the music is good. The music is good in this rum shack. I spot a stool and stand up on it. I'm about to stand tall when I get a woeful crack of something into the back of the head that nearly cleans me off the stool. I duck down and shoot a look around the room, then outside at the locals, then around the room again, looking for the guilty party. Someone has thrown a bottle at me. The side of my head is throbbing. I'm looking for the culprit. He'll get that back and then some if I find out who it was. I don't care if he's Bahaman or Kerryman. Tommy Walsh is looking up at me. I'm half-crouched, holding the side of my head. Tommy looks like he knows something. 'Tommy!!! Who the f**k threw that???' Tommy can't answer me. He's laughing like a drain. Can't get the words out. Instead, he points to the ceiling over my head. I look up. There's a fan whirring round like rotor blades on a chopper. The f**cking thing nearly lobotomized me. I think about breaking it somehow but as Bahama Mama'd as I am I decipher it will probably mangle me if I touch it. It will either land me inside the counter on top of the bar woman or outside the counter on top of the lads. Instead I get down off the stool, still thinking of ways to get the fan back. I look up at it then I look at Tommy. I start laughing at Tommy, who is still laughing at me. Eventually I take my beating. It was time to go home. The Bahama Mamas nearly blew the head off me. Literally.

We had great craic on our team holidays. The reason being in all my years playing with Kerry I never met a bad guy. Plenty of good characters though. Another night in the Bahamas Séamus Scanlon and Aidan O'Shea were playing blackjack in the casino late at night. Aidan is a son of Jacko's. Injuries cost him in his career. Scanlon was a great character. Very popular and down to earth. As the two boys played Aidan noticed the famous tennis player, Boris Becker, was at the same table. He nudged Scan. 'Hey, Scan, look across the table. There's Boris Becker.' Scanlon looked around the table then looked back at Aidan curiously and asked a question only he could ask. 'Who's Maurice Becker?' They're not big on tennis in Currow.

Another year we were in Negril, Jamaica, at a place called Rick's Café. There's a cliff jump there. It's maybe 40 feet high. Scanlon jumped off it. For some reason, he lost composure and started flailing as he jumped. He assumed the seated position on entry and landed on his arse. There were these local dudes, Rastas on the clifftop, smoking weed watching all the jumps. As Scanlon landed on the seat of his pants the four boys were on their hands and knees laughing and pointing towards the water, gesticulating about this mad white guy with red hair who just jumped off. He was a great character.

I was thinking of how I would best sum up on my teammates in a story. I think this one about Star does it best. I was mad to do the jump with Séamus, but I had no shorts. I went back to the hotel, but jumping off the cliff was all I could think about. I couldn't get it out of my head. Star and I and a few more headed back the next day. I was eyeing up the jump. Star saw me. 'Are you jumping?' I started laughing. 'I am,' I replied. He started laughing. 'Can you swim?' he asked, knowing the answer. 'I can't, as you well know, Starry boy!!' says I, laughing. 'Jesus Christ, you're an awful man,' said Star, as he threw off his T-shirt. 'I'll go in before you and wait for you in the water.' All the insurance I needed. We both walked to the queue for the jump. I was laughing hard with nerves. Star jumped. I was next. I leapt off the cliff after him. He waited for me in the water even though the lifeguards were telling him to get out. When I landed I plunged God knows how deep. I fought the water to get back to the top. As I did Star swam to me and grabbed me by the neck. Through pure fear I somehow learned how to swim and managed to keep myself afloat. We swam to the ledge. A lifeguard was giving Star grief for not getting out of the water. 'All right, buddy, sorry about that,' said Star and kept walking. We were laughing our holes off. That was the kind of guy I was dealing with in the Kerry team. They'd break rules to save you from drowning.

My favourite holiday story involves Darragh, though. We were leaving Shannon for New York in 2008. The weather was shocking as we boarded. It was just after Christmas. No more than myself, Darragh can't do long-haul flights without sleeping pills. He necked two not long after taking his seat. His lovely wife Amy was next to him. I was about three seats behind them. The sleepers hit home. Darragh fell into a deep nap. As he did the weather worsened. An hour passed. We never moved. Two hours passed. No budge. Three hours passed. This bird was a dead duck. Four passed and we were still on the ground in Shannon. Next thing Darragh's sleeping pills wore off and he woke with a start. He took a look out of the window beside him. There was snow on the ground by now. He rose from his seat to get his bag, wondering why Amy, his wife, wasn't moving. He was half standing when she told him we were still grounded in Shannon. He thought we had landed on the other side of the pond in JFK, and started looking around at the rest of us in the hope that Amy was joking. He sat back down, glanced out of the window again, then back at Amy, horror and disbelief on his face. He was disgusted. When he saw me laughing he was even more disgusted. Which made it funnier still. Like I said, we found humour in each other's hardships.

14

Cork v Kerry, Part I – Recidivist?

The atmosphere in Páirc Uí Rinn is dark. The floodlights are casting shadows. In the half-light of the evening it's hard to see clearly. Cork are highly motivated. That much I can see very clearly. Last year's All Ireland final went down the wrong hole. Hard to swallow. Later in '09 there was Tadhg Kennelly's autobiography. That was hard to swallow for them too. In fact, it came back up. At the start of that final Tadhg caught Nicholas Murphy with a high, mistimed tackle. In his book there was an insinuation that it was deliberate. In a newspaper serialization that followed there was an insinuation that it was premeditated. There is a difference between something being deliberate and it being premeditated. You might say that is semantics. That's exactly what it is. Semantics are important. You can do something deliberately in a second without thinking about it. Doing something premeditated is different. That takes planning. There's no way Tadhg planned what happened. You couldn't. Why would you plan something like that and risk getting sent off 10 seconds into an All Ireland final? Could you plan to go out in an aggressive manner? Yes. Could that go wrong? Yes. And it nearly did for Tadhg.

Between the jigs and the reels there was uproar in the aftermath.

What happened? I don't rightly know.

Wires got crossed, I think. A man who'd just achieved a lifetime dream by following in the footsteps of his deceased father and his older brother, high on victory and a sense of achievement. A ghostwriter living on a different continent in a different time zone. A conversation had late at night or early in the morning. The Aussie mentality celebrates the manliness and physicality of its own sport. Clearly there was a misunderstanding about what Tadhg did or said or meant. I don't rightly know. If you're on a deadline, as they would have been following an All Ireland final, rushing to finish a book due for release within days or weeks of the final, it's very easy to make a mistake. The telling of the build-up to the final, the preparations, the game, the aftermath of the game, the incident itself, would require time and careful crafting. Speaking over the phone to a ghostwriter in a different time zone in the aftermath of a big victory about a game that the writer may not know well or fully understand is tricky. It's open to all sorts of interpretation and misinterpretation even to the most well-intentioned ghostwriter. There's a big difference between telling a story and writing a story. I know myself I could never tell my story to a stranger and expect the efficacy and accuracy of my own written account. The Aussie and the Irishman couldn't be any more different. Australian culture is markedly different to Irish culture obviously. We are two disparate nations. Disparate geographically, culturally, psychologically and sociologically. This sociological disparity is a telling one. What can be construed as acceptable in one culture can cause uproar in another. Lines got crossed. I felt for Tadhg in a way. He is a completely honest and honourable sportsman. He seemed as surprised as I was.

The outrage was all a bit Irish for me. There was a lot I didn't understand about the whole thing so I kept out of it. Even so there was a lesson in it; ghost-written books could haunt you if you weren't careful.

I can understand Cork being annoyed about it all the same. I also think had Cork won the game we wouldn't have heard much about it.

In February 2010 I was programmed to play at my usual number 10 spot. Aidan Walsh was named at 7 for Cork. I had heard good things about him so I was interested to see what he was about. Half-back is a tough position to play at that level if you're not used to it. When he approached me before the game he was smaller than I expected. It took me a while to cop what was going on. As was a habit of the Cork manager at the time, particularly with whoever was marking me, he made last-minute changes. He had named a dummy team. Eoin Cadogan replaced Aidan Walsh. As late as my last game against Cork in the summer of 2013 he sprang Noel O'Leary just minutes before the throw-in though he wasn't named to play. We all knew it was going to happen. I had to wonder what the endgame was. I can understand springing a forward at the last minute, like Davy Fitz did with Shane O'Donnell in the 2013 All Ireland hurling final. O'Donnell scored 3–03. That's clever. I fail to see how naming a young 6-foot 4-inch midfielder at wing-back, then springing an inexperienced defender at the last minute, works for anyone though. The individual or the team. Unless perhaps he is playing under certain instructions. It seemed to me that Cadogan was detailed to man-mark me. In that case surely the defender needs to know he's playing well in advance? I know when I played at wing-back I wouldn't have appreciated being given a marking job on a dangerous player at the last minute. I found it all very bizarre.

Going into the game, trouble and suspensions were the last thing on my mind. I was 30 years old, Footballer of the Year coming to Cork for a league game in February. The previous weekend I was Man of the Match against Dublin, kicking 4 points from play. I was reaching my peak as a footballer. I had nothing to gain getting involved with anyone. I had plenty to lose, though. Nothing was going to be proven on a dark February night in Páirc Uí Rinn.

The first time Eoin Cadogan touched the ball, nearly 15 minutes in, Donnchadh Walsh and Kieran Donaghy tackled him. One of them accidentally caught him high. He went down holding his face. The doctor was called for. He received treatment for a facial injury, which it turned out needed dental surgery a few days later. A few minutes later Cork were attacking up the stand side of the field opposite the dressing room and their path was blocked. I took Eoin's ground about two yards in front of him in case they switched the play. This was the basis of my game for years. Being defensively aware, not allowing my man to be an outlet or attacking threat.

As the play developed on the other side of the field, he pulled me to the ground from behind. My head was on one side of him, my body on the other. I was struggling to breathe. To release myself I stuck a finger in the side of his mouth and pulled his cheek. It's the most effective way I know to defend yourself and prevent a situation from escalating. No punches, no gouges, no squeezing their windpipe. It works and it's pretty harmless. It disarms immediately. That's not to say it's an acceptable thing to do. But as intended it defused the situation. He let go and I could breathe again. We got up and the ref, Maurice Deegan, consulted with the linesman, as he hadn't seen the incident himself. What was said between them, I don't know. He sent us both off. He didn't say why. I found out later

I was sent off for striking. The ref was going on his linesman's word. If I am to presume he reported me for striking, the guy was seeing things. I didn't hit anyone. I think Maurice Deegan was sold a pup. None of that matters now. I was sent off. Again. Recidivist? I didn't believe so, but it was hard to argue my case.

By the time I had showered Cork were out the gate. I sat there in the false light of Páirc Uí Rinn as kids hammered the plastic dugout behind my head. What a headache.

The Central Competitions Controls Committee called me. I had to explain myself. I was glad of the opportunity. Jack attended the hearing with me. We put together a strong case for my defence. It was easy, really. There was no evidence of me striking anyone. So we defended the case. We produced video evidence and I explained my record of the incident. I spoke for myself, highlighting the earlier incident where Eoin was accidentally struck in the mouth after 10 minutes or so, for which he subsequently received treatment on the pitch. We reached the point of the video where we ended up on the ground, how the referee Deegan has his back turned as it is happening and then the point in the video where we are being spoken to by Deegan. I told the board members that I hadn't hit anyone, that in actual fact I was trying to defend myself and to defuse the situation. In reply to all this evidence I was told by the board that they were of the view that something must have happened off-camera before we were captured wrestling on the ground.

The verdict came in and a two-month suspension was imposed. The decision-making process and the final result were hard for me to accept. It just didn't sit right with me. I took my licks over the years. I never ducked an issue when I was wrong.

The decision to suspend me on this occasion was something I struggled to reconcile. Afterwards I chewed on it, tossed it, rolled it about like a pill in my mouth. The one thing I couldn't do was swallow it. I felt like I was guilty until proven guilty.

I kept my counsel and served my time. Working on *Galvinised* kept me focused. When I came back I continued where I left off, kicking 3 points against Monaghan in our last league game. I enjoyed being watched by the cameras. It gave me a confidence and a sense of security. The game felt easy, like I could do it in my sleep. Throughout the spring, 13 June hibernated in my head.

15

Cork v Kerry, Part II –
All Over the Place

The cuckoo that Mick O'Dwyer spent early spring listening out for came and went. Come summer and the Munster semi-final game in Killarney, I had been sick for a few days leading up to it with tonsillitis. On top of that I'd damaged my ankle in training about a week before the Cork game in an aerial challenge with Donnchadh Walsh, so I wasn't in the best of shape. I slept all day on the Saturday. I had physio in the evening on my ankle and fell asleep on the table. I was pumped with antibiotics. Louise Smith, our physio, did a great job getting me right. By the next day I was good to go. I had missed some training. Jack felt it was best to leave me out. He was concerned about the way I had been man-marked against Cork, and couldn't afford another episode like the one in Páirc Uí Rinn. Neither could I. I didn't mind being left out. I was cold. It didn't matter to me whether I started or not. If I could do what I had to do in 20 minutes all the better. Cork played well on the day and led by 4 points with 15 minutes to go. I came on around that time and got involved straight away. I wanted to win as much ball as possible and get it to Gooch if I could. In tight games there is no one better at finding a way. We snuck a draw thanks to him, Maher, and Bryan Sheehan, who all landed big scores. I was happy with my contribution. I had affected the outcome. The replay was a similar scenario for me. I didn't start. That didn't bother me. The morning of the game as I was leaving the Hayfield Manor hotel for a walk I met my friend Gerry Rochford. He threw me the keys of his Range Rover. I drove out of Hayfield Manor, turned down College Road towards Gillabbey Street, where I used to live. I took a right at the lights at St Fin Barre's Cathedral and drove up to Bandon Road. From there I went straight through the lights and up Lough Road to the other house I'd lived in. I pulled in at the Lough and thought of the laps I ran around it with my buddies Keith, Scruff, Ger Murph and Fergus. I did well to pull a degree and H. Dip out of UCC with those lads around distracting me. Those memories of living in Cork put me in great form. The drive helped me relax and prepare my mind for the battle ahead. I was ready.

In the dressing room just before going out I spoke to the players in a group. That was something I never did. I preferred to be quiet and keep to myself normally. This game was different. I spoke from my heart about who we were and what we were about and what we were going to do when we went out the door, what we had to do. Those words weren't really aimed at the lads at all, they were aimed at me. I wanted to put it up to myself like never before, to challenge myself, to deliver a definitive display for Kerry. Sometimes it is easier to be a sub. You can see what's happening and see ways to make a difference.

I was brought on after 25 minutes or so for David Moran. The problem with Cork in Páirc Uí Chaoimh is if they get a hold of midfield you're in trouble. Especially as a half-forward. You end up chasing around after their half-backs. You have to at least break even in the possession stakes for your half-forwards to influence the game.

It was a great game to play in. Pat McEneaney reffed it. He was always a good referee. I liked him as a person too. He came out with one of the funniest lines I ever heard about myself one time. 'Galvin,' he said, 'if you're not going to trouble you're coming from it.' Trying to avoid trouble I was. I enjoyed the wit but I enjoyed more the fact that he had the neck to say it to my face. We were spiky, contesting absolutely everything. We defended really well and were a threat up front. Gooch put Donaghy in for a vital goal in the second half. Gooch darted past his man, Star created a two-v-one by pulling away from his man towards the back post. Star was already pretty close to goal so Gooch floated an early 20-yard hand-pass into Star's hands with the perfect weight. He caught it and turned in one go. The goalie hadn't time to get out. Star took it, turned and slid it past Alan Quirke. In a game like that goals are massive. Momentum changers. Against Cork in Páirc Uí Chaoimh you need goals to have a chance, because they are very hard to beat there. Up front we were dangerous all day, even though it took a defender to save us in ordinary time. I took a ball from Séamus Scanlon and slipped it to Daniel Bohane playing towards the City End. He worked it inside then back out to Marc, who landed it on top of the net. Watching Marc bomb up the field past me was one of the things that gave me the greatest buzz as a player. I smiled as he ran back out past me, full of defiance.

Cork aren't the rebels for nothing. They laid siege on our goal for most of extra-time. Attack after attack. Wave after wave. We battened down the hatches, soaked it up and countered with a salvo here and there to pick off points and stay ahead. The last few minutes were frantic but we kept control of the game. I found myself playing quite deep late on, keeping them out and trying to break. We won 1–15 to 1–14. Barry John Keane swung it for us in extra-time with the equalizing and winning point. It was a real team performance.

I'd challenged myself in February to make sure we won this game. I wanted to take over the field that day, to be all over the place. When the whistle went I headed straight for the shelter of the dressing room.

The storm clouds of controversy soon rolled in. There was always something. I'd gotten in a tangle with Eoin Cadogan during the game. Declan had taken off on a run in the second half. I took off on his shoulder to support him. As he passed it Eoin intercepted. I fouled him in possession. When the free was given he turned around and stuck his chest out, his shoulders back, and threw his hands in the air over his head. His mouth was wide open but he wasn't actually screaming or roaring anything. It was just wide open. Somehow it irritated me more that he wasn't actually roaring or saying something. He was just pulling his face at me. I had baggage since February. He was right up in my face, looming over me. Impulse took over. I stuck a finger in his mouth and pulled at his gum for a split second. The same way I did in February to get him off me. I'd say I couldn't help it, but maybe I could have. I hadn't parked the February issue. I was walking around with a stone in my shoe for four months. The ref missed it. The TV cameras picked it up.

Afterwards I mentioned it to Éamonn in a room in Hayfield Manor. It was a case of wait and see what *The Sunday Game* would do. If they picked up on it the CCCC would probably act. The *Sunday Game* boys took it up from there. Anthony Tohill is obviously a more sensitive sort than I imagined him to be. My actions particularly upset him.

I know that what I did was wrong, but his contribution

surprised me. He was manager of the Ireland team, a position that requires a certain level of diplomacy. I had played under him for Ireland when he was a selector. He spoke well of me in team meetings. I spent about thirty minutes speaking to him the night of the 2008 final, when I was in no mood to talk to anyone. I always thought we got on well whenever we met. When I finally heard what he had said, it almost felt like I was listening to someone else's words.

The Sunday Game had acquired an authority back then, self-appointed it seemed, to address disciplinary matters in the game. I had no issue with this. What I had an issue with was the selective way they seemed to go about it. You either address all of the issues or none of them, in the interest of balance and impartiality. Who set the agenda in this regard? Who knows?

The only vested interest I had that night was in relaxing with my friends. The previous few weeks building up to the drawn game were intense. I had put a lot of pressure on myself going back to February. I needed to rest. I went out in Cork that night with a few of my closest mates, Gerry Rochford, Eddie, Gus, Ger Murphy – and my brother Ray.

In the following days, the CCCC picked up the slack from there. Another two-month suspension was handed down. The real issue for me wasn't that I had done it, more that I had no control over my impulses at the time. That was the one I had to crack. Those bloody impulses. Ultimately I had no one to blame for my action in June, only myself.

I left for New York with more baggage than a Boeing.

From Brooklyn to Bryant Park via Broadway I walked New York streets for a week. There's a hotel on West 29th Street and Broadway called Ace. I stayed there after spending a few days upstate with my cousin Kevin Moriarty and his wife Karen.

I was relieved to be away from the noise at home. There was no one kicking an O'Neills around on the lawn of Bryant Park on 42nd Street. I watched movies at the open air cinema with strangers. The 2010 World Cup was in full swing. I watched the games in Liberty Hall, a basement space in the Ace Hotel. It was quiet there. The mix of nationalities meant pods of supporters stuck together and supported quietly so as not to upset or annoy others. Spaniards, Ghanaians, Uruguayans, Germans, Americans. No Irish.

I drank coffee on the pavement outside the Failte on 2nd Avenue. I made friends in the short time I was there. Opportunities knocked.

One night I was walking down Broadway near 28th Street when my phone rang. It was a Mayo man called John Reddington, a friend of my friend Gerry Rochford, who'd heard I was in town. I got on well with John. He is a unique character. He bought a racehorse a few years back and trained to be a jockey. In his first race out he won back the cost of the horse in prize money. He has ridden three winners since, at 40-odd years of age. I answered the phone.

'Well, Paul, I hear you're in New York?'

'I am indeed, John. Are you?' He was nearby as it happened. I told him where I was.

'Wait there, we'll pick you up.'

About ten minutes later a Lexus jeep pulled up. I got in. John was in the passenger seat. The driver looked vaguely familiar. 'Paul, this is Joe, a friend of mine from Mayo.' I looked at Joe. He reminded me of someone. I couldn't figure out who. When he spoke I twigged it. He was Joe Walsh, a brother of Louis', as it turned out. Joe is a carpenter and lays timber flooring all over Manhattan. He's been married and in New York for years. A third man named Eugene was in the back beside me. The three were from Kiltimagh, County Mayo. We drove to Soho House, a members' club nearby. I'd read about it in a magazine. I have a thing about hotels. I love visiting them, even just for a look around. No matter what city I'm in I'll seek out a hotel or two. Soho House was on the list, but having to be a member meant it was longlisted. Joe Walsh had the key. So, one lad from a bog road called Penny Lane and three from Main Street, Kiltimagh, landed to the front door. The manager awaited Joe. We were brought upstairs to the best seat in the house. Joe had lain all the flooring in the building. As well as that he had done the nearby Standard Hotel, and all the Ralph Lauren stores in the city, including Ralph Lauren's own home. We had dinner and a few drinks as the lads swapped stories of their childhood, and their adulthood. John travelled between London and the Middle East for work. Joe lived in New York. Eugene was a home-bird. I was a migrant bird. I sat there and laughed at the stories they told, then told a few of my own. Staff tried to move us a few times. That table was usually reserved for special guests. Home was the last thing on my mind.

In January 2010 I had agreed to be the subject of a documentary programme with a production company who had been on to me several times over the previous year or two. I'd said no about three times. In the end I agreed to *Galvinised* because it was an interesting alternative to the many book offers I'd had over the years. I trusted the guys involved. I hoped I would be seen as a committed footballer and a more rounded person than the one who was mad enough to smack a book. I ran it by Jack. He had no issue with it at the time. Ultimately, from a football point of view, I felt being filmed while I played would be good for me. I was right. What football I played in 2010 was better than in 2009. Being filmed while you play is an incentive to be the best you can be, surely? That was what the programme was to be about. Football. I agreed to do the programme on the basis that it would be about a season of football and hopefully an All Ireland win. I couldn't have foreseen the suspensions. That was the last thing I thought would happen. There was nothing much to the making of it. The time commitment was minimal: twelve days' recording in total, spread over three or four months. There was also the opportunity to learn the ropes behind the camera – as well as in front of it. The other reason for doing it was that I knew by then I would be leaving teaching. I always had the idea to own or have an involvement in a production company myself someday.

And today I have a stake in a production company called Scratch Empire, my experience in making *Galvinised* having proved invaluable. I mentioned on *Galvinised* that I had an interest in fashion. I never thought having an interest in fashion would lead to the kind of commentary that followed. It was vulgar, small and sad. I also never thought that I would be seen as someone who was fair game or hungry for attention. In fact, the opposite is the case, but an interest in fashion comes with baggage. Literally and metaphorically. Had I been playing ball I wouldn't have been in New York firstly and there wouldn't have been a need for content to fill the gaps. I'm not hiding from the fact that I do have an interest in fashion, but it wasn't the case that I was jumping up and down asking to talk about it. I'm not like that. I still get asked about *Galvinised* today, people wondering where they can see it. I don't know. I only saw it once myself. When it aired for the first time I was in bed asleep. I got up around 2 a.m. and watched it. I haven't seen it since. I don't know if other players have been asked to make similar pro-grammes. I'm sure they have. As a footballer I found the experience helped my game. You can use it to better your play-ing performance. As a person you can use it to better your

Left: On the hunt: tracking down opponents in possession was something I enjoyed doing. Armagh's Kieran McGeeney was powerful prey in the 2006 All Ireland quarter-final.

Below: Taking on Armagh's Aaron Kernan in the same match. I enjoyed playing against physical teams.

Right: 'You're gonna get it.' Staying close to Graham Geraghty after the Aussies called him out in the parade before the 2006 Compromise Rules series game in Croke Park.

Above: Formidable. Éamonn retired from inter-county in April 2007 and turned his attention to Feale Rangers. He kicked the winning point in the last minute of the County final. He is a formidable man.

Below: My captaincy was short-lived. I knocked the referee's book from his hand as he was about to send me off against Clare in 2008. I was suspended for six months. I would have appreciated the chance to lead the team again, just for a league game, before I retired.

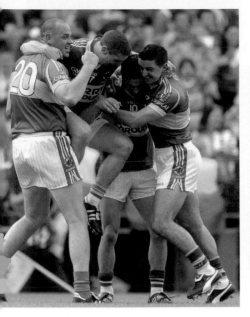

Above left: Unreal feelings: the joy of victory never lasted long with me. At times during 2008 I wondered would I ever experience it again. I was grateful for this moment at the end of the 2009 final v Cork at Croke Park.

Above right: Magic: moments like this with Gooch after the 2009 final mean more than medals. He redefined forward play with his genius.

Below: SAM: Jack O'Connor saw something in me early in my career. I did my best to deliver what he wanted.

Above: It was just banter. I cut my own hair for the 2009 All Star awards. Tadhg was laughing at it. Tadhg is lucky in that he doesn't have to worry about haircuts any more.

Below: Two of a kind: I always got on well with Tommy Walsh. He looked smashing in his tuxedo at the 2009 All Star awards.

Left: Pulling faces: Eoin Cadogan pulled a face at me. I pulled one back.

Below: Break a rib: Jack and I had a pow-wow over my rib injury before the 2011 semi-final against Mayo. We laughed about it afterwards.

Below left: Real deal: shaking hands with Cillian O'Connor after the 2011 All Ireland semi-final. I have developed an affinity for Mayo people over the years.

Below right: You can't beard serious: you probably think I was trying to explain to David Coldrick that our identical beard patches were a coincidence. In fact he was giving me and Ronan MacNamee a caution in the 2012 qualifiers in Killarney.

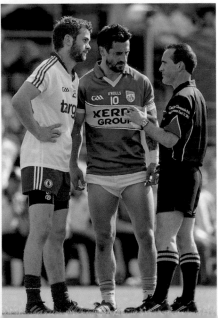

Above: I found myself surrounded at the breakdown against Donegal in 2012. It took me until the second half to get to grips with their system.

Left: In charge: Éamonn on the ball in the County Intermediate Final v Spa, 2012. It had taken us eight years to win it.

Below: At the end of the day. Shaking hands with Cork's Aidan Walsh at Austin Stack Park after an Allianz Football League match in 2013.

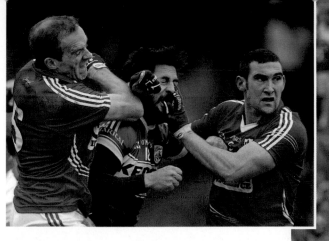

Above: There are all sorts of rules being broken in this photo by my reckoning.

Right: Noel O'Leary tries valiantly to protect me from being hit in the head by the flying football. He was a gentle soul at heart.

Below: End game: my last day out for Kerry was against Dublin in the 2013 All Ireland semi-final. I sometimes wish I could start again.

Sacred Harte: embracing Mickey Harte at the end of the 2012 qualifier game in Killarney. Moments later I was in front of a TV camera. It was an emotional day.

opportunities if you have an interest in television and multi-media production, like I do. Just don't mention fashion in the process. People won't buy that yarn.

In July of 2010 the production company followed me to New York for two days. We filmed some footage and talked a bit about the year so far. The year so far? It was far removed from what it was supposed to be by now. There was less football than I'd envisaged. I tried to keep my commentary as safe as possible. I didn't want to cause any more controversy. There had been enough of that for a TV drama series. I had a little bite at the lads on *The Sunday Game*. I was a bit dismissive of them. Purposely so. I felt they could have looked at the bigger picture in their assessment of the incident in Páirc Uí Chaoimh. There were other similar incidents, which were overlooked. I wondered if what I had done was more dangerous than a choke-hold or a punch, or just less common? I've been involved in a few scrapes over the years. Whatever way I'm wired I was able to deal with them. I was like a pig in a ditch over this one. Stuck. Struggling for perspective, I went to Le Bain at the Standard hotel in the Meatpacking District to find some. You can see the whole of Manhattan, and for miles up the Hudson. It was the fourth of July. Independence Day. I was tempted to stay in New York for good.

By the time I got back to Ireland I had a lot of voicemail messages. Paddy Power offering me work, which I appreciated, newspapers looking for comment, friends looking to talk. Two messages were from Niall Quinn. He had seen me play GAA a few times and invited me to have lunch with Steve Bruce and the Sunderland back-room team while they were in Limerick on pre-season. We met in the Dunraven Arms in Adare. Niall offered me the chance to work on my fitness and train with the

Sunderland lads for a few days while they were in town. I couldn't because of a club game that weekend. It wouldn't have looked right with my Kerry commitments either. We deferred.

Instead, in the lead-up to the Down game, I went to Nottwil in Switzerland to visit the Swiss Paraplegic Centre on an invite from a Kerryman called John Leen. John is a Kerry football fanatic. In Nottwil there is a fitness-testing and rehabilitation centre used by elite athletes: professional footballers, tennis players, sprinters, Olympic skiers, cyclists – all types of athletes use it. Testing is conducted at intervals of the season and used to monitor progress in the lead-up to competition. A battery of tests were carried out from vertical jump tests to VO2 max and more. I stayed on site in pretty spartan conditions, amongst paraplegics and other physically disabled athletes. The Brazilian football team had used the facility in the build-up to the 2006 World Cup. Doctors compared some of my results to those of Kaka. They noted the differences and similarities between us physically. For example Kaka's vertical jump graph showed he sprang really high the first time, not so high the second and similarly low for the third. My results showed three pretty even jumps, none as high as Kaka's first but all three higher than his second and third. This said Kaka was faster off the mark than me, had better acceleration, but that I was possibly more durable. In other words he was a sprinter where I was a long-distance runner. In the end I wasn't overly happy with my results. The time off had had an effect on my fitness. It was a useful exercise to gauge where I was at. I knew I could recover my fitness levels pretty quickly. The only question was would I get the opportunity?

I flew back into Dublin the day before Down beat Kerry at the quarter-final stage. I watched from the sideline. For the first time in the six years since I began playing we wouldn't contest the All Ireland final. Cork went on to win the All Ireland. They beat Down in the final. I didn't know which way was up.

Later on that year I flew over to the Sunderland training ground for a look around on Niall's invite. My hip was giving me trouble. Their physios looked at it. They did tests to check the range. Both were in poor shape. I ended up having surgery on my left one a few weeks later. On my first morning I was in the first-team dressing room, lying on the ground stretching before a light session with around ten of the first team who hadn't played the night before in the Capital Cup against West Ham. A pair of flip-flopped feet stopped beside my head. A hand reached down to my face. I reached out and shook it. 'Wot's ya name, mate?' said a voice. 'Paul,' I replied. 'A'wight, Pool. Whe' ya from?' I got to my feet. 'Am, I'm from a place called Kerry,' I told him. 'Kerry?' he enquired. 'Ya, Kerry, it's down in the south-west of Ireland.' The guy responded instantly. 'I know Kerry, mate. O'im from Cowk,' he said, and slapped his chest with his hand. I laughed. 'How do you know about Cork?' The man's face lit up. He slapped his chest again. 'ROY!!' I laughed again. Standing before me with a big grin on his face was Anton Ferdinand. Roy Keane had been his manager at Sunderland. He was still all they talked about around the training ground, from players to admin staff to coaching staff.

David Meyler was rehabbing from a knee injury at the time. There was no escaping the rebels. I saw him work in the gym. It was no surprise to see him progress in his career. He had a great attitude and was a serious athlete too. Steve Bruce told me they needed reins to hold him back in his rehab from a cruciate injury. The day I was leaving, the team were preparing for Liverpool away. I was in the canteen having lunch with the team. Lee Cattermole was next to me; Andy Reid, a gentleman, on the other side. Anton was at the table too. Cattermole told him I was leaving for London that morning. He asked me how I was travelling. I told him by train. Anton disappeared and came back with a train timetable from nearby Durham station to London and a taxi number for me to call when I wanted to leave. He advised me on which train to get, how long the taxi journey to the station was and recommended places to go in London when I got there.

I know Premiership footballers get a bad rap from time to time. It's cheap and easy to do. Perception doesn't always meet reality. My experience of them couldn't have been more positive. Those I met were more than sound, and a credit to Steve Bruce and Niall Quinn.

I picked up a lot in a short space of time over there. The facilities were leagues ahead of what we had in Kerry, and while the food was similar to what we were used to eating with Kerry, the physical preparations and habits of professional players were different. From the warm-ups, warm-downs and sports science department there was plenty to take in. The head of sports science highlighted an issue Steve Bruce was having with a particular player. Based on his Prozone stats he hardly ever sprinted during games. The players were mapped on a computer screen and manifested as green dots moving around a virtual pitch. When they sprinted the dots turned red and vibrated. The dot representing this player stayed green for almost the entire game. And he was a striker. He was sold soon afterwards. It was educational in many ways and I was grateful to Niall and Steve Bruce for the opportunity to observe.

16

Alarm Bells Ringing

'You left the teachin'?' 'Did you leave the teachin'?' 'Why did you leave the teachin'?' 'Do you miss the teachin'?' 'Will you go back to the teachin'?' Not forgetting my personal favourite, 'What about the teachin'?' If I've heard those questions once I've heard them once too often. What about the teaching? I gave it up. I gave up teaching because one morning I woke up and my alarm clock really irritated me. I stared at it for a while without turning it off. 'DU-DU-DU-DU-DU-DU-DU-DU-DU-DU-DU-DU-DU-DU-DU-DU-DU-DU-DU-.' That's annoying to read and write, never mind listen to. On and on like a klaxon it went. 07.48 a.m. Now imagine listening to an alarm clock every forty minutes of the day. An inanimate object, a clock, ruled my life. The same way the school bell ruled my life. The same way the timetable did. The same way homework did. The same way books did. The same way my principal and vice-principal did. My life was timetabled by clocks. What was I doing with myself? Whatever I was told.

I got a warm welcome in the Sem when I arrived. It was a former boarding school and a famous footballing school. Past pupils include Páidí Ó Sé, Séamus Moynihan, Gooch, actor Michael Fassbender, Supreme Court Judge Hugh O'Flaherty and many other well-known people. Former GAA President and visionary Seán Kelly taught there. Seán is from Kilcummin, football country, but was a noted hurler in his time. We talk hurling whenever we meet. I replaced Father Joe Begley, who was the last priest on the staff. I'm named after Pope John Paul and served as an altar boy for years in Lixnaw. Replacing the last priest on the staff of a former seminary was a natural progression. My style of teaching was probably unconventional. I worked on the basis that there was a kid in every class who was smarter than me. I have great respect for kids. I never just expected respect in return. I worked towards earning it. Towards the end of my time, as my interest in the job waned, I grew a bit more unconventional.

The Sem was different to Críost Rí in that we had our own classrooms. In Críost Rí we moved around from class to class. There are pros and cons to having your own room. You're the boss in your own room, awaiting the students when they arrive. The classroom is your territory. For me there was the challenge of being in the same place for large parts of the day, which I still find difficult today. I always like to have somewhere to go. To combat the stasis I would have good craic with the students. You could have great fun with them, particularly the younger lads. The bolder lads kept things interesting. There was a foreign national boy who was very lively from when he arrived in the first year – one of those kids you hear about in the staffroom. I discovered from talking to him that he loved hip-hop. At the end of the odd class I'd ask him to rap for us. He usually did something by Ludacris. That kept him happy and we got on very well from there on. It was a game trying to get on a level with them.

My room in the Sem was number 11. One day, out of sheer boredom as I waited for my next group to enter the room, I climbed on my desk and pulled myself up on to the steel beams that ran overhead along the ceiling. Clinging on with my arms and legs I stayed up there as the first few kids came in. No one noticed me. More arrived until, eventually, the class was almost full. They took their seats and ducked into their bags for books and copybooks, as kids do, before coming up for air, back down then maybe for the pencil case before burrowing in that for their best pen or pencil. Whatever they were at no one noticed me clinging to the beam like a bat. Thinking I was out of the room a din of noise erupted before I dropped to the floor. 'Open your books, guys, let's go, time for class,' letting on like it's the most normal thing in the world to drop from the ceiling. The look on the boys' faces was priceless. 'Jeeeeccccsus, he just came down from the ceeeeeeilin' . . .' That got their attention.

I kept a football in the press too. Most kids in the Sem were football-mad. As a bonus for doing their homework well, or a good class average in an exam, I would take the ball out towards the end of class and have a game of donkey. If the ball went around the class in one-twos (from me to the student and back) without being dropped I would let them finish up a few minutes early. I found it a good way to keep the boys happy and also to practise my hand-passing.

One day, in early 2010, my boss came to me and asked if I would take a particular student into my third-year Irish class. His behaviour had become intolerable to his own Irish teacher. I agreed. This particular boy turned out to be no real trouble to me. It was clear from his general attitude, though, how a teacher could have problems with him. Often the cross lads weren't that troublesome at all, they just had different experiences of life to the rest of us, and different attitudes as a result. They need you to find their level and to communicate with them. I could do that. In the new year the school had applied for funding to refurbish nearly every classroom. Out went the self-contained benches that you sat into, in came new tables and chairs. This small development changed a lot. The novelty factor was way too much for some. After years of being stuck fast behind small, cramped, self-contained desks the kids now enjoyed new freedom. They could move around. This new mobility meant new noise for me.

One morning in late January a third-year class entered my room. I was wiping down the blackboard to start a new class. A gang of third-year students entered and sat at the back of the room. They began to use their chairs and desks in unison to make as much noise as possible, while my back was turned at the board. Without turning around I stopped wiping the blackboard. Usually this would have been enough for me to get the message across. The noise continued. These boys were normally well-behaved and didn't need to be told anything twice. I knew them well. We got on well. The games continued with the desks and chairs behind my back. This time I asked for silence, again without turning around. The games continued however. After asking for silence more of them joined in to add to the chorus and make an even louder din. I was disappointed that they were being sneaky while my back was turned. The novelty of the new desks had obviously gotten the better of them. If this was to be the new practice I'd be in for a long year.

I felt I had to nip this in the bud. As I wiped the board I thought about throwing the duster in my hand at the back wall. A warning shot. Then I thought better of throwing it and kept wiping the board. I needed to do something to halt this. It was the type of misbehaviour that can escalate and undermine you quickly. Usually, if I really wanted to make a point in class

I'd whisper it. To the class generally or in the ear of an individual. Whispering wouldn't solve this problem. The din grew louder. Without looking I threw the duster aiming for the back wall behind me. It flew to my left at an angle you couldn't imagine. It hit the side wall to my left about two desks down a row of six desks. It landed a few feet away from me. That wasn't all. It ricocheted and hit a boy on the head. If I tried to do it again a million times I couldn't. It was a freak occurrence. I was as shocked as anyone in the class. I immediately apologized. I went straight to his desk and said I was sorry and I hadn't meant it. He knew I hadn't. Everyone in the room could see that. He wasn't even one of the lads who was dragging the desks. From what I could make out the noise was coming from another part of the room. The boy was calm and accepted my apology. I brought him outside and rang the principal to meet me at his office. We waited in a room off the principal's office. When he got there I told him exactly what had happened. The boy told him the same, that I hadn't meant it. We then drove to his house. I walked him inside with my principal and explained everything to his mother first and then his father, who arrived later.

I was disappointed but mostly sorry for the boy. It was irresponsible of me to do what I did, but not atypical of me to do something unconventional. What happened shouldn't have happened. Of course I am sorry that it did.

Someone, somewhere decided to run to a newspaper with the story. It being in the public domain made life more difficult. I heard about a settlement on the radio one night. I was driving home from The Courtyard in Leixlip. Luke Moriarty, a great Kerryman domiciled in Dublin, was driving. Darran O'Sullivan was in the back. The story led the nine o'clock news headlines on RTE Radio One. I was embarrassed. It was an unfortunate accident, but as far as I was concerned the matter was closed when I went to the student's family home to explain what had happened. Hence my surprise when I realized that it was still ongoing more than three years later. While it cost me nothing financially, it did cost me something in terms of my reputation, which is why I need to address it now from my point of view. A newspaper report around that time described the family as being 'very upset' at reports that what happened was indeed an accident. I didn't see this report at the time. I'm glad I didn't. I would have been very upset too.

In the summer of 2010 my principal in the Sem called me in to discuss my contract for the following year. The same hours were offered with the same subjects. Everything was in order for me to continue. Had I worked another year I would be eligible for a Contract of Indefinite Duration, which had replaced permanent contracts at that stage. On the football side of things I worked closely with Gary McGrath and Haulie Clifford with the senior team. We enjoyed success for the first time in fifteen years, winning two Corn Uí Mhuirís and contesting two Hogan Cup finals in the three years since I'd arrived, following a barren run at that level. My future at St Brendan's was secure if I wanted it. I didn't. I told him I wouldn't be returning in September.

By 2010, aged 30, I had nearly ten years of teaching under my belt. That was enough of that. I was spending my days repeating myself. Repetition is a good way to drive yourself up the wall. The onset of social media has affected kids' ability to retain information. I saw this in class. (I also have experienced it myself. Since I started working in social media my attention span isn't what it was.) Repetition and routine wasn't for me. For some people routine is hard to do without. For me it was hard to do. After nearly ten years I couldn't see myself doing one more year, never mind twenty more. Apart from being time-governed every day, I wasn't enjoying teaching any more. People seem to be hung up on this. Like there was another reason for me giving it up. Some of the small-mindedness I have encountered since leaving teaching has surprised me. I had to arm myself for people. 'The holidays' was another common refrain. 'Jesus, Paul, what about the holidays?' I'd stand there and listen thinking, 'Ya, because it's worth spending eight or nine months doing something you don't enjoy, for the sake of the three or four months you spend not doing it.' That didn't make sense to me. What made sense to me was doing something that I enjoyed *all* the time.

I respect teachers, teaching and the Irish language. There must be a more interactive, technology-led way of teaching students Irish. Maybe there is by now. Every week I used to record *Aifric* on TG4 and play it for my junior cert Irish classes. It's a drama series based on the lives of secondary school students in Connemara, dealing with the same issues and challenges students deal with in real life every day. I wondered back then why the programme wasn't on the syllabus instead of one of the many expensive books kids were dragging around after them. All they would have to do is go home and slump in front of the TV and watch it, like they were doing anyway. Make kids watch every episode and incorporate the programme into the junior cert exam paper. If kids want to watch television why not put part of the syllabus on TG4? Or online? A lot of my good friends are teachers and love their jobs and I enjoy talking to them about it. I enjoyed it for most of the time I spent doing it. For now writing, blogging, social media, multimedia, fashion and television offer too many possibilities and opportunities. I might go back to it someday. To teach English. I might still be at it if it wasn't for that bloody alarm clock.

17

Fashionation

Since *Galvinised* I've had many other similar television offers. I turned down 99 per cent of them. I took up one offer. My teaching contract ran to September 2010. By December, an opportunity to write for a national newspaper came my way. Between that and a short pre-recorded music radio show on Radio Kerry I earned well in excess of my monthly teaching wage for a fraction of the work. I only feel the need to state this because it was around this time it began. 'What are you doing with yourself?'

Before I accepted the position at the *Weekend* magazine I weighed up my responsibilities to Kerry. I considered what the repercussions might be. I asked myself if this would affect my focus, my ability to train or play. I was satisfied that it wouldn't. How could it? If anything it had the opposite effect. I had more free time to prepare. I had a much more enjoyable life all of a sudden. Every box was ticked. Writing was a great way for me to switch off from football. The column in the *Irish Independent*'s weekend magazine happened to be about fashion. This seemed to really affect people. A GAA player writing about fashion? That wasn't right. There seemed to be a fascination with this that I couldn't quite understand.

Ultimately, writing for the *Independent* was actually nothing to do with fashion and everything to do with writing. It was an opportunity to write. The column could have been about music, travel, sport or cars. It could even have been fictional. It was about fashion because that was what was required. No big deal. That said, there were a few sidewinders along the way I could have done without: a TV ad publicizing it was a surprise; and there were a few photo-shoots I hadn't banked on. Comes with the territory, I guess. You live and learn. Overall, the experience taught me I had the ability to write. I worked with good people – Gerry O'Regan, a Kerryman, was the Indo editor at the time; Yvonne Hogan, a Corkwoman, was the *Weekend* magazine editor; Bairbre Power, the fashion editor. Gerry and Yvonne moved on, and so did I, after eighteen months or so; Bairbre has forgotten more than I will ever know about fashion. I learned a lot from her about fashion and writing. Doing something different and unconventional teaches you more about life than doing something everyone else is doing. I encountered a degree of ignorance that was eye-opening. Some people's attitude towards me changed. What can you do? Ignorance deserves arrogance. I ignored a lot of people along the way. People wondered what I was doing with myself now I wasn't teaching. What was I doing with myself? Whatever I wanted. And getting well paid for it.

I find fashion interesting from many points of view: visually, aesthetically, creatively, from a business point of view, from a show point of view, from the point of view of brands and brand positioning. Then there are the designers and creative directors who lead and direct the big fashion houses. The transfers and appointments that happen within that side of the industry, the personalities you find, are similar to what you see happen in soccer at Premier League level. Aesthetically there are similarities with sport too. To appreciate aesthetics is to see beauty in the art of something. There are artists in fashion and football.

Fashion is full of interesting people, too. Gianni Agnelli was a leading Italian industrialist and businessman, who owned both Juventus football club and Fiat for much of his life. His nickname was L'Avvocato, the Attorney. Agnelli was a successful man in everything he did, from football to cars and fashion. He didn't so much dress to impress as to confuse. He approached his business deals in an unconventional way. Because of his fondness for fashion and his love of fine Italian suits he is still renowned as a man of impeccable personal style today, a decade after his passing. Fashion was something he embraced throughout his life and used to his advantage. He became the embodiment of an Italian custom called 'sprezzatura', which is the art of dressing well while looking dishevelled and untidy at the same time. His habits or sartorial quirks, which appeared haphazard and pointed towards a disorganized, eccentric man, were, in fact, a weapon in his armoury when it came to business dealings. A sharp mind was at work behind the slicked hair and shades. Competitors would sometimes take him for granted and underestimate his intellect and capabilities. A man sitting across a table wearing a watch over his shirtsleeve is bound to distract and amuse. His tie would hang tied but in two strands, never looped, for a more dishevelled look. Everything looked out of place like it was supposed to. The imperfections created a style that was memorable and a perception that Agnelli, the businessman, was someone you could underestimate. What people didn't realize was that he had them just where he wanted them – busy underestimating him. From there he grew to become the most powerful businessman in Italy and beyond. Cars, football, fashion and business.

What is not interesting about a man like Gianni Agnelli?

Fred Perry, the tennis player, is another interesting man. He quit the amateur Lawn Tennis Club of Great Britain, today known as the Lawn Tennis Association, in the late 1930s to play in the US, where players were being paid. He became a black sheep in England and was never truly accepted again in his own land, being banned for many years from playing at home for deciding to become a professional player. Perry was visionary and soon tennis was a fully professional game. The man himself was rebellious, and considered a womanizer. He was courageous, too – he served in World War II as a member of the US Air Force, and before retiring he recognized his own potential value and registered his own name as a brand. The brand happened almost by chance when he met a former Austrian footballer called Tibby Wegner in the canteen at Wimbledon in 1948. Wegner, just retired, was there to show the then reigning Wimbledon champion Bob Falkenburg this new product he had invented called the sweatband. Perry, not a shy or retiring type, declared himself to Wegner to be 'generally regarded as the best dressed player of my time'. The two struck a friendship and went into business together. The first product made under the Fred Perry brand name was a sweatband, followed by the now famous signature polo shirt. He won all four Grand Slams as a player but conceded in later life that he was far better known for his clothing.

There is a depth to fashion that makes it interesting and current. There are connections to be found between sport and fashion everywhere. There are many to be found here in Ireland. J. W. Anderson is from The Loup in County Derry. He started his eponymous label in 2010. Louis Vuitton Moët Hennessy (LVMH) are the world's biggest fashion conglomerate, who own some of the most luxurious fashion labels from Gucci to Bottega Veneta. They have just bought an ownership stake in his own label and made Anderson creative director at Spanish label Loewe, a luxury sports and leather goods label they also own. J. W.'s approach to design is bold, fearless and unconventional. He was one of the pioneers of the androgynous look that is widespread in fashion today. He bends the rules and disrupts the status quo. His father is former Irish rugby captain Willie Anderson, he who faced down the All Blacks Haka in 1989. Talk about bold and fearless. Black cat, black kitten. Despite being the most coveted, talked-about young fashion designer in the world for the last four years, when J. W. approached potential sponsors and governing bodies here in Ireland for financial help to get started, he didn't get much support. The British Fashion Council, on the other hand, recognized his talent and nurtured it both creatively and financially.

It's a pity he wasn't embraced in Ireland first. The manufacture of clothing was once an industry here. Woollen mills abounded. We made our own clothes. There are still small-scale manufacturing capabilities in Ireland today, but costs are prohibitive. To produce clothes and shoes here is much more expensive than in Turkey, Portugal, Spain or further afield in the Far East. If the Irish government could address this issue somehow and regulate manufacturing costs, it might allow Irish designers to make products here, cutting out all manner of logistical problems, VAT issues and unemployment issues. It could also nurture the design talent that is leaving the country to work in the UK, though I realize market forces dictate this move too. I think it's time we started the conversation about fashion as an industry in Ireland for real.

Sport and fashion are well met. Nowadays there is an emerging trend for top soccer clubs to embrace collaborations with leading fashion houses to create their match-day suits and capsule travel wardrobes. Arsenal may have the most impressive relationship: Lanvin is one of the world's oldest and most prestigious fashion houses. Any suit you see on the back of Arsène Wenger on the touchline, or on the players stepping off the team bus, will have been made by Lanvin, Paris. Chelsea have the same relationship with Hackett, London. José Mourinho wears Hackett on match days. I have met Jeremy Hackett, the founder and creative director of Hackett, a few times and been a guest at his shows. Real Madrid wear Versace, AC Milan wear Dolce&Gabbana, and Bayern Munich wear a suit made by a family-owned German company called Sir Oliver. The Bayern manager Pep Guardiola is an aesthete and keen follower of fashion. One of his closest friends is a Spanish fashion designer called Antonio Miro. The best creative directors and head designers are as sought after in fashion as the best managers are in the Premier League or La Liga. The same principles apply. A creative director of a fashion house must be progressive, visionary, bold and forward thinking in his or her quest to deliver products that drive sales, whilst always remaining true to the brand's heritage. A manager taking over at any of the world's leading clubs must have the same values in his quest to deliver results for the fans, the shareholders, the sponsors, whilst always respecting a club's tradition, history and belief system on how the game should be played.

Until recently there was a fear of fashion amongst men in Ireland. We seem to be less inhibited now about expressing ourselves through clothes.

Once upon a time in Ireland men who dressed well were seen as very masculine. Take the signatories of the Proclamation: Mac Diarmada, Clarke, Connolly, Pearse, McDonagh, Ceannt and Plunkett. Looking at old photos it's clear they had a certain style and direction in how they dressed themselves, their appearance was uniform (in a non-military sense, of course) and had to be in keeping with their message: smart, concise, direct. Every photo I have seen of them is similar in aesthetic: three-piece woollen suits made in Irish woollen mills, four-to-five-button waistcoats, starch white tab-collar shirts and straight ties. Their hairstyles were almost identical too: short, neat, side-parted with a comb. They had a direction and a directional style. They were sure of themselves. They had an identity.

My grandfather's generation, the 'Sunday best' generation, were the same. They dressed up for Mass and took great pride in their appearance. Those men were sure of themselves too. They cared about how they looked. Their suits were pressed, they kept combs and shoe-horns and shoe polish, they used Brylcreem according to Maidhc Dainín Ó Sé's *A Thig Ná Tit Orm*. It was important to be well-presented back then. I ask myself, 'What has changed? When did it stop being acceptable for Irishmen to take pride in their appearance? Where is our uniform, our three-piece suit, our comb today? What is our identity?'

The GAA appears to me to be the organization with the most means and relevance to reinvigorate and rebrand Ireland's identity. Instead, for years, attitudes within the GAA reinforced the view that fashion was somehow unmanly and wrong. Especially on the terraces. GAA players in recent years have discovered themselves. They're more confident and expressive. They realize more and more that appearance is important and can help you get ahead. Television punditry has become a vehicle for people to make a name for themselves and make a career for themselves too. That's not what fashion is about for me, but if there happens to be a reawakening and a new-found confidence amongst Irish men generally because of it then that's a positive thing. The GAA should embrace fashion too. There is enough media interest in it and enough people vying for air time to keep clothing brands and retailers in free advertising all year round. That has a value.

Fashion is aspirational. It can change how you feel and how others feel about you. It can get you the job you want and lose you the job you have. To some it is frivolous; to me it is more than that. It is a form of expression.

Ultimately, my interest in fashion is very straightforward. It has a value, for sure, but more importantly it has values. Something as simple as getting into my clothes every morning brings me happiness. Why wouldn't I be into fashion?

18

Rebellion?

'It really was quite angry in there. I didn't expect it to be so bad. This will take time to recover from,' he says.

'How bad is bad?' I ask.

'Bad.'

'Your hip is arthritic. I've repaired it as best I could. You'll get one year playing out of it; two if you're lucky. You're going to need a full replacement in your early forties.'

The words of hip surgeon Tom McCarthy. He had just looked inside my hip joint. Towards the end of 2010 my groin was playing up and a scan showed I had torn cartilage in my hip joint. The grating of bone on bone had led to some cell leakage, which had hardened to form a cyst. The cyst was preventing proper movement in the joint, overloading the groin muscles and causing tears. The prognosis was worse than I hoped for, but good enough for me to get by for another while.

I came back from the surgery against Armagh. We won up there then beat Monaghan in Clones. We had a two-week break until our next game, against Down. I was eager to play, having missed the 2010 quarter-final defeat. Twenty minutes into the Down game I ran back towards my own goal and felt a tear in my hamstring. I kept running. Benny Coulter won a ball out in front of Marc, I doubled up on him, tackling him with Marc. We won the ball back and I walked to the sideline. Looking back now I did things to my body I had no right to do, going all the way back to my shoulder injury in college.

A scan the day after the Down game had revealed a tear on the tendon behind my knee and and a tear higher up on the belly of the muscle. Neither were too bad, but were enough to rule me out for a few weeks. All this was as a result of the hip surgery. Still, it wasn't too long before I was back with the lads. Then two weeks before our Munster championship game with Cork I felt my hamstring tear again towards the end of a football session. Twice in as many months. Making the game would prove tight, but not impossible. I healed quickly and was diligent with rehab. I doubled my prescribed rehab. We beat Cork in Killarney. I didn't play as I felt my hamstring tighten in a fitness test before the game. After going off injured against Down I was extra careful with it and maybe a little paranoid.

I started against Limerick in the quarter-final. Jack wasn't happy with the forward unit in that game, so for the Mayo semi-final he left me out. I couldn't argue given the amount of football I had missed. Kieran O'Leary and Donnchadh Walsh were going well and deserved their spots. There were extenuating circumstances. I cracked two ribs in training two weeks before the game: I'd ploughed into Brian Maguire in a training match. Whatever way I shouldered him I hit him on the point of his shoulder with my ribs. It felt like I hurt my head and not actually my ribs, for some reason. My head was spinning like something had burst in it. I was short of breath. I kept walking around so as not to give away that I was hurt. It was un-believable. I had more injuries in two months than I had in my whole career. I played the rest of the training game. It wasn't until the following Monday or Tuesday, after a few sleepless nights, I realized I had a problem. The pain wasn't so bad but the lethargy was debilitating. I was shallow breathing and tired, yawning and drawing breath all day. Dr Mike Finnerty organized an X-ray, which showed a cracked rib or two. I had around ten days to recover for Mayo, but training was out.

Although I didn't deserve to start, I made it as hard as I could for Jack in the build-up to the semi-final. The fractures weren't so bad. I missed a week's training then took painkillers and togged out for a final internal training game at Fota Island, the weekend before Mayo, despite being told not to by the doctors. I knew if I didn't play that I wouldn't start the semi. Jack pulled me up after the warm-up. We had a pow-wow. I was going against doctors' orders and Jack's orders to put myself in the frame. Jack pointed out that another belt in what would be a championship-tempo training game in terms of contact and intensity and I'd be out not only for Mayo but also for a potential final. I said I'd take my chances. Jack said I wouldn't. I said I would. Jack said I wouldn't. Jack won. I sat down. My chances of starting were gone. With that my chances of starting any final were slim too. That was why I was being so bullish about the situation. When you get the sniff of an All Ireland all bets are off. Was I being selfish? Yes. Was I being a bit reckless? Yes. Did I care? No.

We had our hands full with Mayo. They were rising under James Horan. They carried themselves with an assurance and an aggression they didn't have before – physically they were much stronger than previously, too. We still had too much. Gooch scored a brilliant goal that was decisive, catching a ball on the 13 and spinning away from a defender in one go before burying it. The forwards played well as a unit. I came on with 20 minutes left and scored 2 points. More importantly I worked for the team, won breaks, made tackles and ran hard. A mixture of freshness from the few injury lay-offs, defiance at being left out, and the promise of an All Ireland final was firing me. The Mayo boys came at us hard. Harder than they had in the past. I got a welcome when I came on. What they didn't know was that I had two cracked ribs and a system full of painkillers. Having gotten to know Mayo people well over the last few years I have an affinity for them. Some of them talk about this curse that is supposedly hanging over the team. The story goes that when Mayo won the 1951 All Ireland they overtook a funeral cortège and a priest placed a curse on the county that won't be lifted until the last member of the '51 team dies. I'm not one for curses or witchcraft. It would frustrate the life out of me to be listening to that kind of talk if I were a Mayo player. Mind you there wasn't much good in that priest either. I wouldn't like to be going to him for confession.

The frustrating thing for me in 2011 was that I played some of my best football when I was fit. I was physically stronger than ever: I rehabbed my hamstring at home, along with a host of other exercises. Louise Smith, our physio at the time, was great in getting me right. I found doing proprioception work a good way to stay strong and explosive. It really helped my balance, my ability to land and spin away off either foot with my back to goal. For all the weights and squatting and dead lifts and max benches I found using dumbbells a useful workout, too. Strong arms were vital to me. Especially in this Mayo game. They protected my ribs in contact. The bigger they were the better. They were my first point of contact for making and breaking tackles, my levers for winning breaks, for dealing with direct opponents under breaks, for collisions. I made them the strongest part of my body.

With my performance against Mayo I had given myself a

chance of starting the final. As a team we were powerful: Anthony Maher and Bryan Sheehan were a dominant midfield pairing; Tomás and Marc were still going well; Darran was in All Star form on the 40. His back-heeled goal against Limerick was the highlight of the championship. We had Dublin in the final. Jack didn't pick me. The way the year had gone I wasn't surprised. Injuries played a part. I have a feeling that 2010 played a part too. One or two suspensions too many. Not enough water under the bridge. Too much patience spent. And I had too much time for Kieran O'Leary and Donnchadh to let the disappointment of not starting show. They deserved to start. I turned my thoughts to the team and being as positive as I could. There was an All Ireland there to be won.

We know now who won it and how: Dublin, by a point, with a last-minute free having been 5 points behind with 8 minutes to go. It was a jarring loss. What could you say? 'Well done, Dublin.' We went home wondering what had happened. A fifth medal had slipped through some of our fingers like dry sand. 2011 seemed to last for so long yet ended so quickly. Everything changed in an instant. We wanted to keep going in that same direction, but we lost our way somehow. Stephen Cluxton showed a sniper's nerve. He pulled the trigger and shot a bullet over the bar, taking us out where we stood. The final whistle went and I felt like I was tripping at a rave. Waves of noise resounded, ringing in one ear and out the other, then back in again and out the other side. Dublin subs whizzed past me in blurry ecstasy, roaring, racing to share the madness with their teammates. We nearly did it. Our fifth All Ireland in seven years. We nearly brought it home again. In the end success proved a stranger and Croke Park a foreign land. We congratulated the Dubs and we meant it. I like Dublin and Dublin people. Guys like Cluxton and Alan Brogan are too good not to win an All Ireland. I walked straight off the field, empty and offended, and I wondered if I'd ever be back.

As a group of players we had to grapple with the nature of that defeat. I kept it simple. They got what they deserved and we got what we deserved. That's what I told myself. They say sport is cruel. Sport isn't cruel. Sport is epic and dramatic. Life can be cruel. The question is, where does sport end and life begin?

By the end of 2011 my body had settled and felt like my own again following the hip surgery. It took a full year to recover. Ireland were going to Australia on International Rules duty. I hadn't been called up to the squad for years for whatever reasons. Earlier that year at a press call in Croke Park, the president, Christy Cooney, who I found to be a nice man, asked me to make myself available for selection. I said I would. No call came, so by early October I made the call.

It was an unusual move by me. I just wanted to compete, to win something again. Kieran McGeeney was a defensive coach in the set-up. I dropped Geezer a line about something else and, at the end, asked what the story was with the squad. Geezer asked me why I wasn't there. I told him because I hadn't been asked. He said the word they got back was that I wasn't interested. I don't know where that had come from because no one had asked me. I registered my interest with Geezer and he passed word to Anthony Tohill. We spoke on the phone the next day. I wanted to test him out, if I'm being honest. I asked him why I hadn't been called up to the squad. He explained how word had come back that I wasn't interested. I explained how I had never been asked, so it was a mystery to me how that word could have gone back. I then told him I had a holiday booked to Dubai for around the time the squad left for Australia, but I would cancel it if the door was open to be part of the squad for

Australia. Aside from wanting to play and win something with Ireland in Australia I saw it as an opportunity to build bridges too. It was a win–win situation for everyone. Tohill hummed and hawed for a while, mentioned my injuries and my fitness and the fact that he hadn't seen enough of me in the year to judge me properly. The best he could do was offer me three trials over the next three sessions and decide then. I went to Dubai.

Whilst there I bumped into my now fiancée, Louise. I went there to visit my friend Scruff. Another friend from Lixnaw, Ger Lovett, lives in Abu Dhabi. Ger came to Dubai to meet me, and I brought him along to meet Louise and her cousin Niamh. Niamh and Ger now live together in Abu Dhabi. Louise and I live together in Dublin. The four of us are great friends. Niamh was in my corner along the way when I was putting in the hard yards with Louise, which I appreciated. Louise changed the game for me. She has this intelligence that I like. I have at least five belly laughs a day with her around. She is a smart cookie. Her family and extended family are great people. Some love football; some love music and singing and know nothing about football. Louise loves music and singing and knows nothing about football. 2011 was a bitch of a year that got better because I met her. Looking back now I wonder if some of the things I did in 2011 were rooted in a kind of rebellion against football, the thing I knew and loved and committed everything to, but which had turned its back on me in 2010. I still don't know the answer.

19

The End of Something

It was a long winter into 2012. One day, a week or two after the Dublin game, I ventured down town. I was in a hardware store in Manor West, buying something for the house. As I stood in the queue an old man spotted me and approached me. He must have been in his late seventies. He tried to say something but the words wouldn't come to him. His emotions got there first. So instead of words he used actions. He grabbed my hand around my wrist and squeezed, looking hard at me. Tears gathered around his eyes but he didn't cry, his lips trembled but he didn't speak. His face said enough. He was hurting, the same as the rest of us. He said nothing in the end and neither did I. He didn't have to. I nodded as if to say, 'I know.' He let go my hand and shuffled away out the door. I don't know who the man was, where he was from or where he was going, but I knew what he meant and how he felt. It was my turn next at the till. The cashier had seen the moment happen. I put down whatever it was I was buying and left talking to myself. Football. What was it all for? Some poor old man distraught in a hardware store? It was enough to make you wonder. It shouldn't be that serious but it is, I suppose. It reminded me just how much Kerry people care about football.

I never really contributed in 2011 because of injury. When I played I felt I was better than before. Like I was still making a difference. But the years were beginning to make a difference too by now. They were racking up: '03, '04, '05, '06, '07, '08, '09, '10, '11. 2012? I wasn't sure. What drove me on was the 2011 final. Especially not starting. You couldn't walk away after that. We were beginning to run out of road as a group. Time was sneaking up behind us, hiding in alcoves and doorways – invisible when we stopped and looked over our shoulders, tip-toeing towards us every time we turned our backs.

2012 was transitional to an extent. A quest to find that elusive balance any team needs to win an All Ireland. Tom Sullivan had retired as well by now. Another hole that had to be filled. He was some player. There was a lot of change, both in playing personnel and in the back room in 2011. We seemed to lose direction as a team.

It appeared to me that teams had caught up to us, or were catching up to us in terms of power and physicality. Maybe Dublin were lucky in 2011. Maybe they were able to go harder for longer and got lucky? New levels of preparation were being employed, new techniques and, as a result, new gains were being made physically, which allowed teams to put the squeeze on us. When you discover and adopt this kind of sports-science-related conditioning the difference it makes to your game, if done correctly, is significant. Doing it right isn't easy, which is why county boards are now sanctioning large sums of money to pay professional sports scientists. No manager will take an inter-county team without a professional strength and con-ditioning coach on board. As a player, you transform both physically and mentally. It wasn't that we were doing anything wrong previously – we were doing a lot right, in fact. I think teams catching up on us coupled with the loss of players every year to retirement was having a draining effect on us. Since '09 we'd lost Darragh, Murph, Tadhg, Tommy Walsh, Mike Mac, Tom Sullivan, Tommy Griffin and a few more. Hard to replace those guys.

We still had plenty, though. We discovered new talent. James O'Donoghue had been precocious underage and was arriving at senior level. He was a cut above most young players. His balance sets him apart. He can turn off either foot, kick off either foot, takes men on all the time, and has an eye for a goal. He learned a harsh lesson against Donegal in 2012. They squeezed him out. But he is not the type to let that kind of setback stop him. The lads enjoy him on the panel too. He is a relaxed character. He missed a session one night in 2012 because he had gone out without his phone and forgot about training. Like I say, a new breed. His best quality is that he is very good in big games.

He'd been on the first Sem team that I was involved with in 2007. That team had Fionn Fitzgerald, Jonathan Lyne and Brian Kelly, who are all now also on the Kerry panel. They are examples of this new breed: young, good athletes who are tech savvy (when they manage to have their phones with them). That might sound like a funny thing to say, but that is the big change I've seen happen in the game over the last few years. The use of technology to record data relating to everything you do on a daily basis – from mood to water intake, diet to sleep, gym to injuries and rehab – represents a new age. I enjoy tech, part of my work lies in multimedia and social media, and technology will continue to play a bigger part in player preparation and per-formance. In the end all this felt like more work for me. All failure is failure to adapt? It wasn't that I couldn't adapt, more like I hadn't time to adapt.

One of Éamonn's big strengths as a manager is how proficient he is in understanding and using new media and technologies in analysing teams, games, preparation and performance. It's likely that you will see GAA managers using real-time analysis data during games from here on – if they are not already doing so. Cian O'Neill has brought a lot of new ideas to the Kerry set-up as physical trainer. He is outstanding at what he does. He lectured sports science to a good few of the young lads on the Kerry panel in University of Limerick, as head of department. The same lads are ahead of the curve in terms of how they prepare. You can see it in them. I'd like to see a few of them stick their heads above the parapet soon, though. There's only so much any strength and conditioning coach can do for you. The best preparation in the world is equal if you don't go out and make it count.

They say Paddy Bawn Brosnan used to drag his boot along the grass across the small square in view of his opponent when he played. He was making his mark. Drawing a line. Literally and metaphorically. 'This is me,' was the message. 'Try me.' I'd love to see some of our young lads drag their boots in the grass someday and say the same. 'This is me.' And play accordingly. I always liked to get to my position before my opponent. Especially in Croke Park. I wanted to mark my territory. I'd carry myself with the weight of every victory Kerry ever had and every headline that was ever written about me or my team. I'd make that weight shine out through my eyes, so they glared as my opponent approached me. I'd shake his hand if he offered it. I could never understand wishing your opponent luck before a game. I wished him nothing but hardship for the day.

Winning All Irelands is testing. If you're not tested on the training ground every evening you go out, you'll come up short. I was tested from the very start. By the Eamon Breens, the Éamonn Fitzs, the Liam Hassetts, the William Kirbys, the Johnny Crowleys, the Darraghs, the Tommy Griffins, the

Aidan O'Mahonys and Brendan Guineys. They were the types of player I enjoyed playing with. They were fighters. We always had plenty of fighters in Kerry. William Kirby was an interesting guy. He did his own thing, showed up, played hard, went home. He never cared too much about opposition. Often he didn't even know who he was marking. Dara Ó Cinnéide is a movie buff, especially taken by obscure, art house works that few people would have heard of never mind seen. He has a whole mental library full of off-beat movie quotes that he might use to synopsize a particular story or event that may have happened. Éamonn Fitz warned me about this when I first joined the panel. He expects the rest of us to know the movie, or to at least have some suitably provocative and cerebral quotes of our own. I usually go for a scene in *Intermission* just to take some steam out of him. There's one where the guys are shooting the film scene and a young local scallywag approaches. 'A' youse makin' a filim?' he asks. The men are curt. 'Yeah.' 'Can Oi be inah?' the boy asks. 'No, piss off,' reply the men. 'C'mon, yiz pricks . . . Oi'll do a dance fo' yiz . . .' With that the young lad starts dancing, doing the 1, 2, 3s to his own music. Cinnéide loves that one. I do the accents and the dance for him. He asked Kirby one day what his favourite movie quote was. Kirby goes, 'Hey, maaaan, you're Shawn Kemp, maaaan!!' That's a line from a sports documentary called *The Reignman* about a former NBA player called . . . Shawn Kemp, funnily enough. Kemp is a six-time NBA All Star. Cinnéide could never get his head around this quote being Kirby's favourite. I mean, is it even a quote? What does it even mean? Who even is Shawn Kemp? To me, it's brilliant. It says everything and nothing at the same time. It says something about William Kirby too. He'd put a hole in you on the field then go dancing in a club. He'd test you in training regardless of who you were. He'd use himself. He'd fight. I'd like to see a few more young fellas step up and use the physiques they have honed in the gym.

There's an argument to be made that winning All Irelands is now about science and spend – that spend equals success. A counter case can be made that says winning All Irelands is more about the rudiments. Both combined are hard to beat. There's a lot to be said for the right physical conditioning. It's hard to win an All Ireland without it, but not impossible. It's impossible to win an All Ireland without fight.

The opening league game took us to Croke Park to face Dublin again. We were easily motivated, but we were a new group too. A few more faces had come through. UCC had a crop of Sigerson-winning players coming through that had a Kerry backbone. Beating Dublin set us up, but we managed to lose to Armagh a week later. Down were up next and we responded well with a win up there, before facing this new Donegal machine in Killarney. On the day there was little sign of what was to come from them later on that year. They were leggy and sluggish. Another win, 2–16 to 1–08, and we were nicely set up to qualify for the league semi-final against Mayo. This was the game that really made us appear vulnerable. We had them beaten the same way we had Dublin beaten in 2011, and conceded late goals to get caught again. I conceded a penalty myself. I'd had my eye on Mayo since the 2011 semi-final. There was something different about them that day. A rough edge. We left them back in to the game and they qualified for the league final, almost despite themselves.

When the championship rolled up Cork beat us in Munster. After that game Éamonn Fitzmaurice rejoined the management team with Jack. There had been a lot of change in our back-room team over the previous eighteen months. Joe

O'Connor had been appointed as our strength and conditioning coach for 2011. He had us all on very specific personal training programmes from November. By the summer he was gone and our programmes changed. Donie Buckley was involved as a coach in 2011, and was also there for part of 2012, but he departed too. He was popular with the players and had good ideas. As a result the existing back-room team became stretched.

Éamonn came in to take up the slack. The turnover of managers and physical trainers in my time involved with Kerry was remarkable. There were five changes and four different managers in eleven years. Páidí, Jack, Pat O'Shea, Jack again, and Éamonn. As a result, there were six different physical trainers in that time: Johnno Keeffe, Pat Flanagan, John Sugrue, Alan O'Sullivan, Joe O'Connor/Alan O'Sullivan and, finally, Cian O'Neill. I didn't find the change in management that difficult, personally, but I found the turnover of trainers tricky. That was just down to me and my body.

The first qualifier took us to Westmeath, where we came mighty close to going out again. We were rattled in the first half. I spoke to the lads at half-time, something I only did a handful of times in my career. We just had to stay in touch and see if Westmeath could close the game out down the stretch. We could make it a lot easier for them by panicking, which we were beginning to do. Let's make them beat us if they can, but let's not beat ourselves was the message. The only other time I recall speaking in the dressing room before a game was in the replay against Cork in 2010. Westmeath stuck a goal right after half-time to give themselves a massive chance. We rose to the challenge and pulled a win out of a tough place. Eoin Brosnan and Tomás were massive. Darran came on and got a typical Darran goal. I knocked over a few points late on to keep us ahead. It was a brave performance. Halfway through the second half everything pointed towards defeat. We limped out of the park in Mullingar, licking our wounds but still alive.

Tyrone lay up ahead, peering quietly through the scrub.

I walked down the stairs from the press room wondering what the hell just happened. One minute I was talking to championship sponsor Tomas Garvey, perfectly composed, the next I was fighting back tears on live TV. Five minutes previously I had revisited the past. We had just beaten Tyrone in the 2012 qualifiers. The last time I lined out against Tyrone in championship football was the '08 final, when I was supposed to be captain. It ended with me on my hands and knees having had the last shot at the final whistle. Beaten every way a man could be. My reaction was a personal one and not a representation of how the team was feeling. Of course, it was an important day for everyone.

Back at the Europe in Fossa as we were having our team meeting I could feel a weight on me. Before the meeting, as Gooch was taking his seat next to me he patted me on the knee and said something that struck a chord: 'Come on now, we need this one.' He captured exactly what I was feeling myself. He said it quietly, in a matter-of-fact way that made it stronger somehow. We did too. We needed it. On the bus I needed some music to help me relax. I scrolled through my iPod looking for the right song. 'Hometown Glory' by Adele? Exactly what we needed.

It was a great game to play in. We played like men possessed because we were possessed. The reality was Tyrone had the better of us a few times but by 2012 they weren't the force they used to be. They were battle-weary. So were we. Our natural ability and the motivation gave us the advantage. Bryan Sheehan set the tone with a few massive hits around the middle.

I got busy early getting on ball, setting up Gooch and Declan for scores, taking one myself and tackling in the middle third. Getting in tackles and turnovers and winning breaks, my bread and butter. If I'm doing these things well I feel I'm playing well. We got on top early and didn't let up. I was affecting the game. My opponent was replaced after 25 minutes or so. Donaghy delivered. He had the hardest job on the field. Balls being rained down on top of him every which way and if he didn't win them the crowd were hanging off him like the full-back. When you're six-foot-five there's nowhere to hide. I have yet to see anyone do what he did at full-forward at his best, though many have tried. His goal was crucial, coming within a few minutes of Tyrone scoring theirs. Aidan O'Mahony and Marc were strong at the back. When Mahony and myself arrived on the scene together Pat Flanagan couldn't tell us apart. He'd call me Aidan. I had to grow a beard in the end to help him distinguish between us. Mahony grows one now and then and the similarity returns. We were similar on the field in that neither of us held anything back. He was a great teammate. I will miss him. Kerry will too when he goes. On days like Tyrone you need a team of O'Mahonys.

Some people said afterwards it was only a qualifier. To me it was more than that. It was an All Ireland final. The atmosphere in Killarney was thick with tradition: one of those days when the ghosts of Kerry's past came out to play with us. The Kerry supporters came out to play too. They were loud and proud. They turned up not knowing what to expect. They got a revival of sorts. They showed class in how they treated Mickey Harte and the Tyrone team after the game too.

The last person I spoke to leaving the field was Mickey Harte. I told him everyone in Kerry was with him and his family. Only a week earlier those accused of murdering his daughter

Michaela on her honeymoon were acquitted. I had met Michaela once or twice over the years. In 2004 I went on an All Stars tour and happened to be seated next to her on both journeys to and from Hong Kong. She seemed to be a lovely person.

Having met Mickey leaving the field, the emotion of the game itself, and its connotations for me going back to 2008, I could have done without the interview. I was whisked off the field at the final whistle by one of the TV3 sports guys. He ran me straight upstairs to receive Man of the Match. It was unlike me to just cooperate like that. Within two or three minutes of the final whistle I was in front of a camera answering questions. For a split-second I lost my composure. I wouldn't have minded but I didn't even deserve Man of the Match. Declan did. He played with that boldness and abandon that makes him great.

At training the next night dummies, diapers, tissues and Johnson's baby powder were taped to my locker by the lads, who were waiting for me to enter. Niall O'Callaghan, or Botty as he is known in the camp, is one of our kit-men and resident comedian. He was in his element. I had to laugh.

We went on from there to beat Clare in Limerick. I was marked on the day by a chap called John Hayes. He was memorable for the fact that he was, in my opinion, the worst footballer I ever encountered at inter-county level yet he had the most to say for himself on the field. An unfortunate combination.

We arrived at a quarter-final with Donegal, who we had beaten well in the league.

Donegal went on to win the All Ireland, beating us on the way. They had the look of champions in the quarter-final. At the same time we probably helped them on their way. Our inconsistency was becoming consistent. We were up and down, capable of great football and mistakes, missing something but no one knew what. Jim McGuinness had taken Donegal to a new place. They carried themselves a little differently, I noticed.

A poor first half coupled with a strong second saw us lose by a point. My own performance mirrored that of the team's: quiet first half, strong second half. Having done well at the break-down in the earlier League game I found myself surrounded by Donegal men on the few kickouts that did come my way in the first half. A few of the Donegal boys got my back up going down the tunnel at half-time. Chirping. They'd had their arses handed to them enough times in Croke Park. Too many times for me to take the chirping too seriously. I didn't say anything back but I put it in the computer for the second half. 'We'll see what they're like down the stretch,' I told myself. My blood was up for the second half. But for conceding a poor goal we would have led at half-time. We dominated for part of the second half, taking the momentum back. Star's goal, with a few minutes to go, gave us a right shout despite having played so poorly on the day. Maybe that was down to them. They learned a good deal from the league game where we dominated them around mid-field on kickouts. Certainly in the first half I felt like a spectator. On their kickouts, everything seemed to go to the other side of the field. The ball seemed to be very far away from me for some reason. I had the same problem with Dublin in 2011. Cluxton went short or to the other side of the field. I was dragged into the corner of the 21-yard line and the Hogan Stand sideline. If ever I felt I wasn't involved enough in a game I'd try to get as physically close as I could to the ball. For the second half against Donegal I cut loose to try to get us over the line. They held out. Just. You could tell they had it in them to win the All Ireland. You could feel they had a belief. We had a belief too. I wouldn't say theirs was any greater than ours. Maybe it was just smarter or younger or fresher. Whilst we lost, we could have won it despite having not played well.

Walking off Mark McHugh asked me for my jersey. I told him, 'No,' and kept walking. It was pissing rain. The jersey was stuck to my back and I just couldn't be arsed. Once I reached the dressing room I sat in my spot for a minute and tried to take in what had happened. Did we perform? No. Could we have won? Yes. Did I perform? Kind of. Could I have performed better? Yes. Could we have performed better? Yes. Did we win? No. Fuck. My jersey was soaking. Wet with defeat. I struggled to get it off over my head. I struggled to get it on over my head for a while when I started out. Once I did I promised no one would take it off me. I set my sights on that number 10 jersey back in 2004 and wanted to make it my own. I never felt comfortable unless I had 10 on my back. Now it was off my back and in my hands. I handed it to Peter Twiss, our county secretary, and asked him to drop it down to Mark McHugh in the Donegal dressing room. I've swapped a few jerseys in my time but I've never asked anyone for a swap. The closest I came to asking someone was with Michael Donnellan after the league final in 2006. Bryan Sheehan had just landed a big free with a minute or so to go. We had the result in the bag. Michael walked past me after watching the free land. I was going to ask him until I heard him talking to himself. He was pissed off, so I let it go. We've all been there. I understood. If someone asks I will oblige unless he has been false on the field, then I refuse. I have no time for have-a-go heroes who, as soon as the final whistle goes, act like we're new friends, like we have somehow bonded because he has spent the game trying to get a rise out of me and now we somehow respect each other. No new friends. I sent my jersey down the corridor to Mark. I didn't know if it would be my last Kerry jersey. It felt like it was. It felt like the end of something. I just wasn't sure what.

20

The Start of Something

Meanwhile, back at the club, another journey was reaching a conclusion. We had been trying to win the intermediate championship for a few years, with some near misses and hard losses being our lot. When I started out in 1996 Finuge were a Novice team playing in Division 5. By the end of 2012 we were senior and playing in Division 1. Getting there wasn't easy. A lost final here, a lost semi-final there, we kept on keeping on until we got there in October 2012, winning the county intermediate championship against Spa after a replay, Éamonn kicking the equalizer in the last minute of the drawn game. He had a habit of doing that. He had a fantastic mentality as a player. We won the replay well. It was at the end of this club journey, February 2013, after the All Ireland club final, that I began to think about another season at inter-county level. Jack retired from the senior job and Éamonn became the manager. The thought of playing for Éamonn, winning another All Ireland together, was too great to turn down while I still had life in me, while the players I knew and trusted so much – Gooch, Marc, Declan, Tomás, Star, Mahony – had life in them. We went at it again. I'm glad I did now.

Kerry's struggles at the start of Éamonn's reign were a test for him. The Crokes players were out of contention. Our intermediate win with Finuge saw us progress to win Munster and contest an All Ireland club final in mid-February, ruling me out of action for the opening games. The club campaign took a bit out of me. I was running on empty mentally and physically. My enthusiasm was low. Lower than the spitting I encountered along the way. But I remained phlegmatic in the face of it. Natural enthusiasm is the best form of fitness there is. I learnt that from my dog, Boo. He is irresistible. If I puck a ball one hundred times he will chase the one-hundredth ball with the very same enthusiasm as the first. I pucked a ball down the green from my front door one day. He had to cross the road to chase it. As he was crossing I saw a van coming around the corner. It was on a collision course with him. He almost made it but the van clipped his back legs, sending him into what might be called in diving, a somersault twist. He landed on his back, before rebounding to his feet in one motion. The van stopped. Boo kept going like it never happened and returned the ball to my feet before the van moved. The driver apologized as he passed by. I apologized for Boo, who apologized for nothing, but kept his beady focus on the ball and waited for me to puck it again. What a warrior. Boo is definitely my sporting hero.

I returned to the Kerry team for the last three league games. We won our last three games to stave off relegation on the last day. That would have been hard to take after eleven years. Relegation would have taken the good out of what we had achieved over the years. We won on the last day in Omagh, which gave us all a lift.

Kerry's poor league form coupled with Finuge's run to the intermediate club final meant my pre-season preparation wasn't ideal. By the summer I was beginning to feel the effects of that. A course of steroid injections in May, six in my back and one in my hip, to relieve stiffness and inflammation in my spine and right hip, had helped get me up and running. My best performance came against Cork in the Munster final in Killarney.

They were a good bit off the pace. Whether that was because of the team they picked, or what, I don't know. Our forwards gave them a runaround in the first half. Declan, James, Donnchadh, Gooch – all caused bother. Our goal before half-time was crucial in winning us the game. Declan won a ball one-on-one. He spun his man and cut for goal. Gooch had already been moving through the centre. Declan slipped it to him and he finished with a side foot into the dressing-room goal like we had watched him do many times in training. I don't think there was any difference between training games and matches for Gooch. He approached both in the same calm way.

It was my last round up against Noel O'Leary. He was rolled out to man-mark me again at the last minute. He hadn't been named to start. It was only during the warm-up he was announced. This was as we had expected; Éamonn had flagged it that week. It was a peculiar habit of Conor Counihan's to name dummy teams. Dummy teams? The name says it all, really.

While the Cork manager might have felt he was negating my influence on the game by man-marking me with a secret last-minute selection, in reality we were always using the arrangement to our advantage. You can't man-mark in the half-forward line and cover space in front of the full-back line; you can't double-up on people like Gooch or Tommy or Declan, or James O'Donoghue or Star, or Darran; you can't track runners like Tomás coming from deep; you can't tackle midfielders if they win primary possession. You have one job and that is to stop one particular player. Even that is hard to do with our forwards. While focusing on that you are hanging your fellow defenders out to dry. The arrangement suited us. The rest of our forwards were delighted with it. As a player given a certain task you have no choice but to do as you're told, I guess.

Going one-on-one against the Kerry forward line is foolish. Conor Counihan did it every time, which was amazing to us. Even if I wasn't on the ball I could still create space for others with good movement, or sometimes by no movement at all, by staying out of the way. If our midfielders got ball within reach of the inside line I'd go short for a pass knowing the ball was going over my head into the space I had left. Then our inside-forwards were one-on-one. I'd double around and make a support run though usually they never needed it. Noel would track my run and the Cork inside-backs were left to their own devices. Half-backs on a Kerry team would never get away with that. O'Leary was playing under strict instructions, it seemed to me. Maybe there was evidence that man-marking me was an effective way to go about things when I got myself sent off in Páirc Uí Chaoimh in 2009? He was a better player than that. This was a guy who played senior for Cork almost straight out of minor. This was a guy who could burst up the field and stick a goal, and did so a few times in his career. Never on me, though. He never seemed concerned with that side of the game in my experience. Liam Sayers, a cousin of my mother's, picked him on his Irish under-17 team to play Australia. He remembers him as a footballer starting out. He could never understand Conor Counihan using him in such a negative manner.

Whilst being man-marked worked to our advantage mostly, I did find it difficult at times. It was a case of accepting it and using my head more than my physicality or aggression, and not getting drawn into any bother. Under breaks was tricky, because anything goes there. Wrestling for every break was counter-productive. For that reason I played from behind on kickouts against Cork, where I couldn't be seen. From there I contested every second break. I'd show no interest in one, contest the next and so on. I couldn't be predictable. Gooch's goal came from one such break. I was still able to influence games.

My last game against Cork was one of my best. It wasn't without an addendum, however. With a few minutes left Brendan Kealy put a kickout to the terrace side of Killarney from the dressing-room goal. I was on the stand side. Cork had won the last few possessions and had all the momentum. We needed this one. I sprinted for the terrace side. I'm obvious in my movements because I have no choice. That makes me visible and vulnerable. Noel grabbed on to my traps with both hands. I was caught in the very situation I'd spent all game avoiding. Now I was out of the play with no hope of winning the ball. He was wide open. I let fly with a shot to his jaw. He'd got me with one back in 2009. Four years was long enough to wait. To be fair, he took it well. I respected him for that. He's as tough as old boots. The ref missed it. I think I deserved to get away with that one.

By the end I enjoyed the meetings with Cork. I developed an insouciance that I carried with me at all times. When that guard of insouciance dropped I was vulnerable. To myself more than any opponent.

What really changed a game that looked lost for Cork in the second half was the introduction of Ciarán Sheehan as a sub at full-forward. We were all pleasantly surprised when he didn't start. We couldn't understand why. The introduction of Alan O'Connor also influenced the game, to a lesser extent. Darragh

Ó Sé has gone on record many times as saying if he could buy any player for Kerry in the transfer market it would be Sheehan. He's tall, strong, fast, can beat a man and kick a score from a distance. His biggest strength is in the air, which he showed when he came on that day. He pulled Cork back into contention. He's now a professional AFL player with Carlton but he wasn't deemed good enough for Cork. Until they both arrived we were well on top, which begs the question, why didn't they start?

That was my last day out against Cork. It was important we won. I enjoyed our battles and respected them as opponents and people. We had always to be at a very high level against them, and I had to be at a level higher than most. They were especially good in a physical sense. I respect Noel O'Leary as a tough opponent, no doubt about that. The biggest compliment I can pay him is that I tried my best to stay away from him. That wasn't easy. My natural instinct is to get stuck in. As aggressive as I was I was smart enough to know that taking him on physically was pointless. I also respect the fact that he doesn't shoot his mouth off in the media. However, I wouldn't be as romantic about our encounters as others seemed to be. I asked my friend, Dr Con Murphy, for his number and congratulated him by text on his All Ireland in 2010.

Any man who wins an All Ireland deserves it. That Cork team deserved theirs. They were a fine side and arguably our toughest, most consistent opponents in my time playing. No other county had as dangerous a provincial rival over the course of the last fifteen years or so as we had in Cork. Tyrone and Armagh, maybe, but that fizzled out quickly. Dublin have had no consistent provincial challenger capable of winning All Irelands. Galway have fallen away in Connacht in the last seven or eight years, leaving Mayo as the top team there and one of the top teams in Ireland. Only Kerry and Cork have consistently challenged for Munster and All Ireland titles.

Ultimately, you would have to say a team with the amount of ability they've had over the last five or six years has under-achieved in winning only one All Ireland. Then again, I might say the same about our Kerry team. But the Graham Cantys, Nicholas Murphys and Alan Quirkes were top players and deserved another medal; Daniel Goulding, Aidan Walsh and Paul Kerrigan still have the opportunity to add to their haul. To my mind Cork's biggest weakness over the last five or six years hasn't been on the pitch but on the sideline. Dummy teams, good players on the sideline, players played out of position, and the same game-plan day-in, day-out. They seemed to lack adaptability. I admire adaptability in teams. I had to employ quite a lot of it myself over the years, particularly against Cork.

Cavan in the quarter-final was a great draw for them. They had a lot going for them: some tradition, youth and nothing to lose. It wasn't a great draw for us, from the point of view that we were expected to win. As it turned out they never really made a stab at it on the day. Their defensive style was difficult for us to play against. I ended up being marked by a nominal wing-forward who spent the game bombing upfield and forcing me to chase him. He handled the ball maybe two or three times offensively – for maybe fifteen runs upfield. Why Cork never tried this with me I don't know, as it would have been a much better way to negate me. Cavan occupied me for a lot of the day, made me run downfield to chase a man who was never going to get a pass. Outside of winning a few turnovers I had little influ-ence on the game. It was clever stuff by Cavan. The game itself wasn't too clever. Croker was half-empty. We were a prelude to the main event. That's where our stock was at.

Mayo drew Donegal in the day's other quarter-final. It was a great day out for Mayo in the end. I felt that day they had an All

Ireland in them. Our game was notable only for how poorly we played. We were slow and disjointed. The Dubs waited up ahead in the semi-final, but there would be nothing semi about it. It would be full-on, just how we like it. It wouldn't last long enough to be warfare, that was our hope. There were snipers everywhere you looked. We had a few in hiding that they didn't yet know about – James O'Donoghue was camouflaged, we'd have to unleash him and come out all guns blazing to stay alive.

'A classic for the ages,' they said. 'The best game of football ever played,' they said. Never to be forgotten, never to be repeated. Kerry v Dublin, the 2013 All Ireland semi-final. Gooch, Brogan, Ó Sé, Cluxton, Flynn, Connolly, O'Sullivan, O'Sullivan and O'Sullivan. And in the end McMenamin, again.

We'd felt we had their number. Éamonn had the Dubs analysed to the death. If ever a game highlighted the importance of good video analysis, this was it. It was an eye-opener when he dissected their game. They had obvious strengths which were formidable, no doubt, but they also had weaknesses that could undo them. We knew we could hit them for goals. Cian O'Neill, our conditioning coach, had us primed perfectly. By half-time we had three goals and expected three more in the second. To their credit they shut up shop. They have shown that they are adaptable and have the character to disallow defeat when it stares them in the face. We had that for a long time with Kerry: too many characters who wouldn't allow defeat. Tyrone had it too. We showed it every year from 2000 to 2014. Most days it was enough. The Dubs are beginning to show signs of the same team personality now.

James stuck two goals in the first half, Donnchadh another, and we were making all the right moves. With the start we had we should have been out of sight at half-time. Three goals in the first half of an All Ireland semi-final? There was a time not long ago when that would have been that. We'd have been thinking of home 10 minutes into the second half. We'd come out after half-time and blitz a team with another flurry of scores. With 20 minutes still left you're telling yourself to stay concentrated.

But by half-time we had conceded as much as we'd scored. We leaked a poor goal and, for all our attacking potency, we were still open at the back. Éamonn knew the score and all the players in our middle third were warned about being aware of defensive shape and not turning the ball over. That was why, as we attacked, I was more concerned with what was going on behind me than in front of me. Had we a good shape? Had we cover if we lost possession? That was my instinct on the field. I always felt more like a defender than an attacker.

The second half. From the off Dublin drove through the heart of our defence for scores but we were clinical at the other end. A decisive moment came when they turned us over on our own kickout, and an attempted point from Diarmuid Connolly dropped short and was flicked to the net by Paul Mannion. Coming on the back of our goal it was a boost for them and knocked the good out of some of our best work. Next play. The pace was rapid. We seemed to be a second ahead of them. All six forwards were programmed in for Stephen Cluxton's kickout from the word go. It was the key to the Dubs' high-tempo game and eased the pressure on their midfielders, who weren't high-fielders but were high octane.

Short kickouts have become a feature of the game in recent years and have negated the influence of wing-forwards like me who feed on breaking ball as there obviously is not as much ball up for grabs and breaking around the middle. My favourite thing to do in the game was to dive in on a breaking ball and win it. Instead, more frequently in recent years I found myself being dragged in towards the full-back line or across the line away from the breakdown, if there even was a breakdown area any more, of course. Short kickouts or fast kickouts (there is a difference) were a source of frustration for me by the end. If you had your homework done and were properly tuned in you could find ways to force the long kick. We had a system that worked very well for us. The problem when dealing with Cluxton was the variety he seemed to introduce by the game, involving more runners, decoy runners and distances to his kickouts as he went. It took keen concentration to not be the one who got caught for a short kickout or, more dangerously, a quick kickout. A short one meant you still had safety in numbers, and territory; a quick one could take players out of the game and get them near halfway with one kick. With a support runner they could be bearing down on your goal in seconds. You couldn't allow yourself to get caught by either, but a short one was the lesser of two evils. I used to get cranky in games if keepers kept going short. You just have to adapt. I adapted by making sure my man never got one.

I went OK in the first half. I got on a bit of ball and made a few things happen. My position and role had changed a bit for the year. It's only from playing the position that you will appreciate the little nuances, the differences between playing at 10 and 12. Small things come into the equation, like my hips. I liked to be able to turn both ways when I received the ball with my back to the goal. Since the hip surgery I wasn't as explosive when turning off my left side. At number 10 I turned off my right towards the sideline, giving me space and passing angles. You could take defenders out of the game. At 12 if I turned right I'd go infield and there was no space and there were no passing angles. I'd end up off-loading to a runner or playing flat passes that weren't taking defenders out. If I wasn't kicking or assisting I could get frustrated, but never for long because there are so many other ways to influence a game from half-forward. The differences between playing high up on the line and going deep had more repercussions for the team than me. I could do either. Staying up and being a threat left the half-backs exposed, going deep gave them protection, but then you had to get upfield in support to keep your man occupied so he couldn't drop off and double up on our inside-forwards. When you're 24 you can do both; when you're going on 34 there's a little more give and take required.

My role was mainly offensive from 12 for the year. After 15 minutes or so the Dublin wing-backs swapped. Donnchadh, Gooch and I had given us a strong attacking platform all year. Physically, I didn't feel great in the first half. I was sluggish. I think the club campaign and my rushed pre-season caught up with me. I had been taking muscle relaxants for my back and hips. I was busy and got on plenty of ball but I didn't feel as sharp as normal. My legs felt heavy. At half-time I drank a lot of water and got a rub from Eddie and drained my legs by the wall. I felt much sharper in the second half. This wasn't unusual for me over my career. I popped over two points after half-time and we were still in control. I wasn't happy with my contribution at the breakdown. Not that there were too many kickouts put up for grabs. By the 55th minute I was sitting in the Hogan Stand, substituted. The last 15 minutes were lost to me.

Dublin achieved some momentum through their substitutions. They raised their intensity levels and kicked on. A flurry of scores put them ahead. Two late goals put some make-up on the final score. Kevin McMenamin's goal in the 69th minute – after we had just kicked a narrow wide at the other end which would have put us ahead – won it for them. Beaten at the same time, at the same end, by a goal from the same player that beat us two years earlier. They said 2011 would never be repeated. This wasn't a repeat but the sense of déjà vu wasn't going away.

21

Defying Life

It was my first night back training with Kerry, in March 2013, and I was arriving with two young fellas in tow. Not normal procedure but these weren't normal circumstances, and Donal Walsh wasn't a normal guy. He was tall, mature, confident beyond his 15 years. And he was sick. Not that you could tell. His attitude was healthier than my own, or many of the fighting fit footballers that wore the Green and Gold with me. A few days earlier a close childhood friend of mine, Trevor McKenna, rang me to see if I would meet this young local boy who had been given only weeks to live. He was literally on a deadline and wanted to say hello. Or goodbye.

The first time I met him was at his house in Ballyvelly, outside Tralee. The second time was a few weeks later, picking him up with his friend, Cormac Coffey, to bring them to Kerry training in Austin Stack Park. I togged out and left the lads with Niall O'Callaghan, the Kerry team's go-to guy, who looked after them, as well as he does everything else, while we trained. Afterwards they ate with us at the Kerins O'Rahillys club, though by then Donal was cold and had no appetite. I was going to ask him if he wanted to drive the car, but he had fallen in

Paris a few days earlier and broken his arm, so he couldn't. He was weakening and had lost some of his spark from when I first met him. He was paler and thinner. Donal and Cormac were typical Tralee town lads. They loved sport – and fashion, funnily enough; I think Donal wanted to meet me more because of fashion than football. Cormac was a big football fan – he was wing-back on the Kerry minor team this year – but Donal and I would talk more about fashion than football. I told him to tell all his friends that they should go and learn a little about fashion, enough to talk to girls about some shops, labels, collections, designers, magazines, or whatever was relevant. If they did that they would go far in life, and they'd do well with girls too. I was only half-joking. Donal enjoyed that, even if I think he already knew that much himself. He loved shopping and clothes, and while he would buy for himself he was always thinking of others. One of the last things we spoke about was his shopping trip to Paris. I'm sure he told me he bought some Gucci. He had expensive taste. He would have done very well in life, and that is the hard part for his family and friends, no doubt. He had everything at such a young age. He would have made a great rugby captain. He had all the qualities required – maturity, self-confidence, awareness, intelligence, good communication skills, and height. He was a tall boy, like most rugby players need to be. He had a caring side, which great captains must have too. Great captains care more for those around them than for themselves. Roy Keane, for all his hard edges, cared deeply about his team and teammates, you can be sure. You could see Donal cared about people too. Maybe in a different way. More openly. That is a rare quality in a man, especially an Irishman.

I was trying to get a sense of who he was away from his parents and amongst his friends. I asked him a few questions to try to draw him out. The usual type you might ask a young lad to try to get a handle on him, to figure out who he was – a messer, a serious sort, a leader or a follower. The evening I called with Trevor he was in great form. I asked him if he'd had any night out on the town lately. He told me a story about an occasion with a gang of his friends. One of the group had too much to drink and was sick. Donal called him a taxi. A decent gesture. Not only that but he got in the taxi with him and took him to his own house around ten minutes outside Tralee. He put his buddy to bed upstairs, laid him on his side with a pan and towels on the floor by the side of the bed, in case he was sick again. He filled him a pint of water and charged his phone. The final touch was to leave the bathroom light on so if he woke he could find the bathroom in the dark. That was the Donal Walsh I knew in the short time I knew him. A light in the dark. His message to young people was to look for a light if ever they found themselves in darkness, to see the good in life, to ask for help if they were suffering from mental health issues. That message was so pure that I think he had to die young so that the message he carried would remain pure. So that it would resonate and last amongst young people. He died so his message would live and save lives. His death only strengthened what he had to say. When I left the house that night I kept telling Trevor he was going to be OK. I thought he would defy his illness and death itself to survive. In the end Donal Walsh didn't defy death but maybe he defied life.

22

Leave on Time

Life had changed a lot for me by the end of 2013. My personal life had taken me back to Dublin. I was splitting my time between there and Kerry. I'd hardly left Kerry from the previous March when I returned to the squad. Louise was on the road down every weekend to see me. When the season finished, I moved up. Life was good. Éamonn and I chatted briefly about 2014. He mentioned the possibility of playing at centre-back. This piqued my interest. I always felt more comfortable playing half-back from when I was in college and under-21. Jack played me there on a training camp in Portugal, and I went well. That was in 2010. I'd have enjoyed a change of position around then. Killian Young broke his leg the weekend before the Dublin game in a scuffle with Kieran O'Leary. Two of the nicest guys you could meet. They hugged each other and fell the wrong way. It just goes to show, some fellas have no business fighting. I thought playing centre-back might happen, but Éamonn went with younger blood, and understandably so. Time was doing a number on me by now – 33 pushing on 34. It would have been a risk to take. Killian's loss was felt. He has the legs and the tackling ability to make a difference against a team like Dublin. Plus, he had experience. It meant a late reshuffle at the back when our match-ups were already in place. We fielded four relatively inexperienced defenders: Shane Enright, Mark Griffin, Fionn Fitzgerald and Peter Crowley.

The condition of my hips and back meant I found it difficult to do every on-field session and still maintain proper physical shape. This physical deterioration was hard to accept. I had started doing Bikram yoga from November and was feeling the benefits of it physically and mentally. My back felt much stronger and more flexible, and the range of my hip joints improved significantly.

Tomás retired around November time too. I heard about it on Twitter, where everyone hears everything these days. I took my time with that one. We didn't talk for nearly a week. He was busy with media commitments and the rest. It scared me a bit, to be honest. Tomás. That was my room-mate gone. Talking to him about retirement was a bit too real for me. If time was tip-toeing up behind my back all along it had just caught up and tipped me on the shoulder. I could feel it. It caught up with Tomás a few months earlier, if the truth be told. It wasn't so gentle as to tip him on the shoulder either. It knifed him in the lower back. Not a week before the All Ireland semi-final against Dublin he spent a night in the Santry Sports Clinic after an epidural. The previous two nights he'd laboured in pain at home. Flat out. His back wouldn't move. He couldn't move. Up or down, left or right. The epidural brought him around after a few days, and he made the Dublin game. You didn't hear about it afterwards. The Ó Sés don't offer excuses in defeat, only con-gratulations. In November 2013 Tomás turned around and walked away. I thought about turning around too. I kept going another while. Time hadn't knifed me yet.

Life had become a balancing act, a race and a rush: constantly thinking ahead, organizing, trying to get a hold of training schedules, planning trips, booking flights, return flights, trains and return trains, preparing bags for training then bags for travelling, packing and unpacking, coming and going. Then doing it all again. In between all this I was training and trying to give the commitment required to play at that level. The way I was living had me wondering if I would fall short in everything I was doing.

My own website thisispaulgalvin.com had taken off. Almost three million visitors in the two years it was live. There are much bigger operations and numbers than that, but for a two-man operation it was intense. I was advertising for five or six brands of barbering, haircare, clothing and cars, writing copy, researching, reading, writing product reviews, and keeping myself informed to ensure all content I posted was relevant. I was selling products through my site also and was invited onto the ASOS affiliate program to sell products on their behalf. My social media platforms – Twitter, Facebook and Instagram – were feeding traffic to my site. I had to keep those updated to keep site traffic high and advertisers happy.

Sportspeople can be selfish. I was. My schedule in 2014 meant I did Bikram on a Tuesday in Dublin, travelled to Kerry on the Thursday to train, did the weekend session and went back to Dublin on the Sunday. I took off one Thursday and told Louise I would see her again the following Thursday. That was how the training schedule worked out. She supported me because she understood that was how it had to be if I was to play for another year. She wanted me to do it.

We played Cork in the McGrath Cup final in Mallow one Sunday. I came on at centre-back and played pretty well. That was my last game for Kerry. I travelled to Kerry as usual on the following Thursday. We trained on the Thursday night and played Dr Crokes on the Sunday in Fitzgerald Stadium.

I was late. I didn't leave on time.

For the first time I can remember with Kerry I was late for a training session or game. I was late arriving to the ground, late for the team-talk and late for the warm-up.

It wasn't like I was on the road travelling. I was at home all morning, working online. That gave me more enjoyment. I was lost in it. When the game came I was a fraction off it. Too busy with life to be properly prepared. That wasn't going to change. If anything I would get more busy. The concern for me was that fraction and not being able to recover it because of work, travel, injury, age or life. All those little fractions add up. The law of accumulation comes into play when you least expect it and flattens you. Time hadn't knifed me, it just tripped me up.

From the dressing room in the Fitzgerald Stadium on Lewis Road to the Brehon hotel on the Muckross Road the idea settled in my mind. I'd walked down Lewis Road many times with a pep in my step alongside Tomás, or someone, after a victory. He was gone down the road before me now. I can only recall losing one game for Kerry in the stadium. That was against Dublin in the 2010 league. I don't recall ever losing a championship game there. I sat through a short meeting out of respect for Éamonn.

As I left the room Darran asked me if I was calling for tea. We had arranged to call at Gooch's house after the game. I said no and kept walking. I felt bad afterwards, but my thoughts were somewhere else at the time. Darran is a good guy. I grew close to him over the years. The last few words I spoke to a Kerry teammate were to him about a cup of tea. We shared a good many of those over the years and laughs to go with them. I went home and slept on it. I rang Éamonn at lunchtime and told him. The time had come. I'd had enough. Enough rising and falling. Enough driving. It was time to stop the madness.

23

The Media and Me: Sky

Growing up I read newspapers a lot. Every Sunday I would read the *Sunday World* and the *Sunday Independent*. The sports section received the most scrutiny. Con Houlihan's column in the *Sunday World* was my first stop. His knowledge of sport was vast, yet it was his understanding of vernacular that I really enjoyed. If you ever fall into conversation with Darragh Ó Sé you will see he has a keen understanding and comprehension of the vernacular of different regions within Kerry and around Ireland. This makes him a great storyteller. And a good texter too. He can capture people and stories through understanding their place and dialects. All the Ó Sés are good storytellers, and Con Houlihan was the same as a writer. He used his column to commentate on a range of topics from sport to political life, from coursing to community, and captured the essence of games, players, people, towns, villages and times by understanding the vernacular. He gave you a piece of his mind every Sunday and left you wondering where he went and who he met every other day of the week.

I popped into the Palace Bar in Temple Bar one day because I heard that was where Con could be found the odd time. The snug was his domain. I was with my buddy, Eddie. I got chatting to the proprietor, Liam Aherne, who told me Con was in hospital at the time. We stayed for a while. I drank a few cups of tea before we were joined by Tommy Wright, who played on the Offaly teams of the seventies and eighties. He owned Messrs Maguire before selling it on to Sean Quinn. Con was an irregular in Messrs. He'd only call the odd time if he needed an odd drink. Brandy and goat's milk was his cure, and Tommy was the only publican who stocked it. The goat's milk that is, not the brandy. Con would stir the curdled goat's milk with his finger while Tommy served Guinness. We were joined in the Palace by a local taxi driver. He was a brilliant character. He had a grey beard so long it swung like a pendulum either side of his belly-button when he walked. He told us a story about the Yank who bought a new house in Walkinstown. This Yank took off on foot one day to find some new furniture for the pad. Walking down the street he met a native Dub. '"Excuse me, sir," says the Yank, do you know if there's a B&Q in Walkinstown?"

'"Be-jaysus, I'm not sure," says the Dub after a short pause. "But there's two Ds in Dundalk."' It took Eddie and me a good many minutes to stop laughing. We thanked Con Houlihan for giving us that laugh.

I enjoyed his depictions and descriptions. It was only later in life I really began to appreciate Con's talent for his craft of writing. My Aunt Nuala bought me his book *More Than a Game: Selected Sporting Essays*. I still pick it up when I feel the need to brush up on my knowledge of just about anything, but especially writing. Dion Fanning was another writer I enjoyed reading as an older teen. He brought something slightly more exotic – his pieces would be addressed 'Dion Fanning: London'. I knew men who had gone to London and were never heard of again. Dion was writing home from London. In a newspaper. About the Premier League. I was impressed. His father Aengus was a character I admired from afar. He played minor football for Kerry in his time before cricket became his passion. Cricket. That in itself made him interesting. Páidí told me one time that Aengus wanted to meet up with me for lunch. I'm sorry we never got round to it.

Locally I found Owen McCrohan of the *Kerryman* interesting in his point of view. I like to analyse people's viewpoints and opinions. Often the people writing give themselves away and you can move on from them very quickly. You have to be open-minded about media commentary. The truth is the truth. I have often taken on board pieces written about me that have had a grain of truth to them. You'd be foolish not to. There have also been times when I have faced down journalists who have taken liberties with me. Some might say you'd be foolish to do that. There is no one in the media world, with the exception, perhaps, of Hector Ó hEochagáin, that I have any regular contact with. I never mastered the media game. I'm not sure why. I may have been a bit too blunt in expressing myself at times. I grew cautious over the years. In the end I had no relationship with anyone in the media. Hector is a good guy to talk to and good craic more importantly.

Writing myself has helped inform me. I always try to write from a positive place. If I have negative feelings towards someone for a particular reason I forget them or have it out with them face to face depending on the circumstances. To me Paul Howard is Ireland's finest writer today. He has a sports journalism background but his works of fiction are unreal. There is a depth to his work that staggers me still. These days I don't read newspapers much. Whenever I find myself the subject of commentary and speculation it is frustrating and turns me off something I used to enjoy. One day a national newspaper ran two false stories on the same day. One related to the Sky–GAA deal – apparently the reason I wasn't with Sky was because we couldn't agree a fee; but at that point there hadn't even been a conversation between me and Sky – and the same paper on the same day put words in Louise's mouth about me. There are so many nonsensical stories that it's hard for me to take any of it seriously any more. Someday I will take it seriously and take the appropriate action.

These days you'd more likely find me reading a dictionary. On my first date with my fiancée Louise she asked me what I was reading. I happened to be reading the Collins dictionary and thesaurus at the time. She laughed, not realizing I was serious. I got embarrassed because I thought she was laughing at me. Then she got embarrassed because she couldn't stop laughing at the table, and I obviously wasn't getting the joke. I sat there trying to be cool and nonplussed. I thought about pretending I actually was joking for a minute, but it had gone too far. She started asking me the definitions of obscure words just to test me. You'd be surprised how intense that is on a first or second date.

I like to read dictionaries. Or refer to them. Of course I don't sit down and leaf through a dictionary every day, like a normal book. Now and then I might spend an hour leafing through it. Nearly every day I find myself checking up the meaning of words, though. A word will either pop into my head or I will see something online and check it up on the dictionary app on my iPhone. I really like words. Simple words have helped me rationalize the craziest situations, events and people in the past. I like exploring synonyms too. The language of fashion alone is very intelligent. You would need a dictionary to get a handle on it.

There is a lot of learning in dictionaries and thesauruses. Especially if you like to write. I like to stay informed by reading magazines and blogs too. I respect the trade of journalism in essence, and I respect journalists who respect me. There isn't much you can do about ignorance. I treat ignorance with arrogance, because that is what it deserves. The pen is mightier than the sword they say. That may be so, but achievement trumps them both. Wouldn't it be great to have all three in your scabbard?

A while back a story was floated in a few newspapers that I had done something I hadn't done. For that reason I kept a close eye on what was being said and written about it. Two journalists stuck their heads above the parapet and made definitive statements on what had happened, saying that I had indeed done it, not before adding the dreaded addendum, 'allegedly'. It crossed my mind to call them. I resisted. Why? Because I knew how the conversation would go. I'd pull one of them up on what he had written, ask him if he realized that some people believe what they read. He'd say, 'Well, if you actually read it, you'd have noticed I wrote "allegedly" as well.' I've had these conversations. Allegedly. The most useful, yet useless word in the English language. It's the type of word you see written a lot . . . but you hear spoken very little. In this instance it was supposed to be my saving grace. Allegedly. Because that's just how conversations about what is written in papers go, right? Reason is employed where allegations are made. When people read about allegations they stop and think for a minute and then withhold judgements, preferring instead to seek out proper evidence before making a decision or a judgement one way or the other. Not likely. To allege something is to declare it without proving it. That's all some people need, it seems. What can I say? 'F**k you, allegedly.'

'And you never got the Sky job?'
The man on the street stops me. Nice man. Means well. Everywhere I go for weeks I'm being asked about this Sky deal.

The GAA had a new broadcasting deal with Sky, who now show GAA games live in the UK. It wasn't something I was pursuing. It's not something I was interested in. In the end I was wondering to myself what was going on. The question I would ask is, what does the deal mean for players on whose backs these broadcasting deals are being brokered? Will we see an increase in the mileage rate that was introduced with the euro in 2002? Will we see a more condensed playing season that doesn't involve players doing four months of pre-season? If these two issues alone were addressed I'd see Sky being a very positive thing. I doubt that 'increased profiles' in the UK and 'exposure to new markets' mean all that much to GAA players, though. Especially hurlers, some of whom mightn't be recognized in many villages around Ireland because of their helmets, never mind in any village around London Town. Let's talk in real terms. How does this Sky deal better the living conditions of players?

I suppose that's more a question for the GAA than Sky. Perhaps it does in ways I don't know about. What's important is that the players themselves seem to be happy with the arrangement and the excitement it brings. I'd probably enjoy it myself if I was playing. But I hope it does benefit them in some real way because players deserve more than they're getting at the moment. Pundits are the real winners. For now I'll stick with the players on this one. I'd like to see them make a few quid out of the deal.

Punditry is now so sought after it's almost a career path. Maybe it should be on the CAO application form. A pundit is someone who has been admitted to membership of a scholarly field. Maybe we should all have to qualify as pundits, then? Especially if we're getting paid for it. It's an industry nowadays. My name was favourite with the bookies anyway. Favourite for what, I don't know. Presenter? Pundit? Who knows? Papers picked up on that. I was to be the new something at Sky. Before I knew it I was getting cards of congratulations in the post, phone calls and texts, tweets upon tweets. Not to mention the man on the street. The last time this happened a story appeared on the front of the *Sunday World* saying I was about to be the new something on *Xposé*. You can imagine my delight at the new line of enquiry. 'When are you starting on Sky?' First I had to explain that I knew nothing about any Sky gig. That in itself was proving problematic, because then you have to explain to people who've read it in the paper that it's possibly not true. Then you feel you have to explain what you think might be going on to help ease the sense of confusion and disappointment in the air. Such a waste of time. I made no comment on it as it was speculative. Maybe I should have. Now, after appearing as favourite to get the still unspecified job, I had to explain to well-meaning, supportive people why I didn't get a job I didn't apply for or want, whilst trying to explain the new social media symbiosis between the bookie and the pressman at the same time. Jesus H. Christ on a High Nelly. Where was 'allegedly' when I needed it?

24

Disruptive Thinker

Being part of a team is the same as being part of any business organization or corporation. You have a manager, colleagues, competition, promotion, demotion, different departments requiring different skill-sets, leaders and followers, strengths and weaknesses. Within that you must make yourself a valuable team member whatever way you can. Having a vision and ambition is important in moulding a role for yourself and making a valuable contribution. Further to that you must look ahead and find ways to adapt and improve to remain relevant in the future.

I started out as a sub in a Kerry team that had lost some big games in the previous few years. It was widely felt at the end of 2003 that Kerry football was in a bad place and that All Irelands were decades away. I felt lucky because in that bad place lay opportunity. Not only that but from the inside I could see exactly where that opportunity lay. I knew what the competition was like in the squad, what the strengths and weaknesses were, and what was required to become a valuable commodity within the team. From watching opposition teams it was clear that a certain skill-set was needed. I had that skill-set; Jack O'Connor moulded me according to his system of play.

I was lucky also that several young players came to the fore around the same time as me. They were of a similar mindset to me. We were insurgents and we were starting the insurgency at home in Kerry. We had to disrupt the traditional mode of thinking within the county with regard to how we, Kerry, should play football and the type of player that should wear the Green and Gold. We had ball players aplenty, but maybe not enough players who could play without the ball. Our traditional way of playing possession-based, free-flowing catch and kick had been overtaken. New methods based around physicality, aggression, tackling and intensity had disrupted us. These qualities had nothing to do with possession of the ball and everything to do with non-possession of the ball. On a good day with thirty-plus possessions in a game you'll still only have actual possession for maybe 40-odd seconds in total of a 70-minute game. For me it might be less than that again because I rarely took plays on the ball. You spend more time without it, obviously.

A new breed of disruptive thinkers infiltrated the game at management level, led by Joe Kernan and Mickey Harte, who saw the margins that could be gained by improving and working on their game without possession. Jack saw that we had to adapt to new methods and to new standards of practice. He needed new, open-minded players to do that. I was one of those.

So while many said that traditional Kerry football was in trouble, we saw a new way of playing. Jack identified the areas where he felt I could offer something different, and I went about working on those to make myself better at them: getting into the right zones to win ball for us in the middle third; using myself to tackle and win ball back from the opposition; making myself physically strong, matching the aggression of the opposition; and using my head, anticipating and pre-empting, reading and covering. All these things essentially happened without the ball. I trained myself to be very good without the ball. Before I could think about being good with the ball I had to become good without it, because for me that was where the opportunity lay. I had to look at the game a little differently, with a disruptive mindset. Maybe I took the disruption too far at times, but there were plenty others who did the same. That was part of the strategy. You need an aggressive strategy in business and sport.

There were things I wasn't so good at, but there were others on the team who were very good at those things, so I didn't worry about them. I tried to become very good at what was needed. Over time I up-skilled in order to remain an important member of the team, improving my kicking, my speed, my game-management and my creative play. I can see parallels between disruptive thinkers in sport and in business. Assessing from within, identifying talent, identifying opportunity, making yourself valuable to the team or organization, up-skilling and providing something that wasn't readily available to your bosses, perhaps, making your own niche and creating your own rules and expectations, terms and conditions. Disrupting the status quo in other words.

There were a few disruptive thinkers in the group. None more so than Gooch. He has an innate unorthodoxy that I saw at close quarters. He played from behind defenders when every-one else played in front, or he'd start in front, spin in behind his man and roll back out in front on the other side. When most forwards would come down the line at me for a pass, he would step towards the line then spin back in towards the D. He stood still where other forwards would run, he ran where others would stand still; having the nerve to stand still and wait and wait and wait until the right moment is a rare quality. Most forwards will make the first move and the defender reacts,

Gooch plays hardball and makes the defender make the first move, then he reacts. The defender will move towards the ball then realize Gooch hasn't moved at all, so he turns around to look for him. And when he does, he's dead. That's when Gooch strikes. He moves in circles when everyone else moves in straight lines. He takes a bounce or solo when others kick, he kicks when others can't see it. That bounce or solo was never for show, but almost always when he sensed a goal. Only then. That bounce or solo bought him time or allowed him to spin back the way he came because on his way out for the ball he saw a runner on the way in and he knows if he can just hold for that extra second, commit some more defenders to him, then slip that runner in, a point for himself becomes a goal for the team. So he slips the runner in. Why take a point when a goal will do? And then, for all the subtlety and sensitivity to situations, there is the hardness. When he was caught, tackled, marked, triple-marked and brought to his knees he could stand back up again and kick a point just to be defiant. That's hardness. He never touched the ball for the first twenty minutes of the 2004 All Ireland final. He finished with 1-05. Patience. No panic. He has this cold composure. He sees things differently and un-conventionally. In business that is called disruptive thinking. In sport it is called genius.

Once the Kerry team got going I had all the knowledge I needed right beside me on the training ground, or within the company, if you like. I didn't have to look at the opposition or listen to talking heads. Marc Ó Sé, a defender, came along and wanted to score more points than the corner-forward he was marking. Aidan O'Mahony wanted to take guys on physically, to impose himself because he knew he was stronger than most. Declan O'Sullivan had a radical, rebellious mind. The more you try to dominate him the more dominant he becomes. I was surrounded by these insurgents who saw 2001, 2002 and 2003 happen, and turned the experience of those years upside down for the next decade. Towards the end of my career I played with my back to the sideline instead of the end line so I could see more of the field and give defenders more to think about in terms of my movement. Would I go down the line away from goal, down the line towards goal, across the field, behind his back or out in front? I was adapting to new conditions in my own body, to my age and to the age of my opponents. In doing so I was trying to disrupt the game.

In business today I work a lot in social media and multimedia through my website, thisispaulgalvin.com, and my social-media platforms, advertising for brands and retailers. I see how the insurgency of social media has disrupted the traditional advertising game. I see how the retail space can be similarly disrupted. One of the brands I advertise for is a chain of barbershops called Sam's Barbers in Dublin City. Barbershops have the potential to be much more than just barbershops. Clothing and coffee and magazines and music can add a lifestyle element and diversify the retail space and the business model, as well as a ready-made customer base already coming through the door.

Audi Cork are another brand partner. Denis Murphy is the bossman there. If I were the Cork football manager he would be the first call I would make for counsel. Reads the game well – the car game and the football game – more importantly he reads people even better. Audi are the most innovative and forward-thinking of all auto-manufacturers. They do so by being creative in how they approach the design process, and more and more so the marketing process. I work with Audi Cork on their marketing and social-media strategy to help them grow their presence online, which essentially comprises a new customer base that didn't exist ten years ago. There are things happening today in football, as in business, that weren't happening a decade ago. All success is successful adaptation. Being adaptable, flexible and open-minded helps to create your own terms and conditions for success where possible. If you can't do that, just disrupt the game and play by your own rules.

25

8 March 2014 – Life is a
Funny Old Game

Today is Sunday, 9 March 2014. The time is 2.02 p.m. on my phone. I just remembered that Kerry are playing Tyrone today in the NFL at Fitzgerald Stadium. Football and Kerry was once all I thought about. Now it's something I hardly ever think about.

I am writing this as I sit on Delta Flight 91, 30,000 feet above the south coast of Greenland, on the way to New York. Liam O'Sullivan, another Kerryman from Renard in the deep south, is with me. I am part of a new team now. Liam, along with another Kerryman, Paul O'Sullivan (also from Renard), and a native New Yorker, Mike Donaghey, formed Scratch Empire, a multimedia production company and creative-collective based in Brooklyn, New York, which specializes in creating online content, music video production and post-production, building websites, animation and graphic design. Donagheys and O'Sullivans. The more things change, the more they stay the same. Liam and I are flying over for a business meeting. Scratch Empire want me to help expand their business operation into Ireland. I sometimes work out of a space in the Guinness

Enterprise Centre, where a second cousin of mine, Eamon Sayers, is manager. It's a fertile, dynamic environment to be in, full of opportunity and may suit Scratch's needs. Tomorrow we all meet in Brooklyn for the first time. I'm put up in the ROW NYC hotel near Times Square. After a few days I realize it is the old Milford Plaza where we stayed years earlier with Feale Rangers.

It's 2.34 p.m. now. Half-time in Killarney. I hope Kerry are winning. Éamonn will have taken some time before talking to the lads. He'll be calm and measured, whether they're up or down. The lads will be taking stock. Wet with sweat, or with the rain we got to know so well coming in off the lakes and mountains south-west of Fitzgerald Stadium. Some lads will be sitting alone in silence, others standing in groups talking, some sipping water, others eating bananas or Jaffa Cakes. I couldn't look at food at half-time when I was playing. I needed to play on an empty stomach.

2013 turned in Tyrone. Kerry's current situation needs to turn too. Or be turned. Backs against the wall is easy, because you have no choice but to stand your ground and fight. But it's not my fight any more now. I fought because what's the point otherwise? What's the goal? To see how you get on? To make friends? Or to win? Maybe I took it all too seriously. I took it to heart and in the end my heart wasn't in it any more. A bigger part of me is happy where I am right now. Instead of heading for Dick Fitzgerald Stadium, I'm headed for John Fitzgerald Kennedy Airport. New team, new teammates. I eventually hear the Kerry result on the Tuesday after the game at a business lunch in a restaurant called Seven on 7th Avenue, right across the road from the Affinia hotel where we used to stay with Kerry when we visited New York. We'd gather in Niles, the hotel bar, every evening and laugh about last night then laugh some more about tonight and what was to come. I pass the door of a deli next to the Affinia that Éamonn, Tommy Griffin, Marc and myself would raid for food before bed. We'd go in and try to outdo each other with New York accents. Every sandwich would have to have 'salaaami', 'pastraaami', 'aaaanchovies', 'tomaaaato', with extra Swiss cheese, all the regular American sandwich ingredients just to see who could sound most American while sounding utterly Kerry at the same time. Good times.

At lunch I sit next to a Tyrone man, Fay Devlin. Fay is a successful contractor in New York, a friend of my cousin Kevin Moriarty. I end up doing my first piece of business for Scratch Empire with another Irish businessman, Cormach Murrihy. He is a steel engineer. As it goes he contacts me a week later with another job. In the short time I know him he is already one of the more interesting people I have met. There is a reason these guys are already successful. They're all about getting it done. That suits me fine. Within weeks Liam and Mike score a major video project with Miller Lite for Scratch. We're sitting around a table upstairs chatting business and football. My cousin Kevin is at the other end of the table. I kicked ball with him and my other cousins – Séamus, Tommy, Derek, and Declan from Curraheen – as a young lad when I hardly knew what football was. They had an O'Neills football back west. We had O'Neills sliotars on Penny Lane but no football. We'd call back to visit the rest of our relations every Sunday and I'd kill the time until we reached the house of the O'Neills.

Kevin and the rest of the guys here represent the Rockland GAA club. Kevin will bring the under-14s to Ireland later this year for the Féile. They want the best for Rockland, a small community in Upstate New York that I have known about now for twenty years or so. My cousins, Richie, James, Kerry and

Rose, came to Ireland and brightened every summer only to leave again to this faraway place called Pearl River, Rockland County. My Uncle Dick and Aunt Mimi have lived there for forty years now. My dad's other brother, Sonny, lived near there for even longer but eventually came home. Kevin is from my mother's side of the family and lives in Orangeburg, NY, now with his wife Karen and three boys, Colin, Darren and Eoin, not far from Pearl River. Colin came home in the summer of 2014 and starred at the under-14 Féile tournament for New York, like my cousin Richie did in 1994.

Memories race up and down 7th Avenue. Whilst there I proposed to Louise in a corner room at the Bowery Hotel overlooking the Bowery and Soho areas with a ruby I bought in Catbird, a vintage jewellery store in Williamsburgh. She said yes. More memories.

At the end of our lunch I heard talk of the Kerry–Tyrone game amongst Fay and Cormach, and tuned in to find out who won, without asking. My heart lifted to hear the result. Kerry.

Epilogue

We Can't Start Again

'You and me – why, we're all that's been. The anger of a moment, the thousand pictures, that's us. This land, this red land, is us; and the flood years and the dust years and the drought years are us. We can't start again.'

The Grapes of Wrath
John Steinbeck

All good things come to an end, all great things don't. All great things live on. That is what I think. All great things live on. In your heart and in your mind. And if you're great enough in the hearts and minds of others. Kerry football lives on. It endures. Therefore those of us lucky enough to be part of its story will too, in some shape or form. On a wall or on a plaque, in someone's memory, in old photos that were once new but will gather dust as the years pass over them. So, really, through it all there's nothing anyone can say or do to touch you, to hurt you, to change you, to make you any more or less of a man than you think yourself to be, than your achievements say

you are, or that your teammates say you are, or that the character you displayed while doing it says you are. I don't need
anyone to validate me.

I take with me medals and memories. I have plenty of both.
I'll count the memories every day and the medals now and
then. I don't know where they are. I hope my mother has them
somewhere safe. I have the count in my head where I've always
kept it. I know my medal count off by heart from when I was
12 years old. Hurling and football. The only medal I haven't
won in Kerry GAA is a county minor football championship. Of
the championship games I played in from '04 to '13, we won 80
per cent, lost 13 per cent and drew 7 per cent. I don't know if
winning is all that matters in sport, but I know it's all that
counts. I don't know if I won a lot or lost a lot, but I know I tried
my very, very best – and maybe that counts more than anything.
I don't know if I was good or great, but I know that I never set
out to be good, I set out to be great. That counts to me.

So what have I learned? I have learned that in sport you
shouldn't be desperate for success but desperate for the work
that inevitably brings success. There's a difference. In the end I
had to go because I was desperate for success but couldn't
commit to the work it takes to bring it. When that happens you
have to do the honourable thing and go. I go with nothing but
gratitude and thanks for everything that has happened to me
over the years. The medals, the memories, the men I soldiered
with, the man I became. I leave with pride and honour and my
head held high, not because of anything I won or anything I did
or that I was any better than the next man, but because I stood
my ground with some of the greatest players to ever play Gaelic
Football. My teammates. I leave with the pride of knowing
when the going got tough I never hid. I could have run and
hidden. But I didn't. I couldn't. That defiance that has been in

me since I was a young boy wouldn't let me. There were a few times over the years when I wished it would let me. I asked myself why I was bothering with a game that wasn't giving back what it used to, that was taking more than it was due. Ultimately the defiance and stubbornness would win out and I'd fight some more. That same defiance combined with Kerry football made a man of me. So I have to be grateful for that.

I write these words, eventually, because I have to. I owe it to the people who matter, to my family and friends, to those I soldiered with and those I soldiered for. There were issues that had to be addressed for myself. Issues that I kept my counsel on while I was playing, lest I create any more headlines or controversy that would reflect poorly on the Kerry jersey. I put up and shut up and waited. This is not a catharsis – nor is it to cleanse or to cast stones – but to close a chapter and move on.

And after all this what do I even know? I know that there are actually limits to what you can achieve in life and in sport, but that great people and great players don't see those limits. I know that the surest way to improve yourself is to learn from your teammates, not your opponents or pundits or experts. Watch your teammates closely, amongst them you'll find every ingredient you will ever need to be the best footballer, hurler, sportsman, competitor and person you can be. I know that doubts may come, but that they will go just as quick if you can face them down and dismantle them. Accept them, then attack them, break them down into small pieces and leave them on the ground behind you as you walk on to the next challenge. I know that if in doubt, practise. Practise kills all doubt.

I know I made mistakes. I know I learned from some and not from others. I know the value of saying nothing. I know the value of the noise that surrounds me. There was plenty of that. Too much, but I couldn't do anything about the talking heads.

Let them talk. Noise has a value too, if you can package it. Some of that noise added to me, some took away from me, some was fair, some unfair – all of it forms part of who I was and who I eventually became. I know too I have many more supporters than detractors. I know that most people are very good. I know that those who tried to take advantage of me along the way are too small to be mentioned here. And I know that now the time has come to say goodbye to all that. To the Kerry dressing room. To the Kerry jersey. To my teammates. To my friends. I gave them everything I had in me and they gave me much, much more.

There's plenty I don't know too. About myself. About football. About this life we're all existing in. Existentialism says that people are entirely free and are responsible for what they become through acts of the will. I like that. I try to just be myself. My father's advice. I like where that has taken me so far in life.

Regrets? People think it's necessary to have no regrets to be happy in life. It's a thing to say – 'No regrets' – like we're all James Deans blazing through life perfectly, not giving a shit until we die young. To me not giving a shit only means being happy with who you are. I am very happy with who I am. I think it's inevitable you will have some regrets in the end. It's not wrong to have regrets. You must be able to face them and accept them and make sense of them if you can. Then let them off. They'll only harm you otherwise. Regrets can be your friend or your enemy.

I know that if you follow your heart in life you'll always find your way. It won't lead you astray. In the end what does any of it matter anyway? Regrets, no regrets, four All Irelands, five All Irelands, six All Irelands. Ten years, eleven years, twelve years.

In the end, I know this. There is only one regret that matters.

The one that runs through every sportsman or woman when it's all over. Like someone has just turned on a tap inside you and a feeling runs through you like water from a well deep in your stomach. You let the tap run for a minute or just a few seconds and your mind wanders back to a day, a person, a game, a win, a memory, or a moment and you smile. Or maybe you begin to cry? Then you turn that tap off and keep forging ahead, driving on, asking yourself not, 'What if?' but, 'What's next?' It's only a fleeting regret and it has a beauty to it. A longing that tells you that you must have done something right on the way to where you are right now, at this moment in time, to feel that regret you feel for those few seconds. You must have had some success. You must have done something important, something worthwhile, something that people will remember, something that people enjoyed. Something that brought you happiness. At least for a while. That happiness now sates the hunger that once consumed you, quells the defiance that once drove you and soothes the scars you may have suffered along the way.

Regrets? My only regret is that I can't start again.

Notes

All references on page 124 can be found in *Final Whistle* by Paddy Russell, with Jackie Cahill (Mainstream Publishing Company/Random House: Edinburgh, 2008):

    1   p. 16, l. 27 and p. 197, l. 15
    2   p. 18, 3rd paragraph
    3   p. 187, l. 13
    4   p. 196, l. 31

Acknowledgements

Over the course of my career there were many people who helped and influenced me. Of course I must start at home.

Thank you to my parents for the values you instilled in me. When you tell a young boy to be his own man, to believe in God and always to try to be honest in his dealings, this is what you get. You may not have bargained for all of it, but when the time comes to cash in our chips, at least we'll have great stories to tell and value for our values.

To my brother Raymond, a man's man. Thank you for being who you are.

To my sisters Tina, Ciara and Catriona who kicked every ball. Thank you for the support.

To my extended family who travelled the country, and often from overseas, to watch us play, thank you. That meant a lot.

Thank you to all my coaches and trainers in both codes at every level, club and county. Had I not been directed along the way, I could have taken a wrong turn.

Thank you to the Kerry County Board, the Kerry supporters and my close friends who stood their ground with me over the years.

Thanks also to my teammates and friends in Lixnaw and Finuge GAA. I wouldn't have had it any other way. Thank you for the laughs and the learning. If I could I would write another book and change the ending. I hope this one does you guys justice.

To Feale Rangers and UCC GAA, without you I wouldn't have been able to compete at the levels I did.

I must, of course, thank the men I played alongside in the Green and Gold of Kerry; forever bound by victory.

To Denis, David, Brian and all the lads at Audi Cork. Keeping the peace and fostering cross-border relations for three years now. Thanks for the support.

To Barrister Aaron Shearer for the contract advice.

To Eoghan McDermott and Aileen Gaskin at the Communications Clinic for your time and patience spent dealing with everyday requests and enquiries.

To Joanne Byrne, thank you for the friendship and support over the years. Up Kerry.

The decision to do this book was a tough one, and long in the making. Writing the thing was comparatively easy. Special thanks to Eoin McHugh, Brian Langan and especially Alice Youell at Transworld Ireland for your help, support, and diligence in making it happen. Mostly, though, thank you for your honesty and integrity; without those this book definitely wouldn't have happened.

Finally to Louise, my hero. Thank you for coming along. I love you.

Picture Acknowledgements

Every effort has been made to contact copyright holders where known. Those who have not been acknowledged are invited to get in touch with the publishers. Photos not credited have been kindly supplied by Paul Galvin.

First section
Pages 4/5: the Kerry senior hurling team, Croke Park, 30/08/98: © Ray McManus/SPORTSFILE, 009433.
Pages 6/7: Liam O'Toole, PG and John Kelliher, Cork semi-final, 1999: courtesy of the *Irish Examiner*; UCC's Éamonn Fitzmaurice and Fionán Kelliher, Munster final, Limerick, 1999: courtesy of the *Irish Examiner*.

Second section
Page 1: PG and Kieran McGeeney, All Ireland quarter-final, 5/8/06: © INPHO/Lorraine O'Sullivan, INPHO 00192796; PG and Aaron Kernan, All Ireland quarter-final, 5/8/06: © INPHO/Lorraine O'Sullivan, INPHO 00192743; PG and Graham Geraghty, International Rules, 5/11/06, Ireland: © INPHO/Donall Farmer, INPHO 00202228.
Pages 2/3: PG and Éamonn Fitzmaurice with Bishop Moynihan Cup, Austin Stack Park, 11/11/07: © Stephen McCarthy/SPORTSFILE 273184; PG as Kerry captain at Munster semi-final, Fitzgerald Stadium, 15/06/08: © Stephen McCarthy/SPORTSFILE 304090;

Micheal Quirke, Killian Young, PG and Aidan O'Mahony, All
Ireland final, Croke Park, 20/09/09: © Brendan Moran/
SPORTSFILE 379484; PG and Colm Cooper, All Ireland final,
Kerry, 20/9/09: © INPHO/Lorraine O'Sullivan, INPHO
00374163; PG with manager Jack O'Connor, All Ireland final, Croke
Park, 20/09/09: © David Maher/SPORTSFILE 379522.

Pages 4/5: All Star award winners Tadhg Kennelly, and Footballer of
the Year Paul Galvin, 16/10/09: © Ray McManus/SPORTSFILE
RP0079415; Tommy Walsh and PG with All Star awards, 16/10/09:
© Brendan Moran/SPORTSFILE RP0079382; Eoin Cadogan with
Declan O'Sullivan and PG, Munster semi-final replay, 13/6/10:
© INPHO/Dan Sheridan, INPHO 00437500; Jack O'Connor with
PG, All Ireland semi-final, Croke Park, 21/09/11: © Brendan
Moran/SPORTSFILE 549882; PG with Cillian O'Connor, All
Ireland semi-final, Croke Park, 21/09/11: © Brian
Lawless/SPORTSFILE 549846; Ref David Coldrick, Ronan
McNamee and PG, All Ireland qualifier, Fitzgerald Stadium,
21/07/12: © Diarmuid Greene/SPORTSFILE 668990.

Pages 6/7: PG, All Ireland quarter-final v Donegal, 5/8/12:
© INPHO/Lorraine O'Sullivan, INPHO 00619350; Éamonn
Fitzmaurice and PG, Kerry County Intermediate final, Austin Stack
Park, 28/10/12: © Stephen McCarthy/SPORTSFILE 695702;
Aidan Walsh with PG, Allianz Football League, Austin Stack Park,
24/03/13: © Brendan Moran/SPORTSFILE 735597; PG, Paudie
Kissane and Noel O'Leary, Allianz Football League, Division 1,
Austin Stack Park, 24/03/13: © Brendan Moran/SPORTSFILE
735620b; PG and Noel O'Leary, Munster final, Fitzgerald Stadium,
7/7/2013: © INPHO/James Crombie, INPHO 00715744; PG, All
Ireland semi-final, 1/9/13: © INPHO/James Crombie, INPHO
00735838.

Page 8: PG and Mickey Harte, All Ireland qualifier, Fitzgerald
Stadium, Killarney, 2012: © Michelle Cooper-Galvin.

Index

ABOUT THE AUTHOR

Paul Galvin is among the all-time greatest Gaelic football players, and was a stalwart of the Kerry inter-county team from 2003 until his retirement in 2014. He also plays football with his local club Finuge, and hurling with Lixnaw. Galvin has won four All Ireland medals, eight Munster medals, and three National Leagues, as well as three All Star awards. He was Footballer of the Year in 2009.

Paul is also founder and editor of thisispaulgalvin.com, a fashion and lifestyle website. More recently, he has taken on the role of style editor for Ireland's biggest online magazine for men, www.joe.ie.

Twitter – @pgal10
Facebook – Paul Galvin
Instagram – pgal10
Contact – thisispgal10@gmail.com